ABANDONED PENNSYLVANIA

INDUSTRY AND ENDINGS

SUSAN TATTERSON

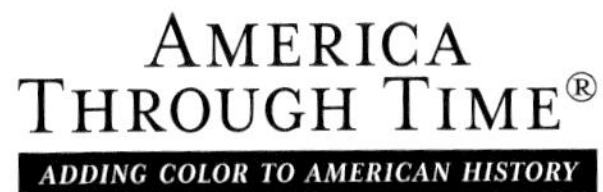

As always, for my "Huckleberry," especially this time, for the nagging!

America Through Time is an imprint of Fonthill Media LLC
www.through-time.com
office@through-time.com

Published by Arcadia Publishing by arrangement with Fonthill Media LLC
For all general information, please contact Arcadia Publishing:
Telephone: 843-853-2070
Fax: 843-853-0044
E-mail: sales@arcadiapublishing.com
For customer service and orders:
Toll-Free 1-888-313-2665

www.arcadiapublishing.com

First published 2023

ISBN 978-1-63499-475-0

Typeset in Trade Gothic
Printed and bound in England

CONTENTS

PREFACE

Pennsylvania's history is intrinsic to our understanding of America's expansion. As the second state in the nation, much of America's early industrial history can be traced back to Pennsylvania and its two largest cities, Philadelphia and Pittsburg. Not only was the Declaration of Independence signed in Philadelphia in 1776, it was also the capital city of the United States from 1790–1800.

More than two centuries later, evidence of much of this history is slowly being erased from our present-day landscape. The images in this book were created well over a decade ago, and when I began researching the locations, I was shocked to find that all but two are vanished and the remaining two, Richmond Power Generating Station and the York County Prison, are more than ten years along in their deterioration—and closer to the same fate as the others.

Preservation and historical societies work valiantly to keep history alive, but all too often their efforts are in vain, as Mother Nature and vandals are unforgiving in their reclaiming of untended sites. Richmond Power's decline is disheartening, to say the least. A 2020 YouTube video, created by an urban explorer, is evidence to the extent of the water damage that has occurred. Below the turbine hall stands what I call the never-ending stairs, and where I once stood to photograph them is now several feet under water. Senseless graffiti defaces what was once touted as the "most handsome station in America." There is still hope, albeit slim, that the 100-year-old Beaux Arts showcase for new technology will be repurposed. Only time will tell.

The Inn at Buck Hill Falls is perhaps one of the most beautiful, although haunting, abandonments I have photographed in my fifteen years of seeking them out.

I still cannot fathom how such a naturally beautiful location can fall to the wrecking ball. Nor in fact will I ever understand the demolition of sacred sites; there is something inherently wrong, regardless of religious affiliation, with the demolition of church altars—these exquisitely detailed repositories of faith are architectural treasures, filled with stunning mosaics, European marble, and superb stained glass. As a society, perhaps it is time to give more consideration to what we so carelessly allow to be destroyed.

The locations featured in this book span Pennsylvania's industrial, recreational, correctional, and educational past. Many were the first of their kind in some realm, and they all share a common thread: their dereliction and their metamorphosis into light and texture-infused entities make them photographic delights. With the complete absence of human existence and intervention, they take on a life of their own and possess a mythical quality. They tell their stories with light, color, and decay. They inspire us to imagine what went on within their walls and they have led me, personally, on a wondrous and thought-provoking journey into America's history.

I truly believe no creative body of work is created in a vacuum, and I am fortunate to have friends who share my passion for abandoned structures. I prefer to photograph alone; I enjoy the solitude these abandonments offer, but I also recognize the danger in my solitary exploits. I smile each time a well-meaning person says, "be careful," and I think of Stephanie, a friend who joined me in exploring many of the locations included here, and her patience with my antics. We now live on opposite sides of the country, but her constant "be careful" is always with me. I am not careful; it is not in my nature to be so. I often test the limits of sensibility to create the photograph I see in my mind's eye; sometimes they work and are worth it, and sometimes not so much.

Regardless of the risk involved, my greatest hope is for the photographs on the following pages to communicate, visually, the rich and varied histories these places share. It is impossible to capture the feeling of standing within their walls. I have attempted, however, to capture their spirit, hence the title of my website: Spirits of the Abandoned. Many, if not all of them, are off limits to the public, and I am grateful to have accessed them while they were still standing and to share what hides behind their shuttered facades—may they inspire your imagination as much as they have mine.

Keep Adventuring!

~ Sue Tatterson
Gold Canyon, 2022

THE INN AT BUCK HILL FALLS

For decades, the remains of the once-grand Inn at Buck Hill Falls loomed over the idyllic Poconos Township of Baxter. Once the lifeblood of the township's villages, the inn fell into disrepair during the late 1980s and closed in 1990. Residents, tired of what they considered an eyesore and a danger, raised the more than $2 million required to demolish the stately, more than century-old, 400-room resort. Demolition began in December 2016 and was completed by early 2017. An illustrious past and ongoing work by Pennsylvania Preservation could not save the meandering 1,000-acre site from extinction. The inn's presence is now only a fading memory, honored by online history buffs and urban explorers.

During its glory days, so alluring were the inn's facilities, it hosted the likes of movie stars and magnates—including Walt Disney, who was enticed by the lawn bowling competition. The "grand dame" of Poconos resorts boasted an impressive array of amenities including an amphitheater, a twenty-seven-hole golf course, a bowling green, horseback riding, tennis courts, an outdoor pool measuring 165 feet long by 65 feet wide, which had an attached 50-foot-wide wing with diving boards, and an indoor pool with a retractable glass roof.

The history of the inn began in 1900 when Samuel E. Griscom, a Quaker, inherited the land from his father. From his first visit to the wilderness area with his sons in August of that year, he became enamored with the picturesque landscape and bewitched by the solitude the mountainous region offered. Griscom partnered with fellow Quakers, Charles and Howard Jenkins, and on December 31, 1900, the Buck Hill Falls Company, named for one of the stunning waterfalls in the area, was formed.

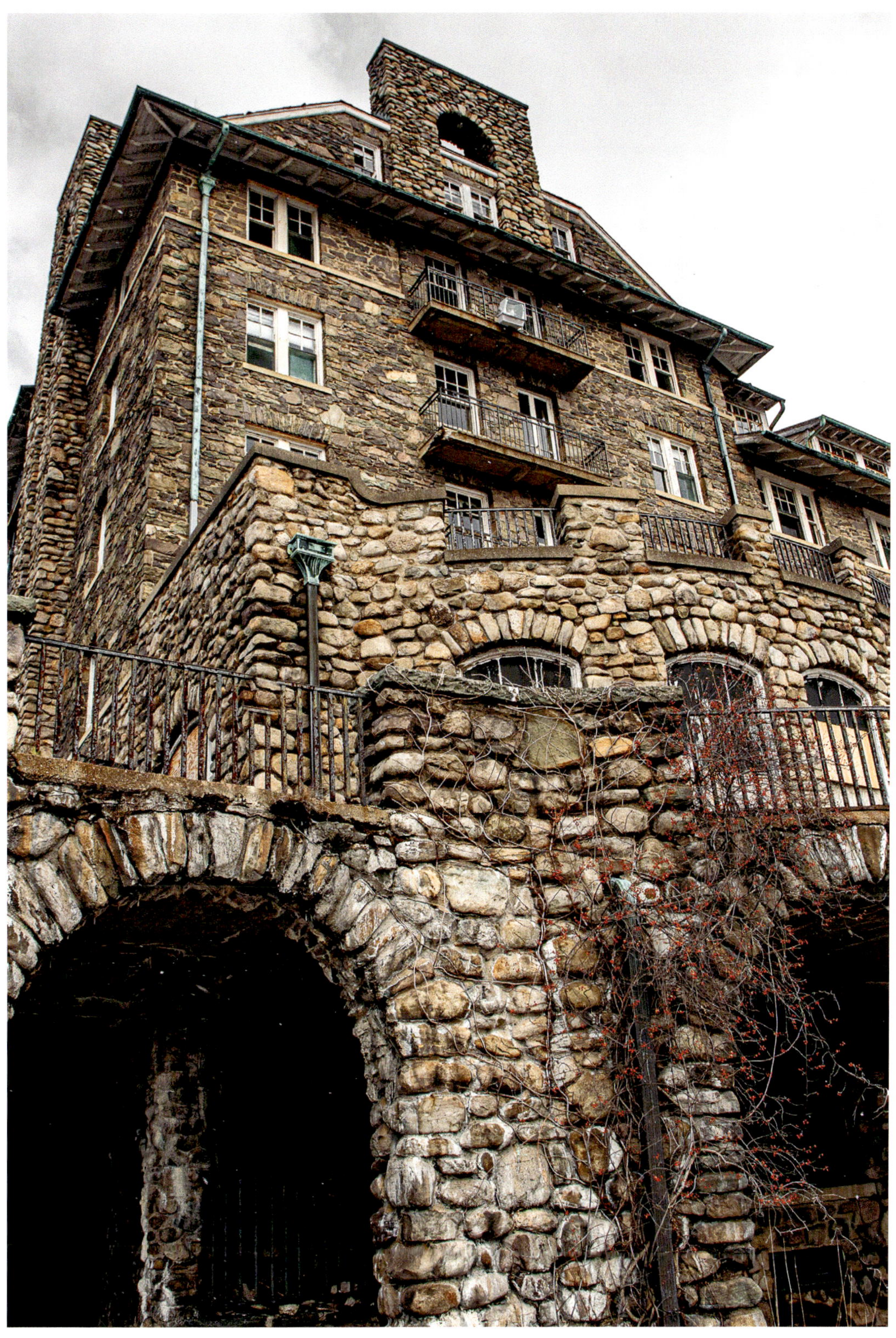

The imposing stone facade of the Inn at Buck Hill Falls.

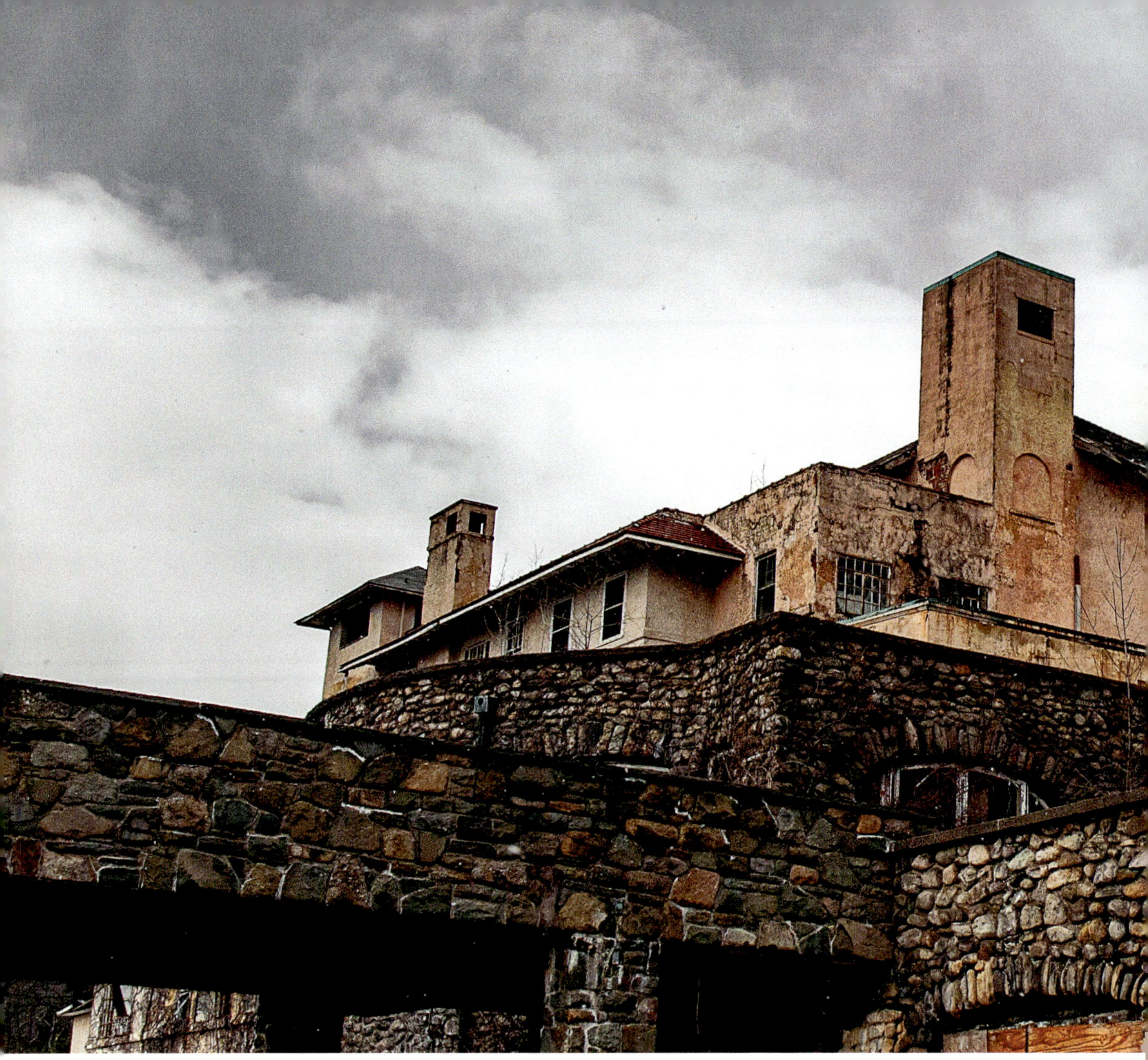

At the time, the Poconos area was fast becoming a popular getaway for prosperous New Yorkers. In less than a year, forty-three lots had been purchased and the rapid growth of what would become the celebrated inn began. The company hired the Philadelphia architectural firm of Bunting and Shrigley to design the facilities and Olmsted and Associates—the landscape company headed by Frederick Olmsted Jr., the son of Frederick Olmsted, the famed Central Park landscape architect—to complete the planning and implementation of the lush grounds.

In 1923, after more than twenty years of constant expansion, the iconic four-story Pennsylvania stone hotel was added. Built in the Mission Revival style, the structure's graceful arches welcomed wealthy and famous visitors for decades to come. In 1935, economist Rexford Tugwell hosted a conference at the inn as part of the New Deal's Resettlement Administration. Eleanor Roosevelt was in attendance, and according to the guest register from June 6, 1935, she stayed in room 534.

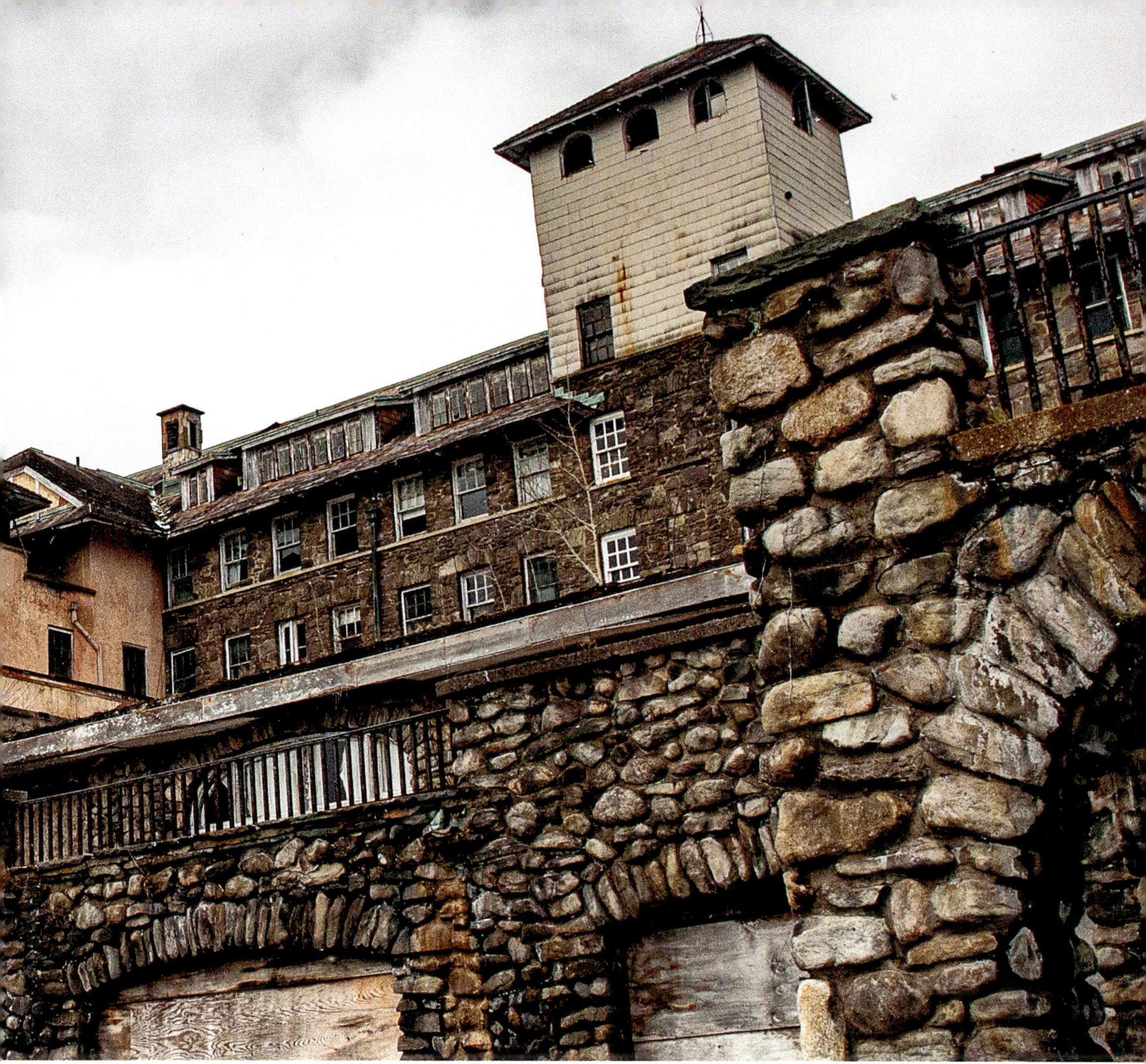

The inn's decline, along with many others in the region, began in the 1960s and is credited, largely, to the rapid expansion of the airline industry—New Yorkers suddenly had access to more exotic locations at affordable prices. By the late 1970s, the Buck Hill Falls Company could no longer afford the operational costs and in 1977 sold the inn to its president and CEO, Walter Sabo. Little more than four years later, Sabo sold the still struggling inn to Astrid and Jacob Kueller.

The Kuellers believed the revival of the inn depended on marketing the declining resort as an ideal location for conferences. While their plan was not enough to save the Inn at Buck Hill Falls, their efforts did not go unnoticed; in a 1985 edition of *Inflight* magazine, the inn was named as one of the top ten conference centers in the country. Only five years later, in 1990, Jacob Kueller would close the doors of the financially struggling resort once and for all.

The eventual shuttering of the once-bustling resort was, sadly, inevitable, and after a decade of desertion and decline, the inescapable rumors began. Fueled by an MTV episode of *Fear*, a reality program that ran from 2000 through 2002, stories of murder and hauntings took on a life of their own, as they seem wont to do when their impetus is an immense, derelict edifice.

The title sequence of the *Fear* episode alludes to multiple on-site murders and reports of mysteries hauntings—none of which are true. The damage, however, was done, and the internet rumor mill fed upon the fabricated stories of death and the supernatural, causing the inn to become a popular destination for thrill seekers and vandals. According to a 2006 article in *The Pocono Record*, since the airing of the 2001 *Fear* episode, between fifty and 100 trespassers had been apprehended each year.

Rarely is Mother Nature the sole reason for a building's demise, and in the case of the Inn at Buck Hill Falls, this proved undeniably true. The increased level of interest was blamed for several fires that devastated the outer buildings, and the vandalism of the interior all but sealed the once "grand dame" of Poconos resorts' fate.

In July 2017, after decades of false starts at redevelopment, some as recently as 2014, when sealed bids were called for, the last stone walls of the historically significant behemoth succumbed to the wrecking ball. Today the former site is owned and managed by the Buck Hill Conservation Foundation. The last enduring vestige, the former East Room fireplace, stands proudly on the 16-acre parcel of land where the inn once stood and has been designated as a "Clean and Green" space. The fireplace hearth bears the inscription "The Simple Life and Friendly Cheer May all those find who gather here"—a more deserving and accurate accolade than the one bestowed by the illusion created by "reality" television.

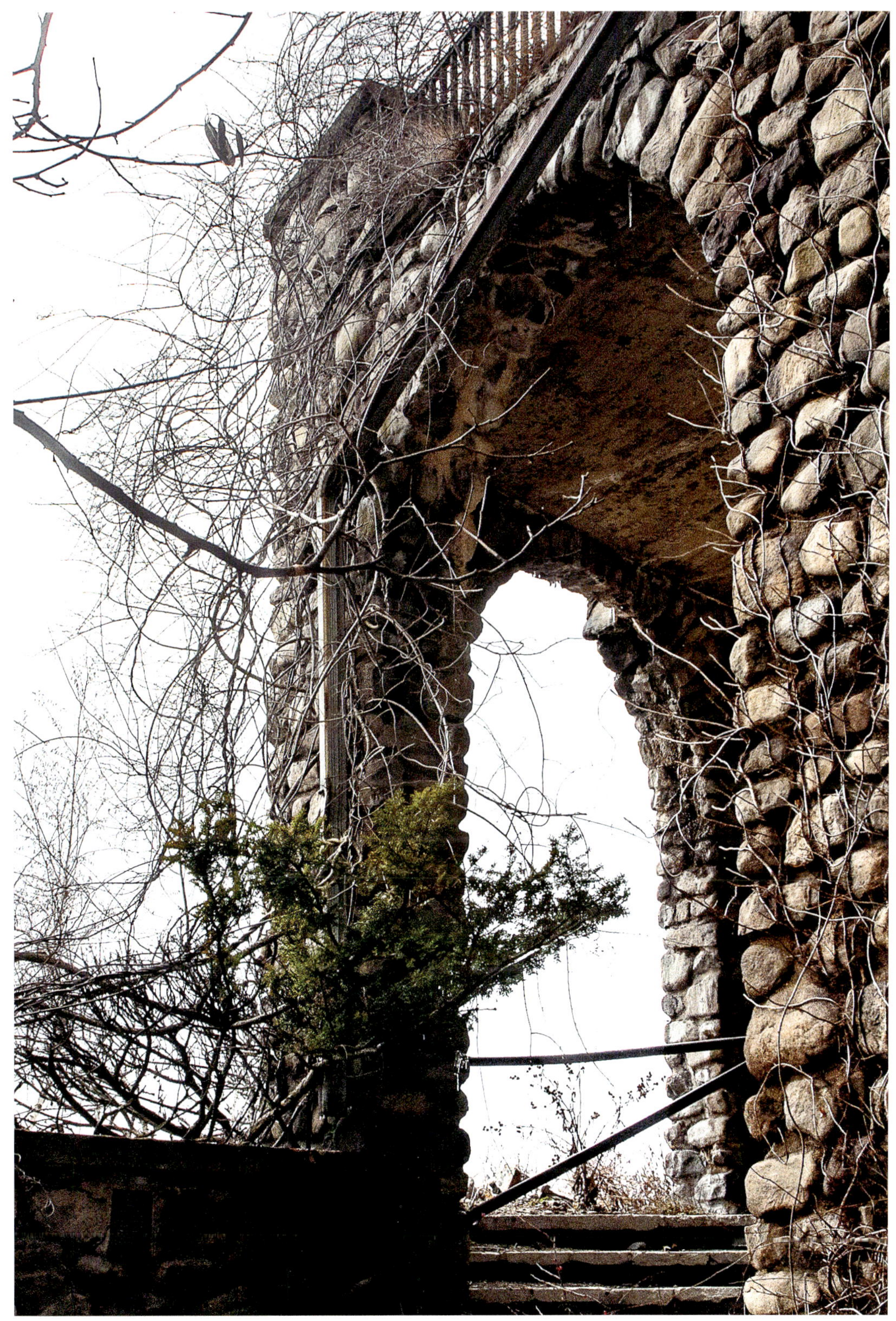

Graceful stone arches greeted guests.

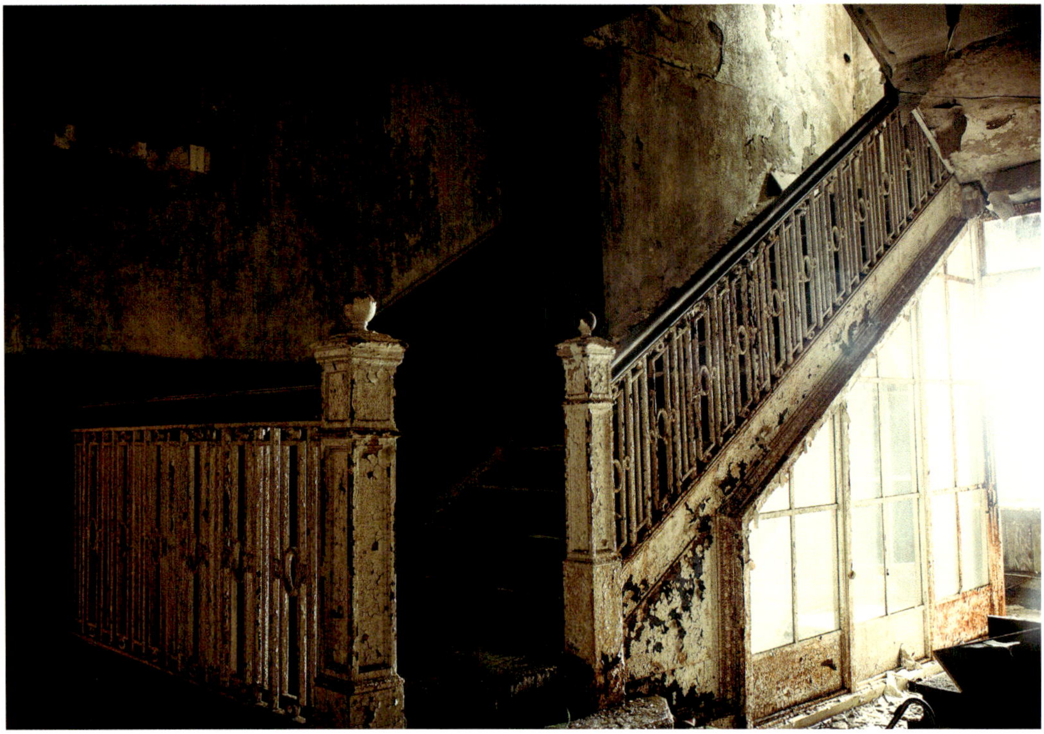

A haunting light falls on a decrepit stairway.

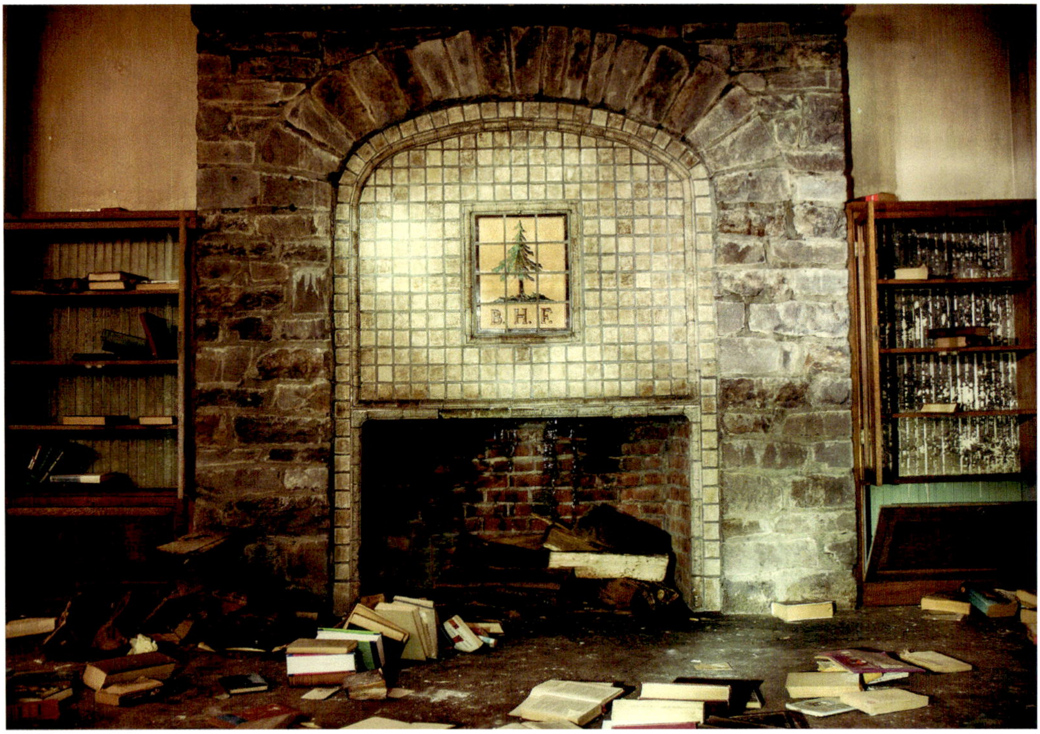

The fireplace in the library.

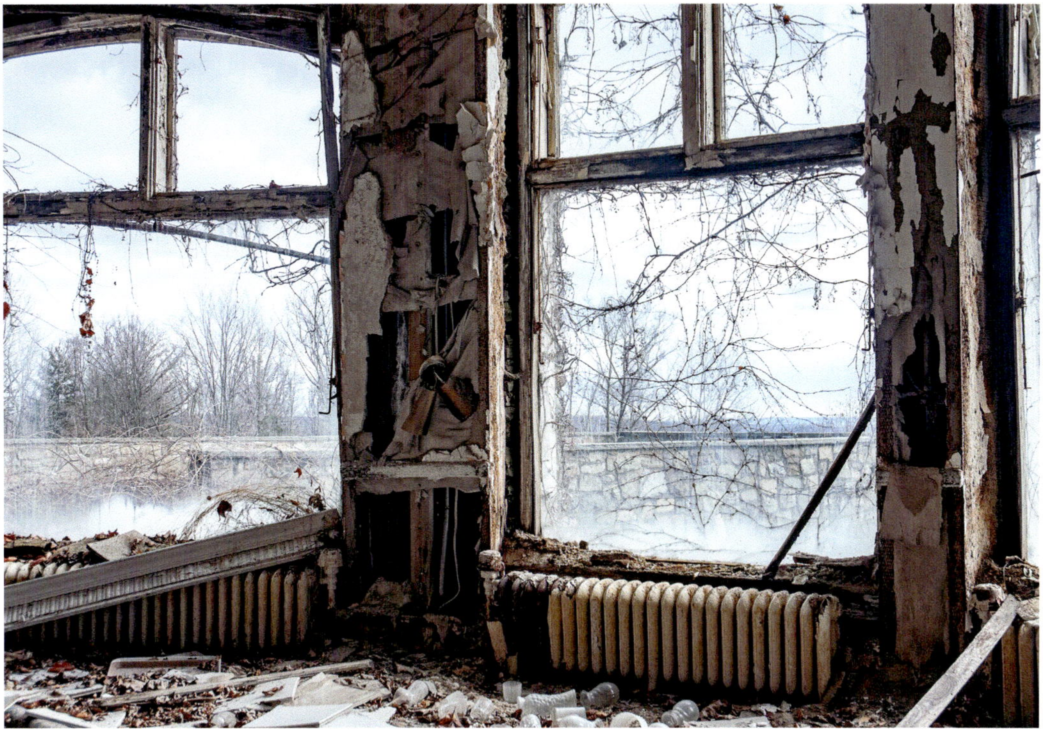

Water damage is evident in many of the rooms.

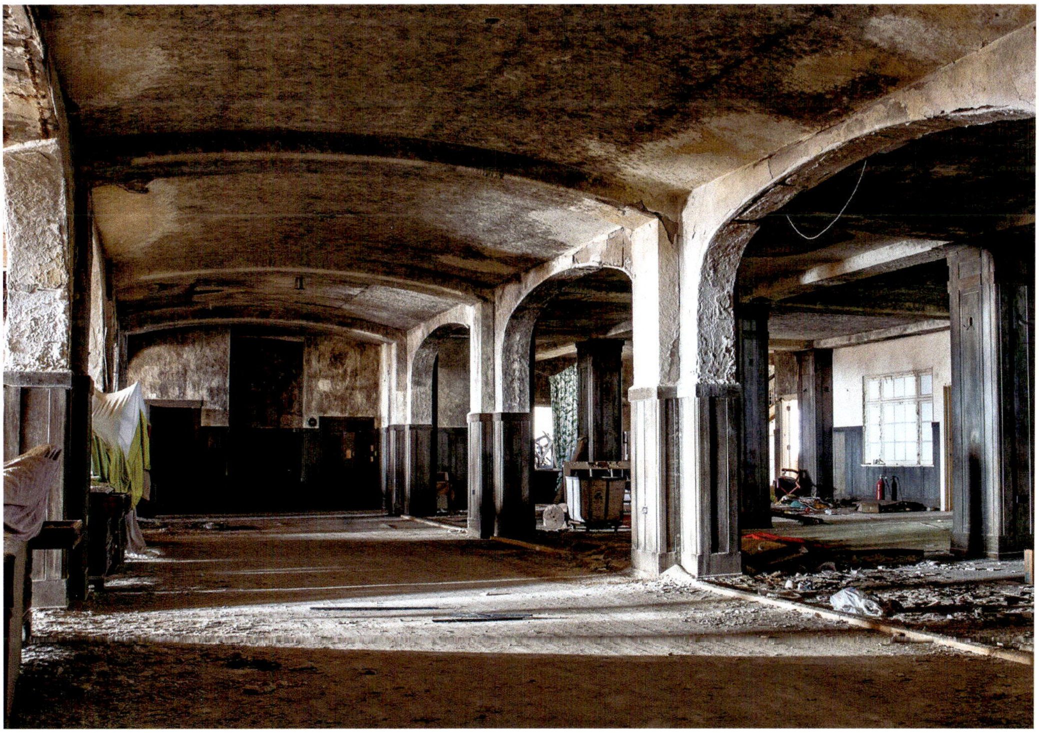

A wide hallway in the east wing.

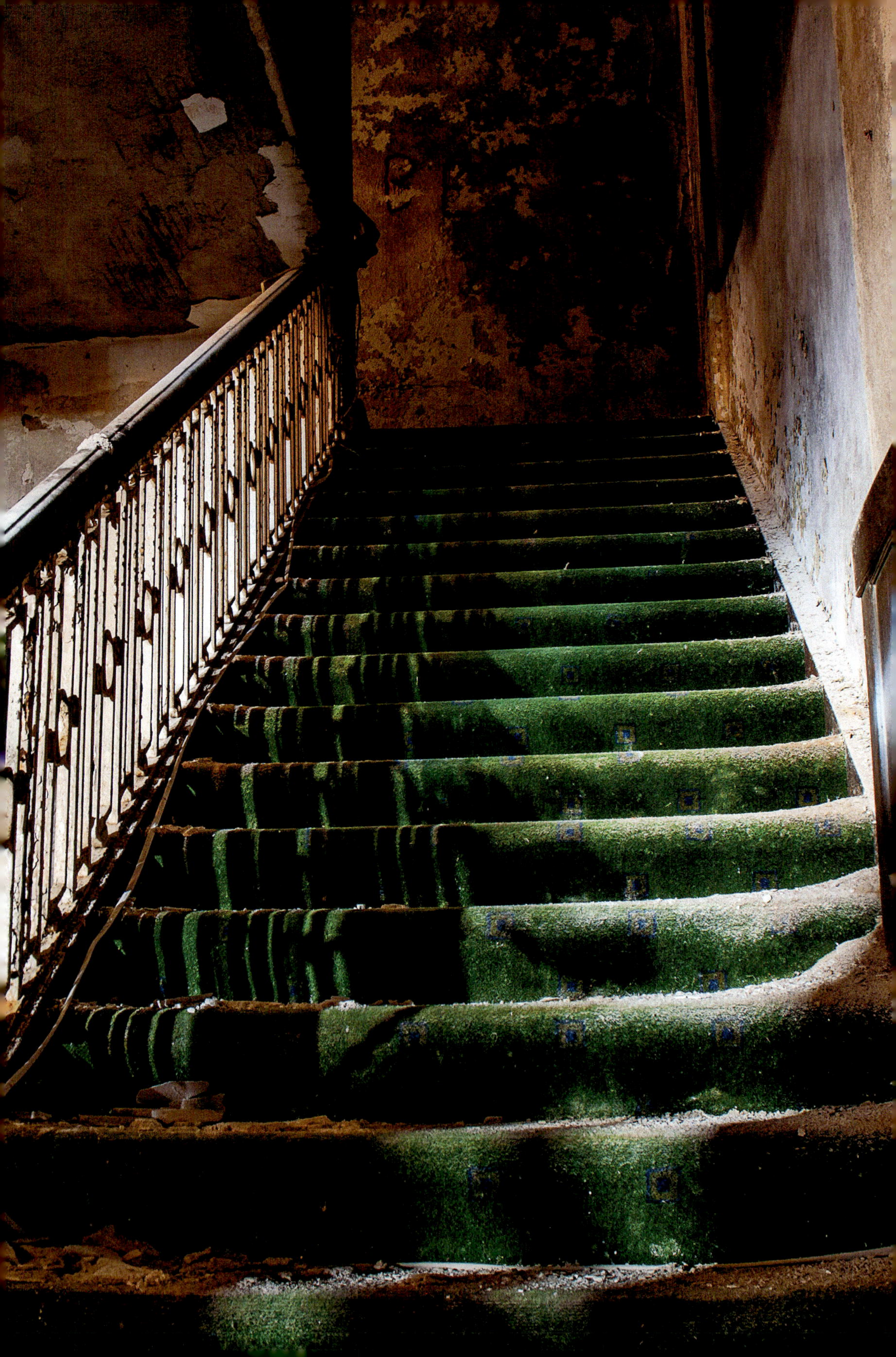

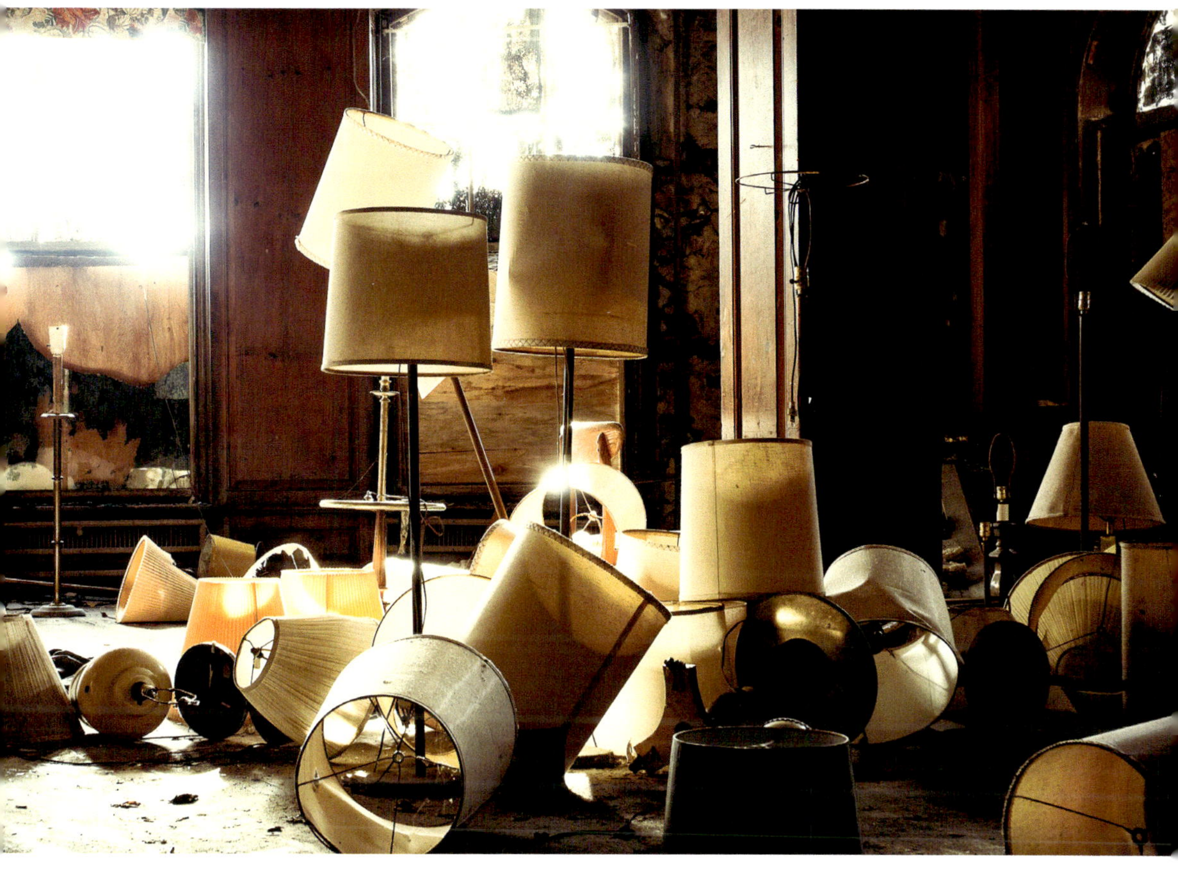

Above: Discarded lampshades glow in the afternoon light.

Opposite page: Dust gathers on the rich, green-carpeted stairs, while a creepy warning is graffitied on the landing.

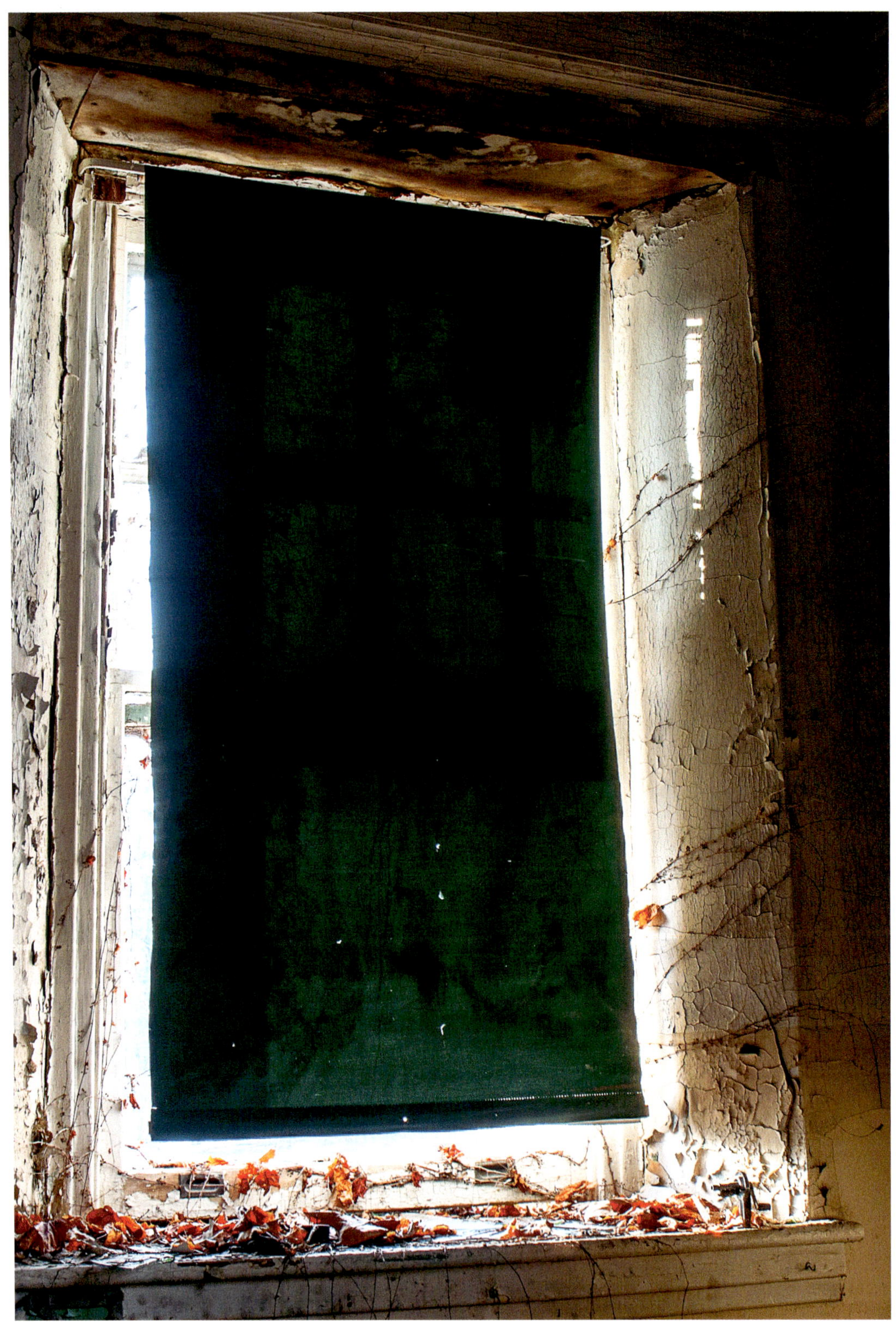

Nature reclaiming a windowsill.

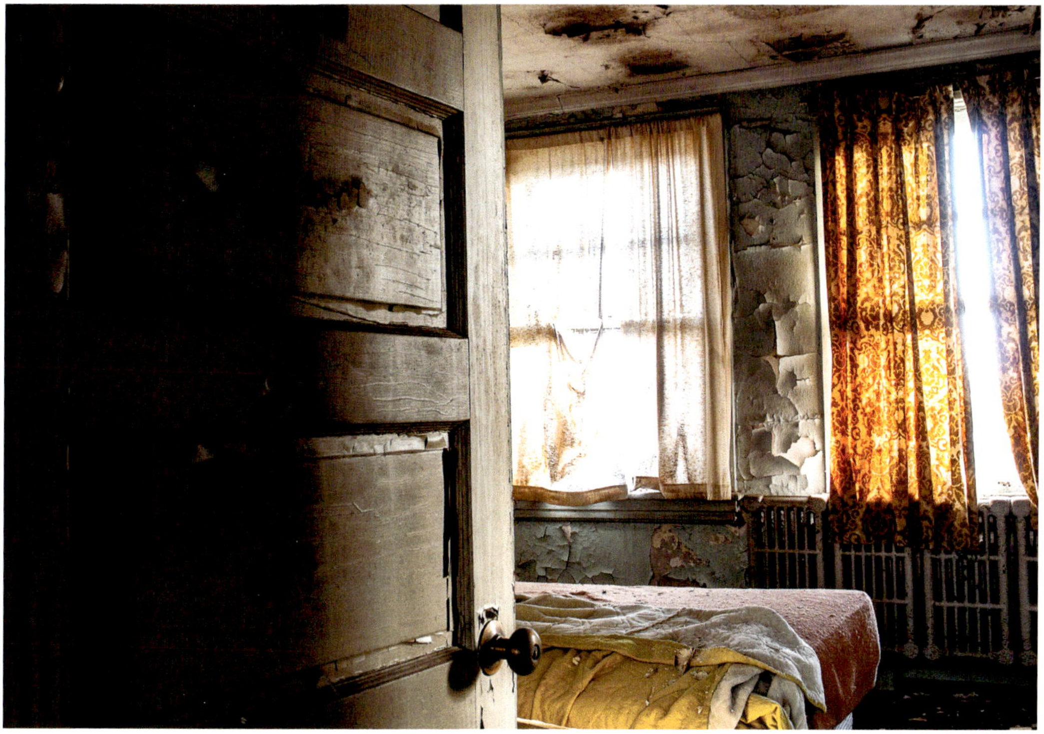

An open door reveals a decaying guest room.

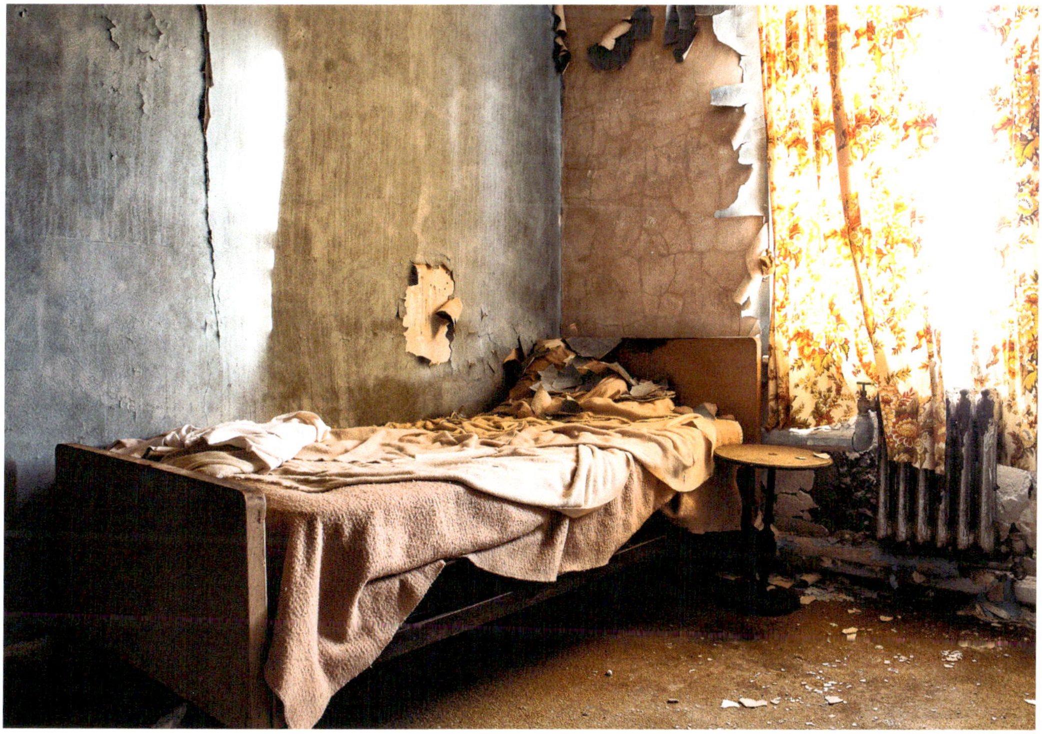

Sunlight streams through a brightly colored curtain into a guest room.

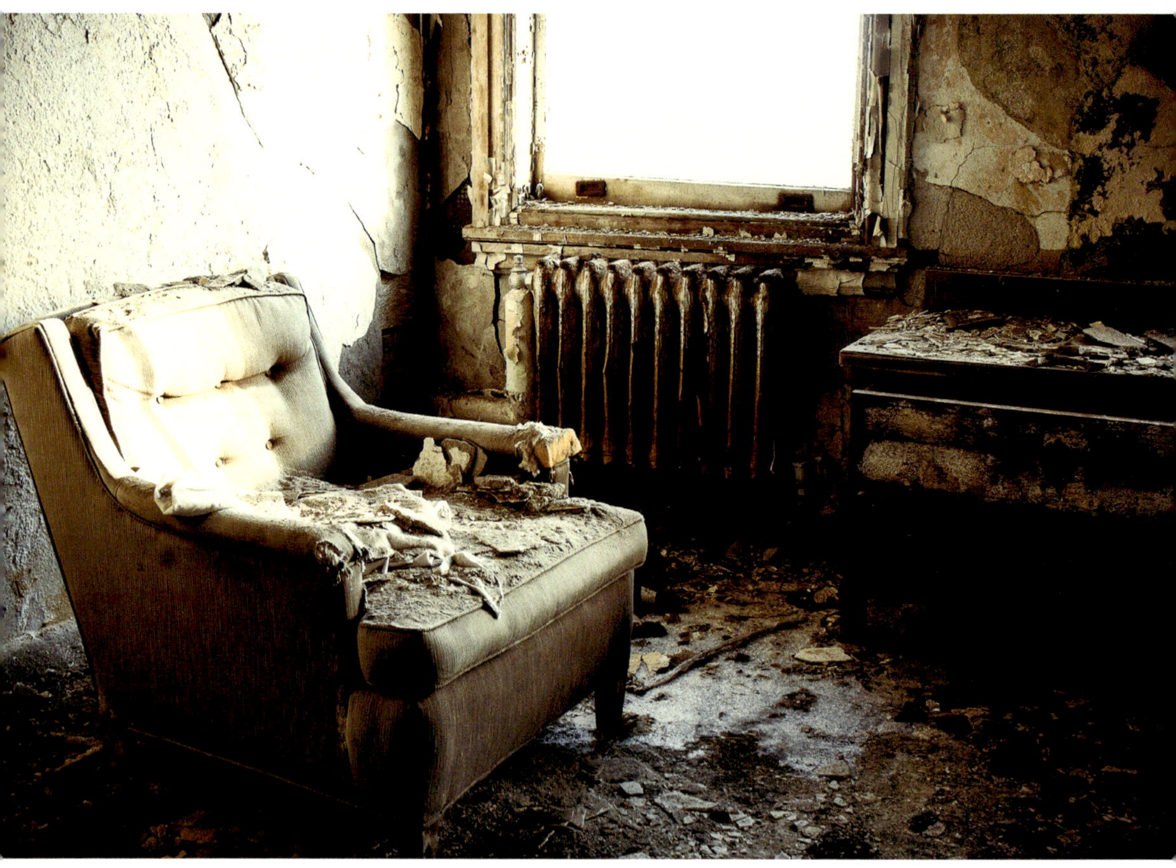

A once-comfortable armchair now surrounded by filth.

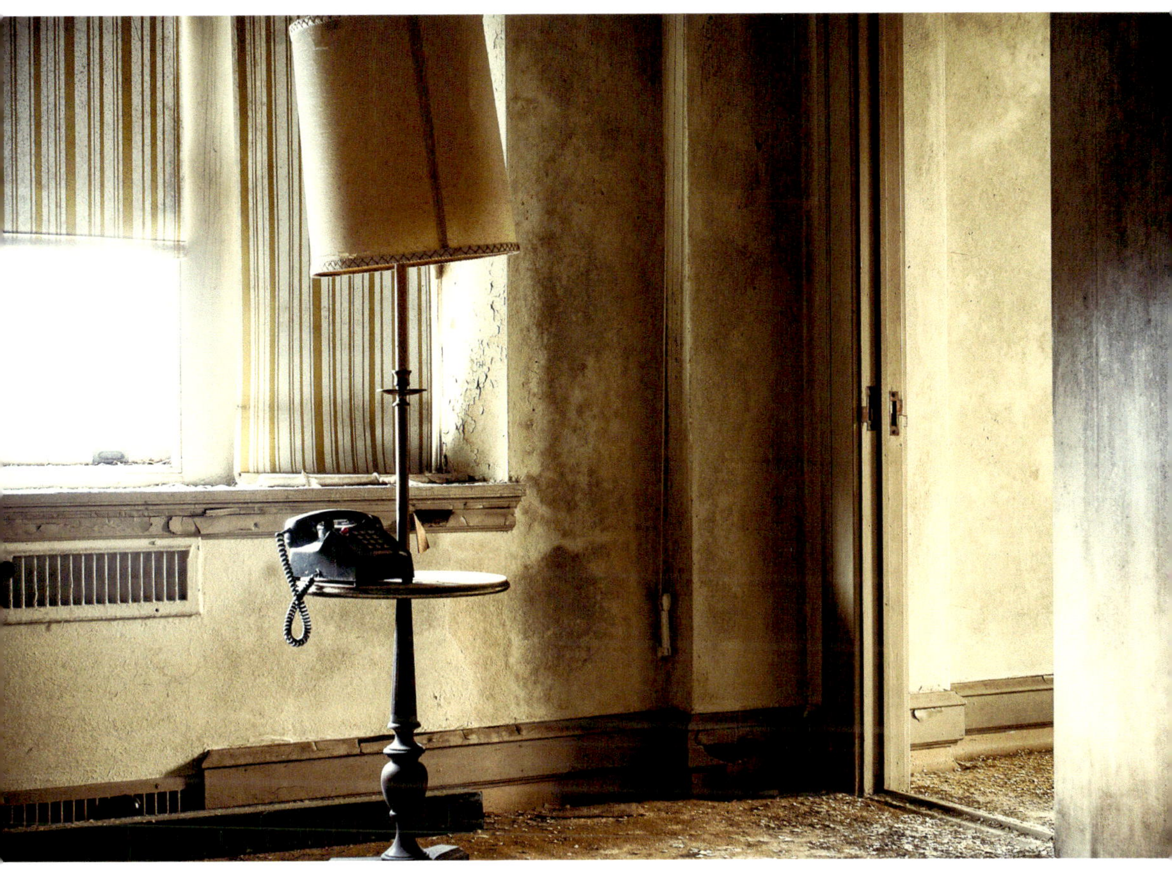

A disconnected telephone; a relic from another era.

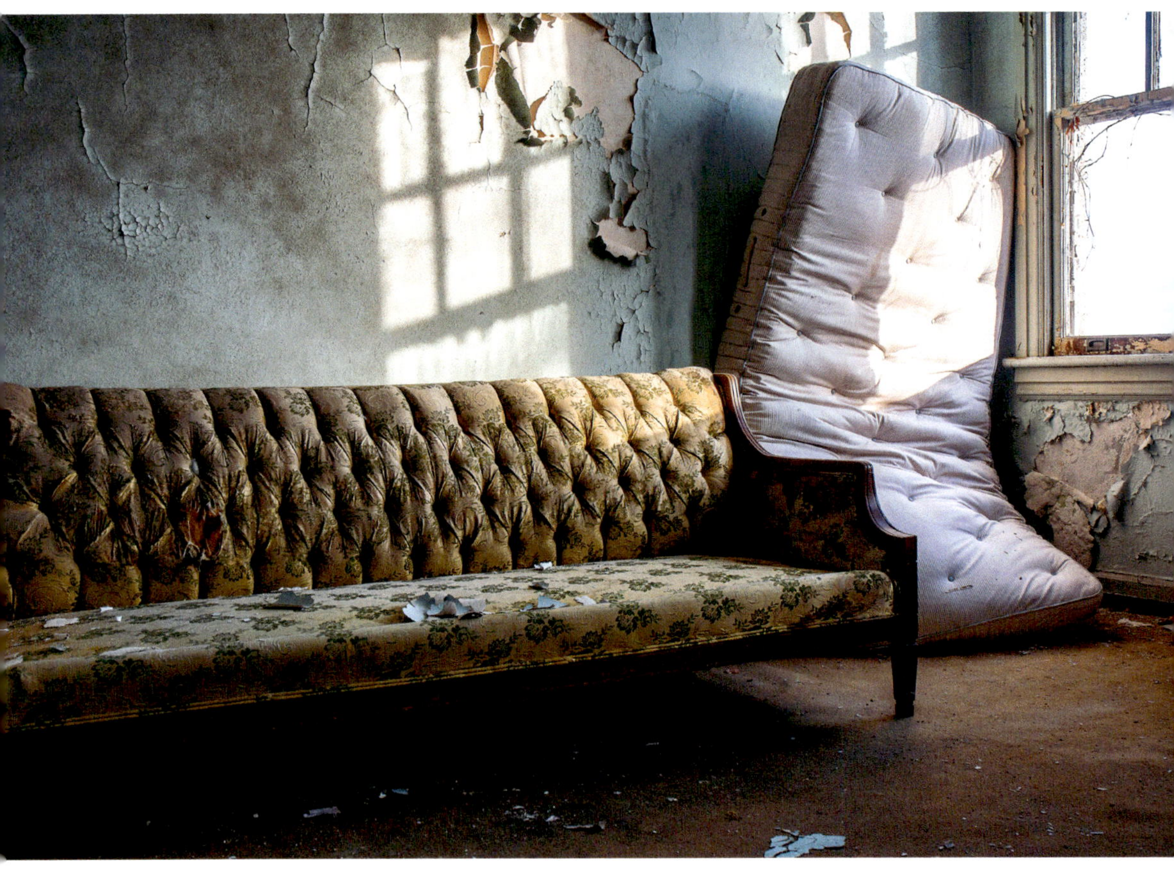

An expensive chaise lounge, left to rot, along with a mattress in one of the guest suites.

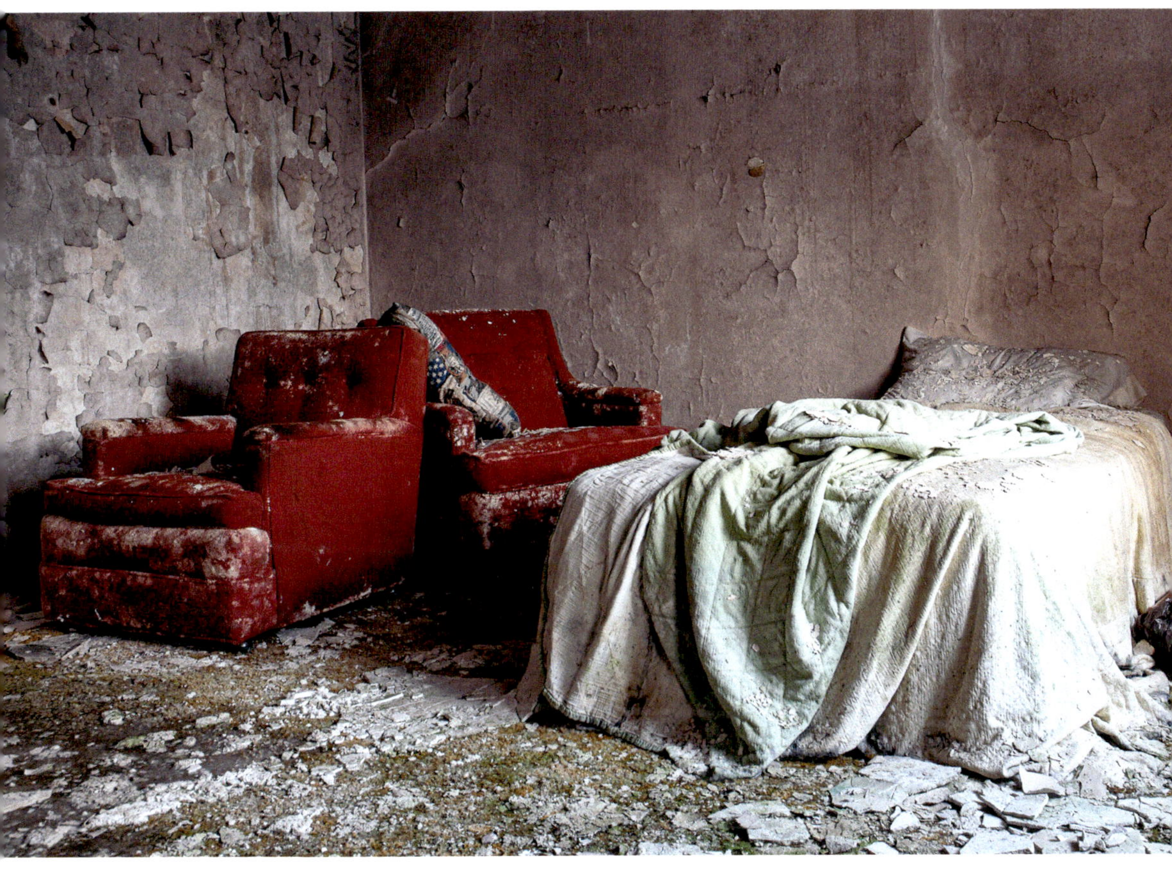

Plaster and peeling paint cover bright red armchairs and a sagging bed.

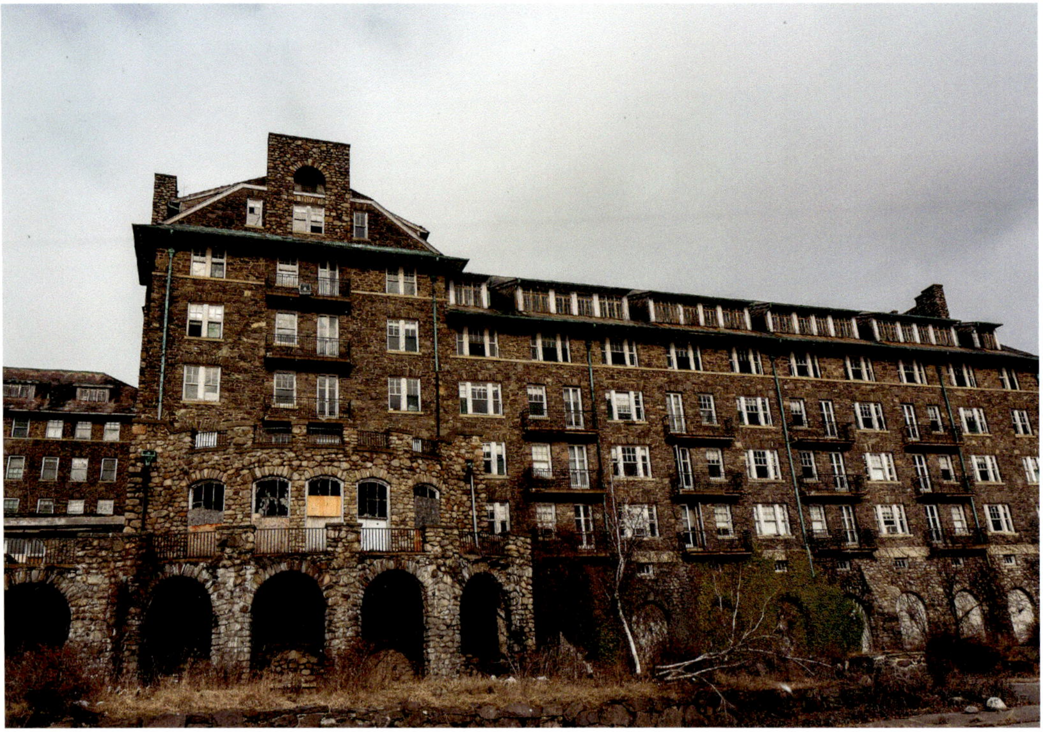

The main building of the inn consisted of three wings.

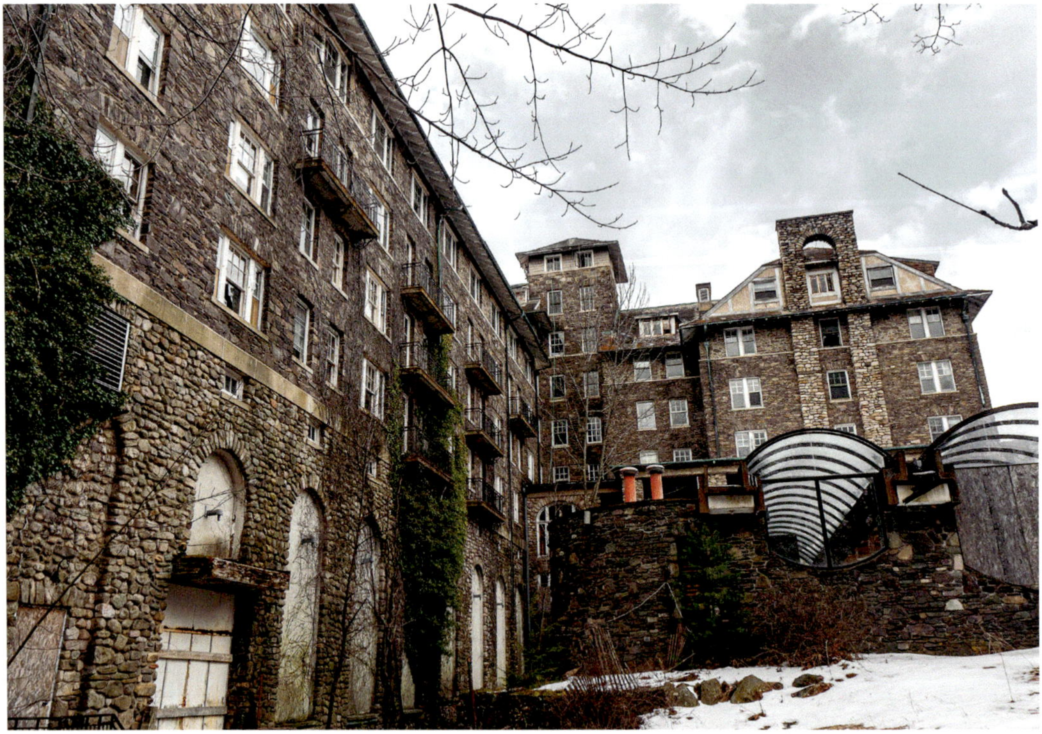

The main building overlooking the indoor pool.

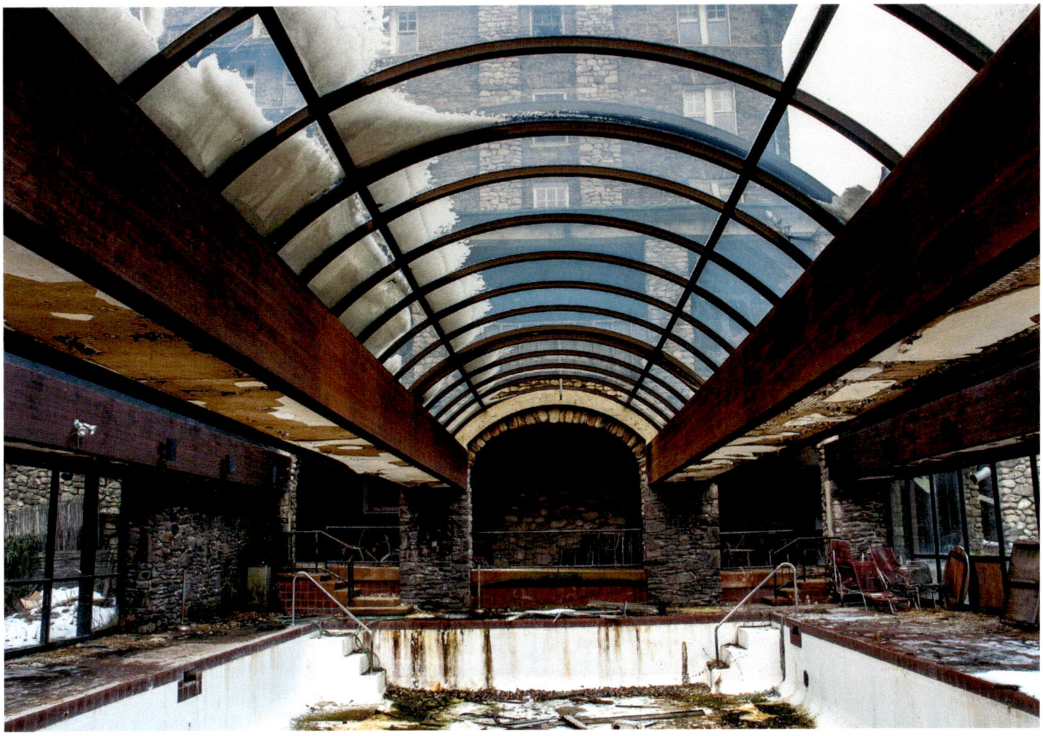

The glass-enclosed heated pool with a vista-dome roof.

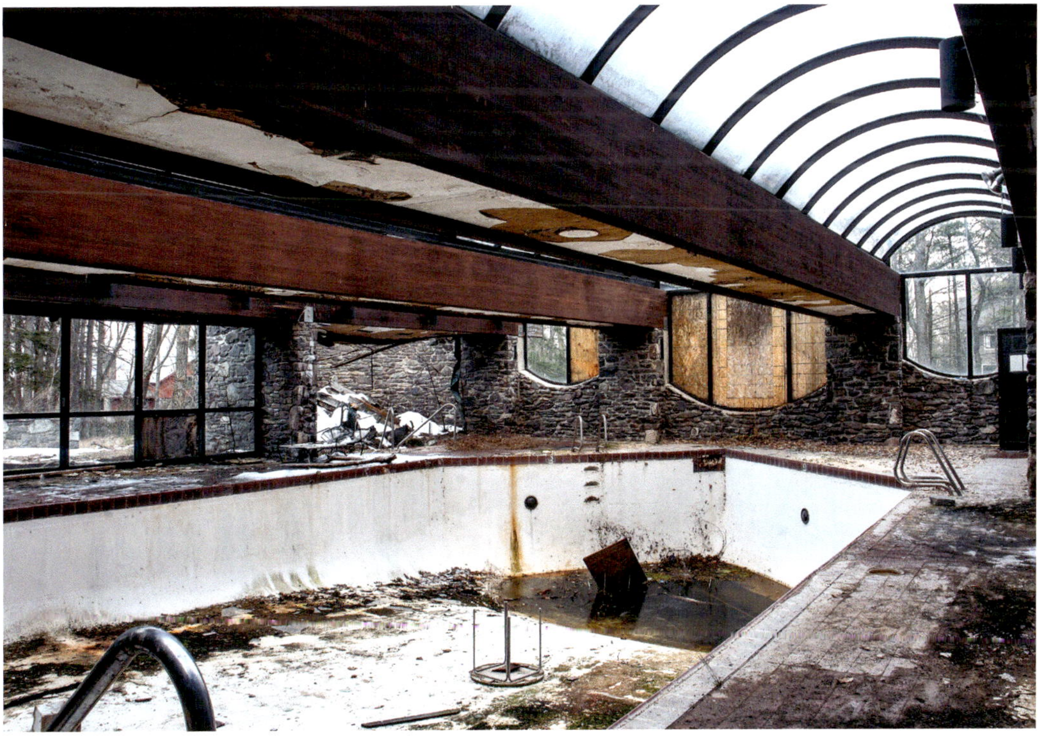

What remains of the once-stunning indoor pool area.

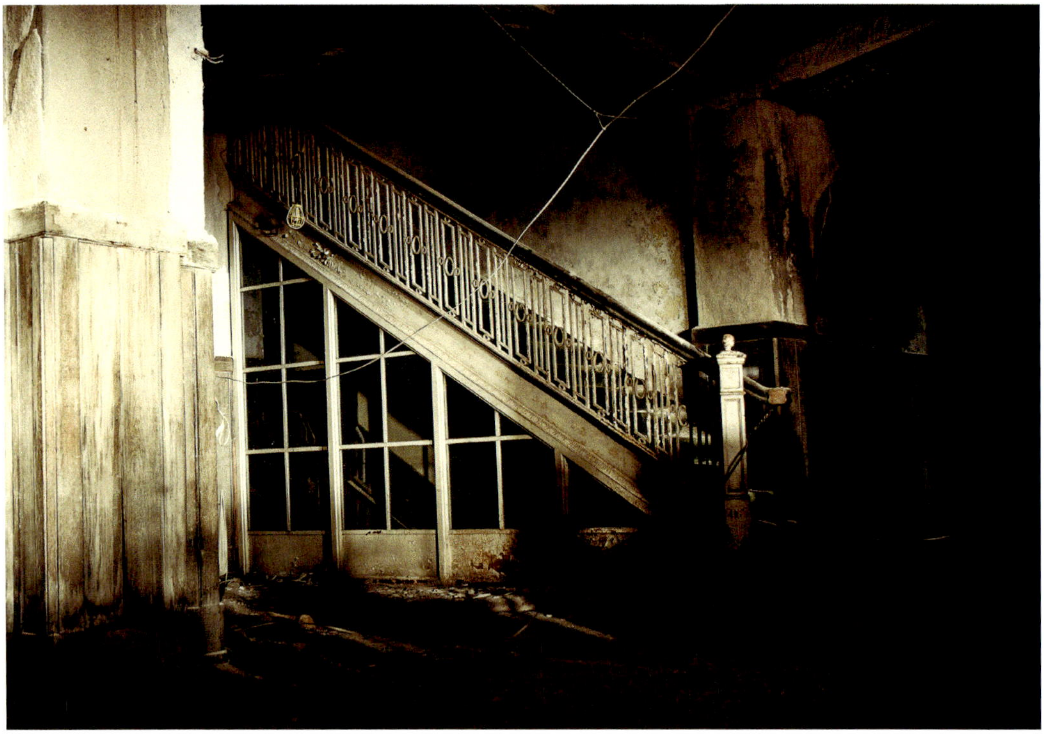

Wires hang from the ceiling in an eerily lit hallway.

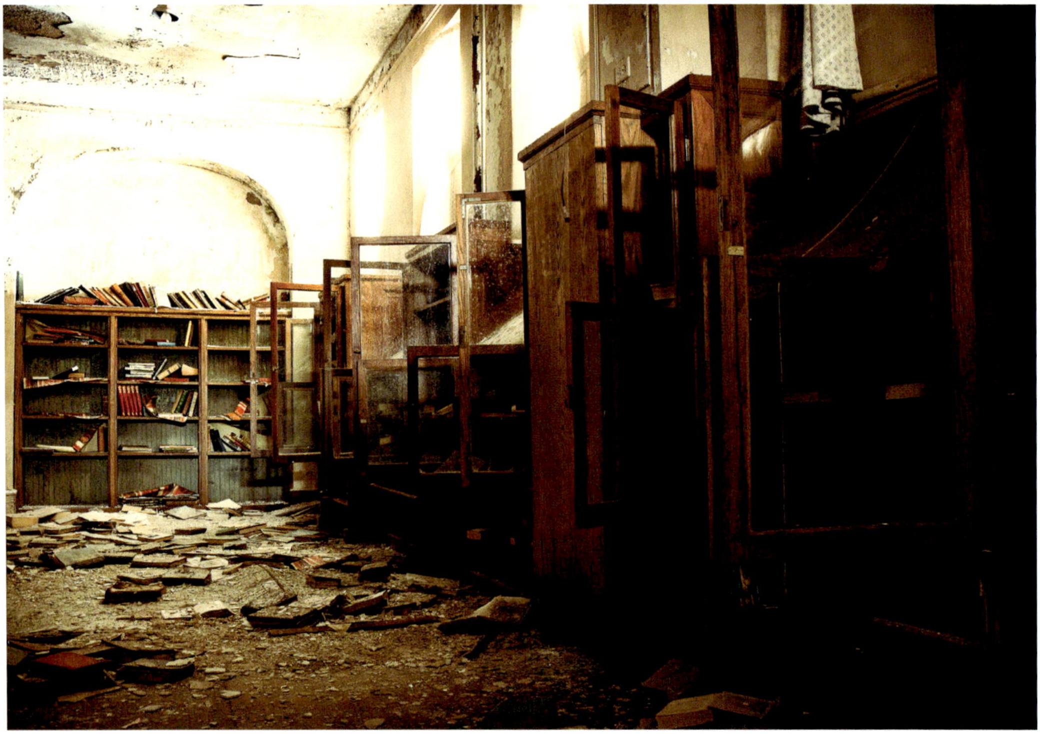

Books strewn over the floor in the Greenleaf Library.

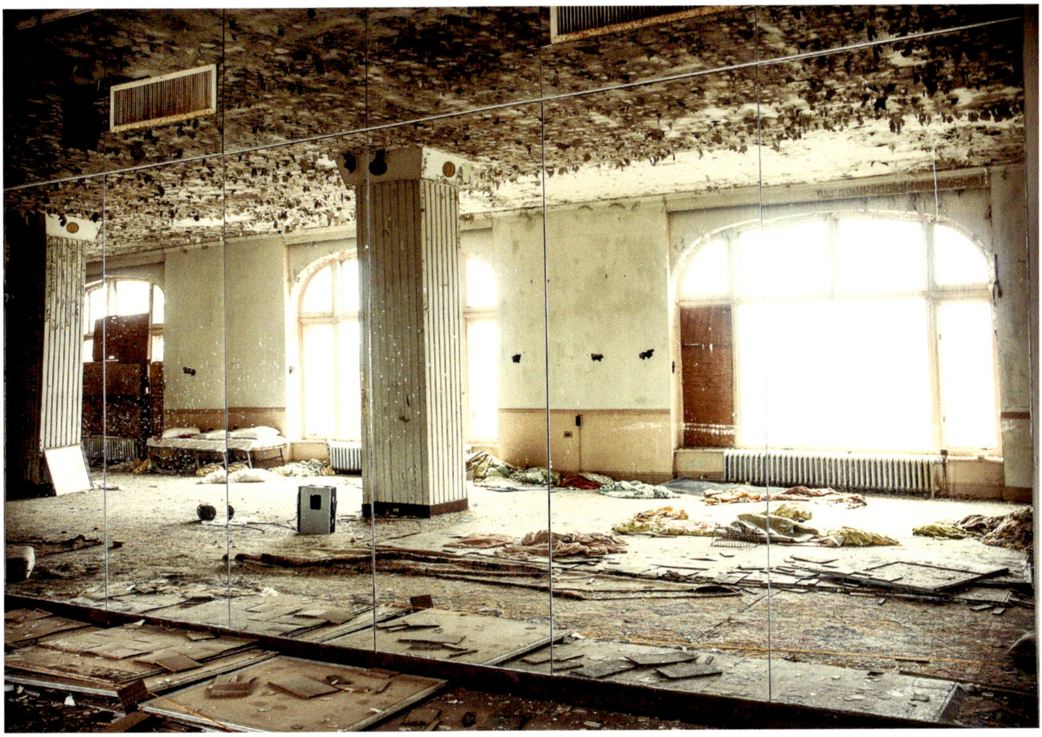

A mirrored room, possibly used for dance rehearsals.

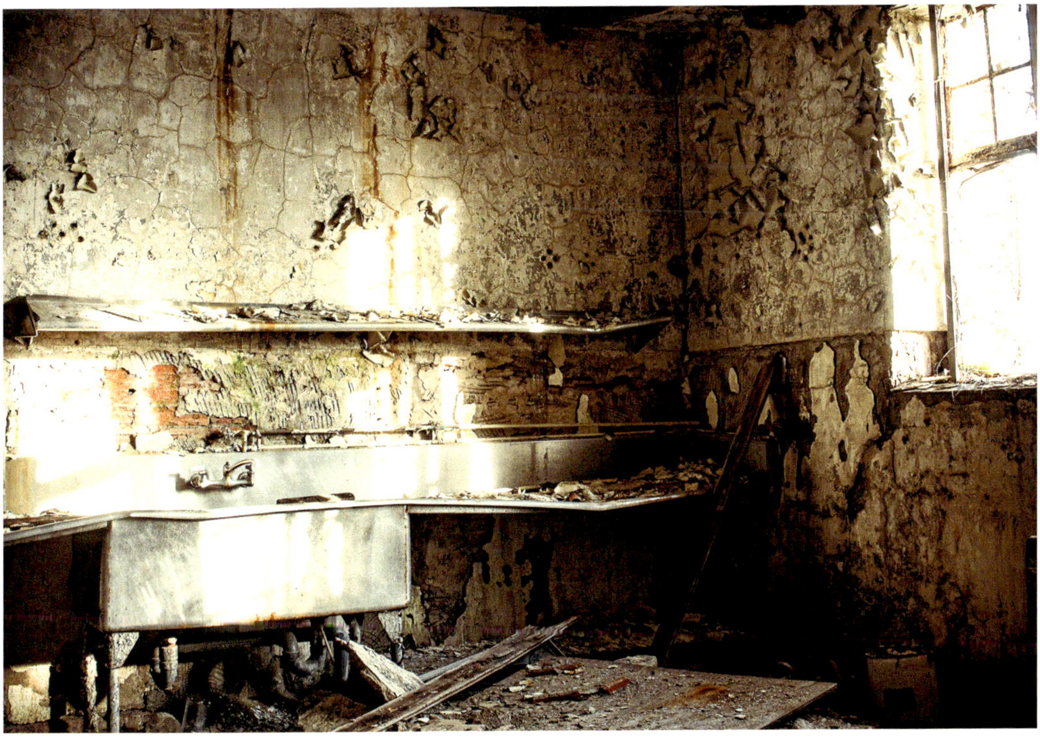

A laundry trough surrounded by decaying walls.

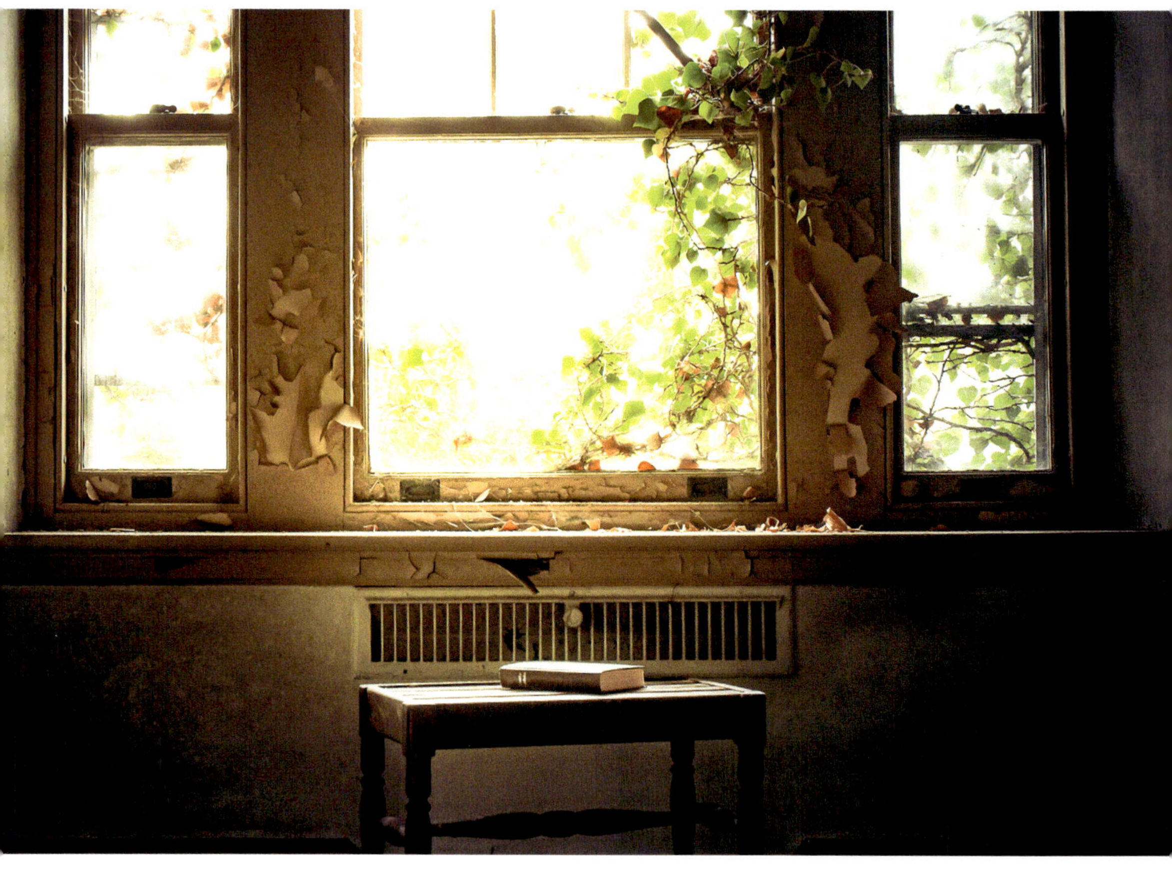

A solitary book in the sunlight creates a peaceful scene.

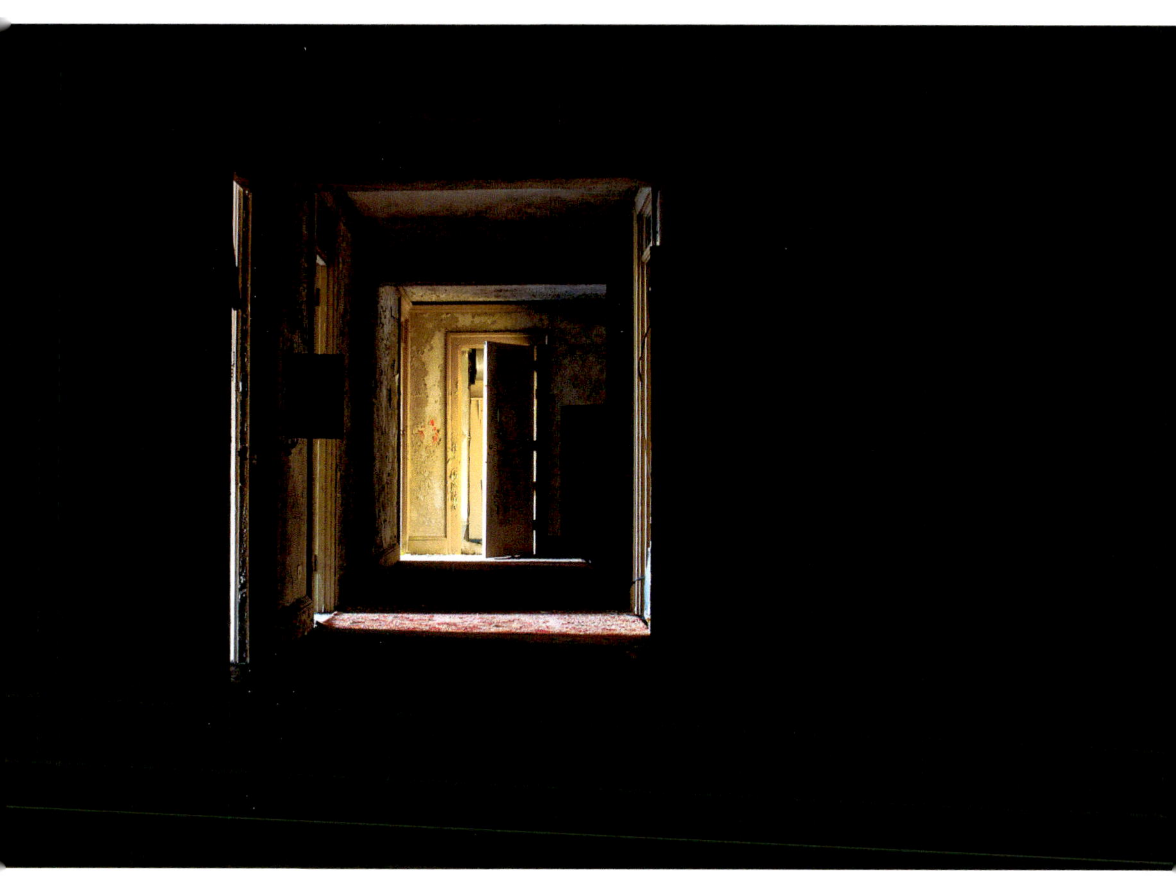

A darkened hallway leads to a brightly colored door.

RICHMOND POWER GENERATING STATION

Rising resolutely from the banks of the Delaware River, the Richmond Power Generating Station, a former giant of Philadelphia's industrial boom, awaits its fate. Conservationists favor an adaptive-reuse approach, while current owners, Excelon, remain non-committal on the station's future. The immense monument of a bygone era, designed by architect John T. Windrim and chief engineer of the Philadelphia Electrical Company (PECO), W. C. L. Elgin, was once touted as "The Most Handsome Station in America." Today, the Beaux Arts-inspired cathedralesque structure faces ongoing deterioration from natural as well as man-made elements.

During its heyday, the state-of-the-art plant powered Philadelphia's ever-growing industrialization as the city claimed the title "Workshop of the World." Turbine Hall, a 125-foot-high imposing towering glass and steel cavern, was as much a showcase for new technology as it was utilitarian. The coal-devouring goliath was converted to gas in the 1970s, and by the mid-1980s, it became obsolesced with the decline in Philadelphia's population, industry, and employment.

Deterioration set in and led to the historic edifice being sought after by Hollywood location scouts. The number of times the Richmond station has actually been used for film production becomes confusing when researched as most of the filming seems to have occurred at Richmond's "sister" plant, the Delaware Generating Station. Richmond Power is credited with playing host to the *Transformers II* production, as well as *12 Monkeys*. Interestingly, the station that once provided power is now in fact powerless, and massive generators are set up on site to provide the Hollywood blockbusters with the power needed to create otherworldly sets.

Merciless intrusions by the elements and scrappers over the past decade are taking their toll, and signs of serious decline are threatening the building's structure. Water cascades through the shattered areas of the glass roof and rust is enveloping what remains of the once progressive machinery. Hope still remains though, as the neighboring Delaware Power Station, in the same state of disrepair, has recently been purchased for redevelopment as event space and water view apartments. With perseverance and foresight, the future of the Richmond Power Generating Station need not be bleak.

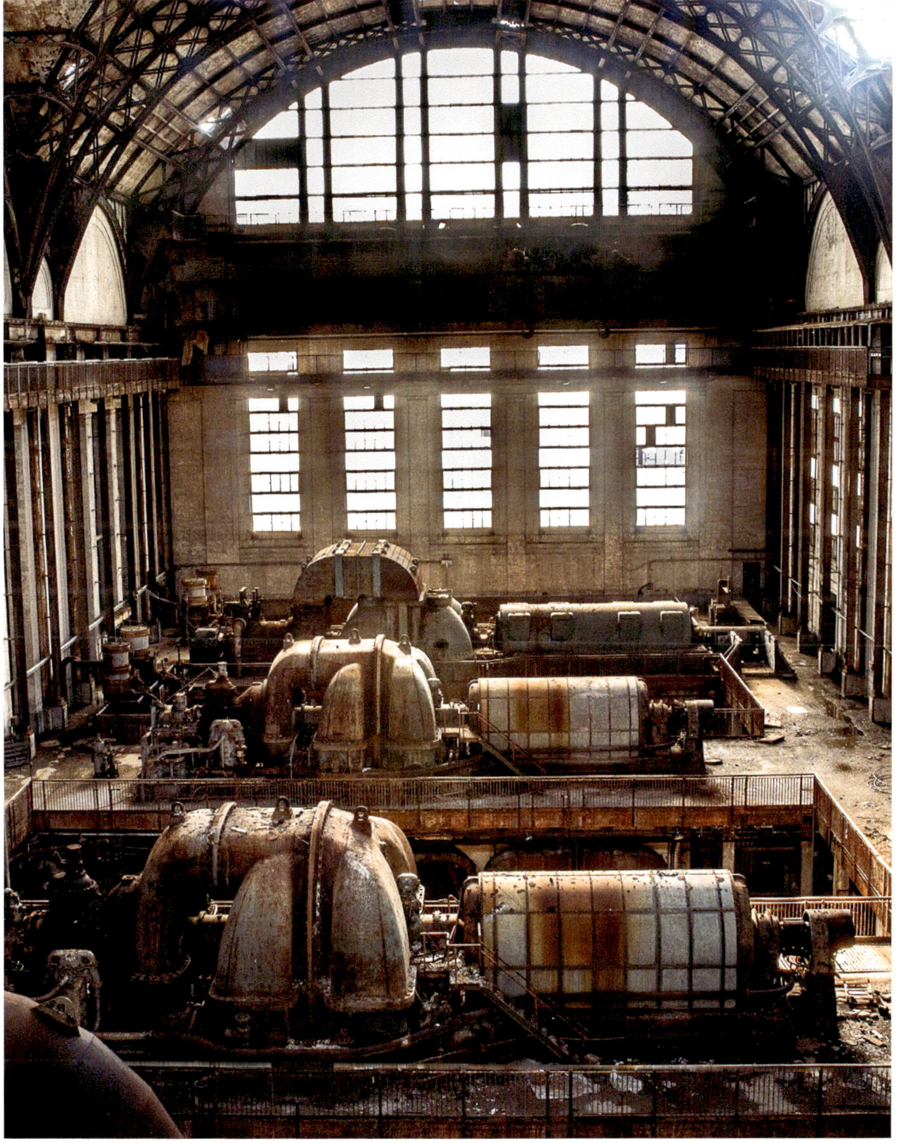

Richmond Power's turbine hall.

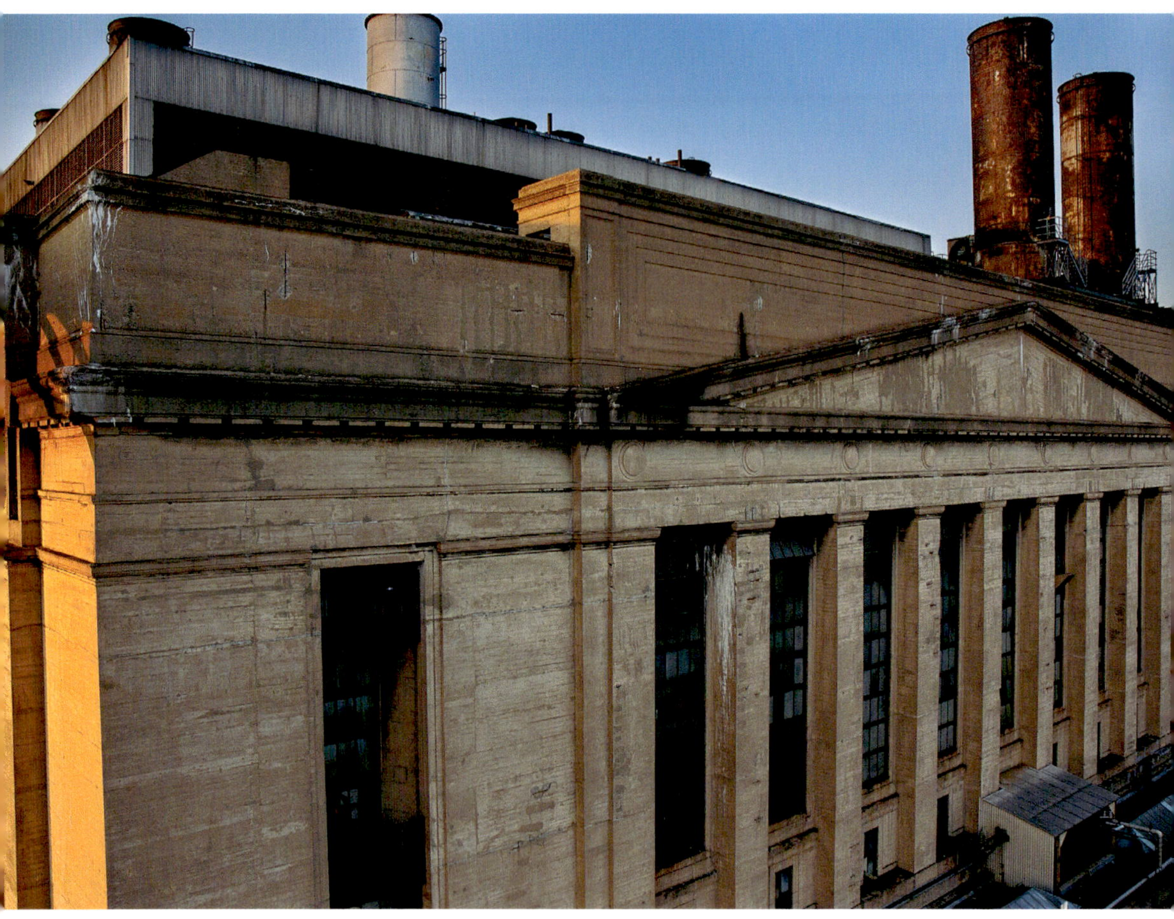

The imposing Beaux Arts-inspired exterior.

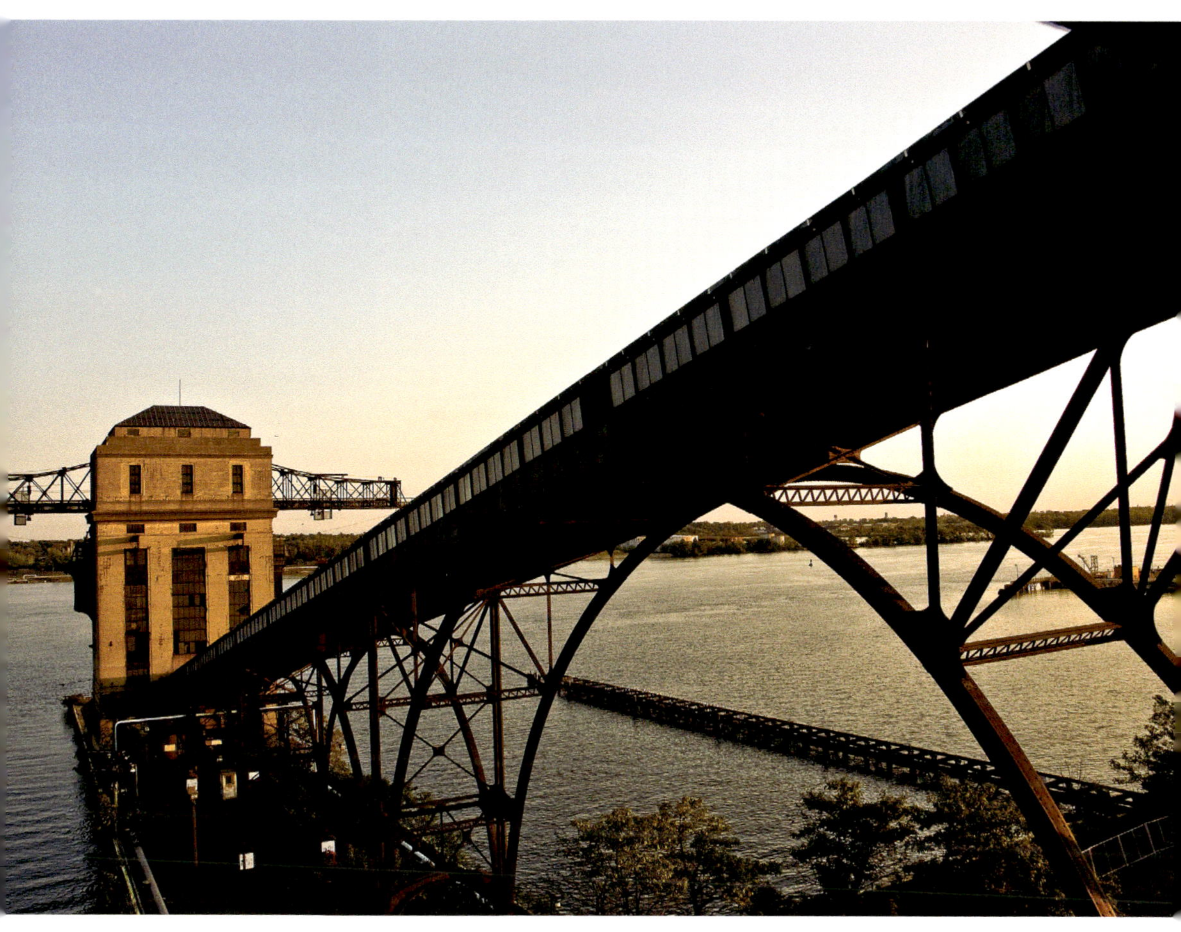

A view of the steel-framed coal conveyer.

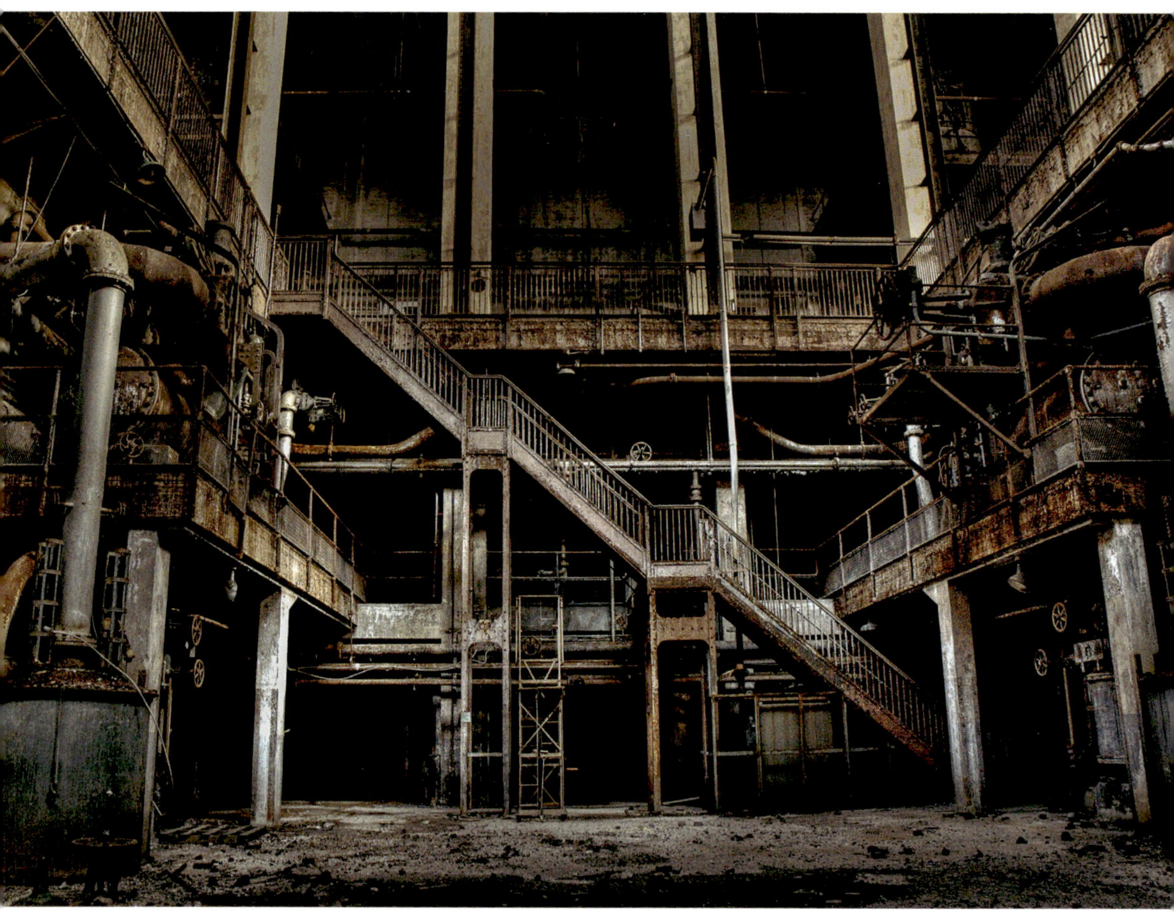

Never-ending stairs complete the industrial portrait of an icon.

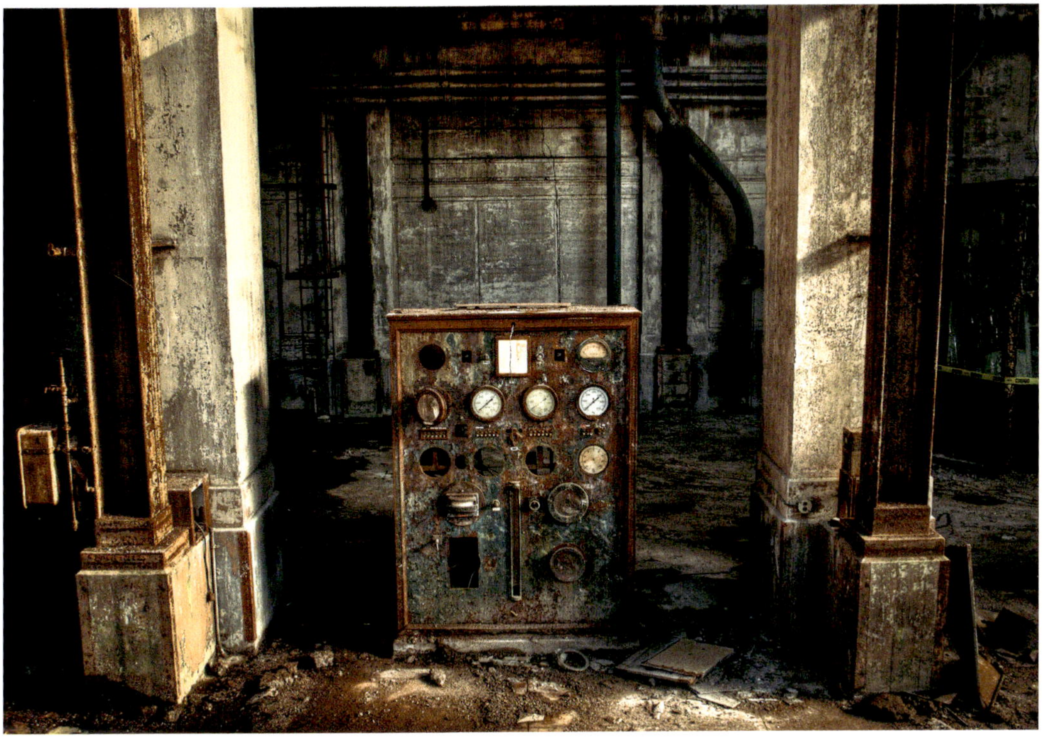

Antiquated machinery that could be reimagined as a time machine.

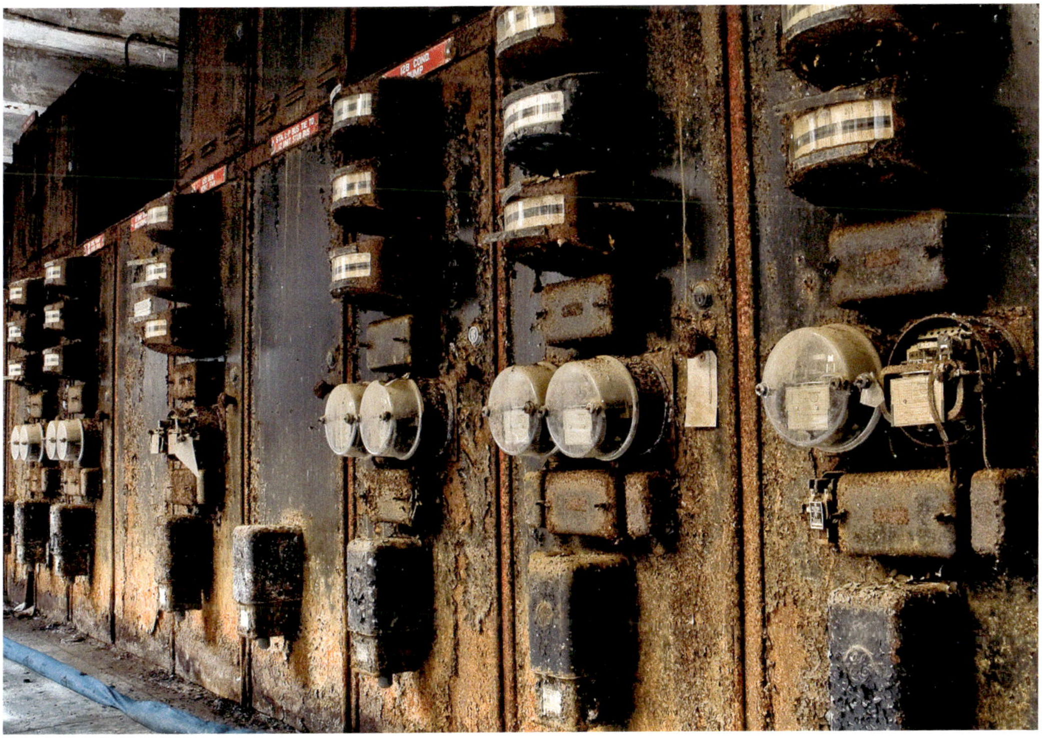

A section of the plant near the main control room.

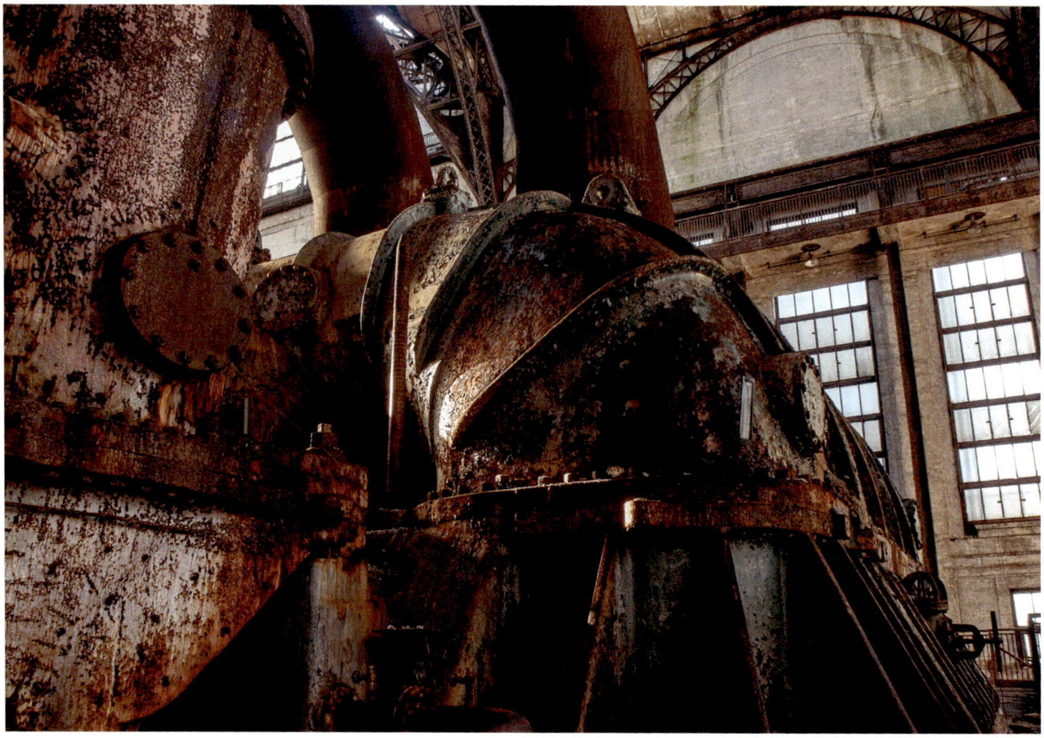

A close-up of a turbine.

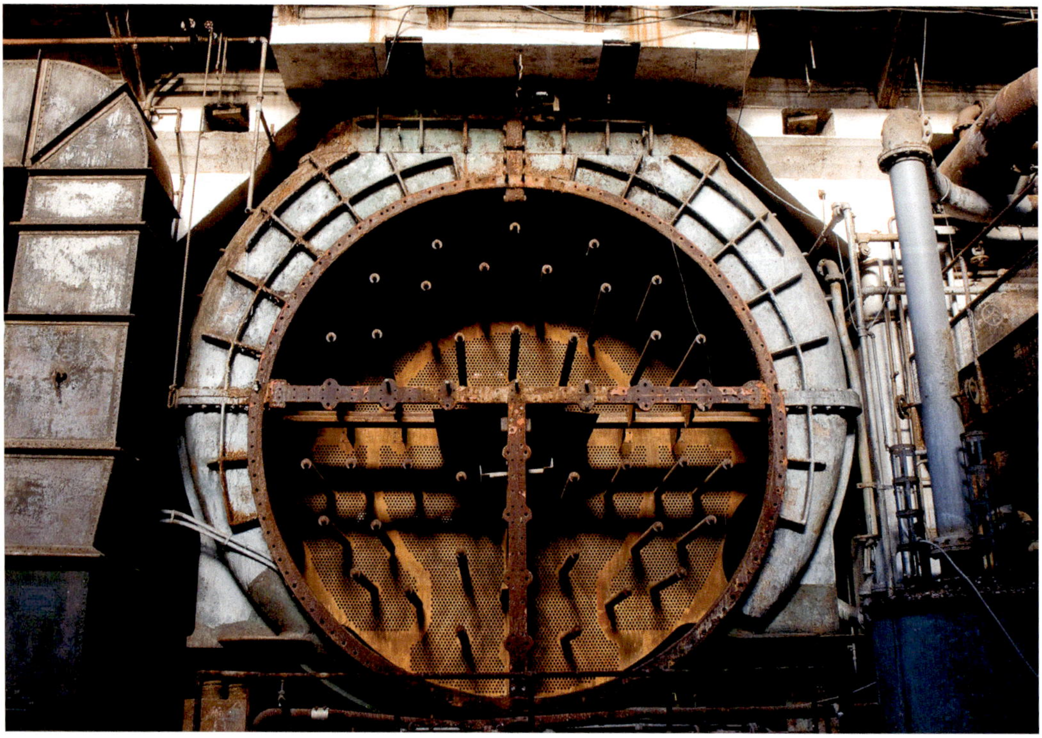

The abandoned industrial machines create the perfect setting for movies like *Transformers II*.

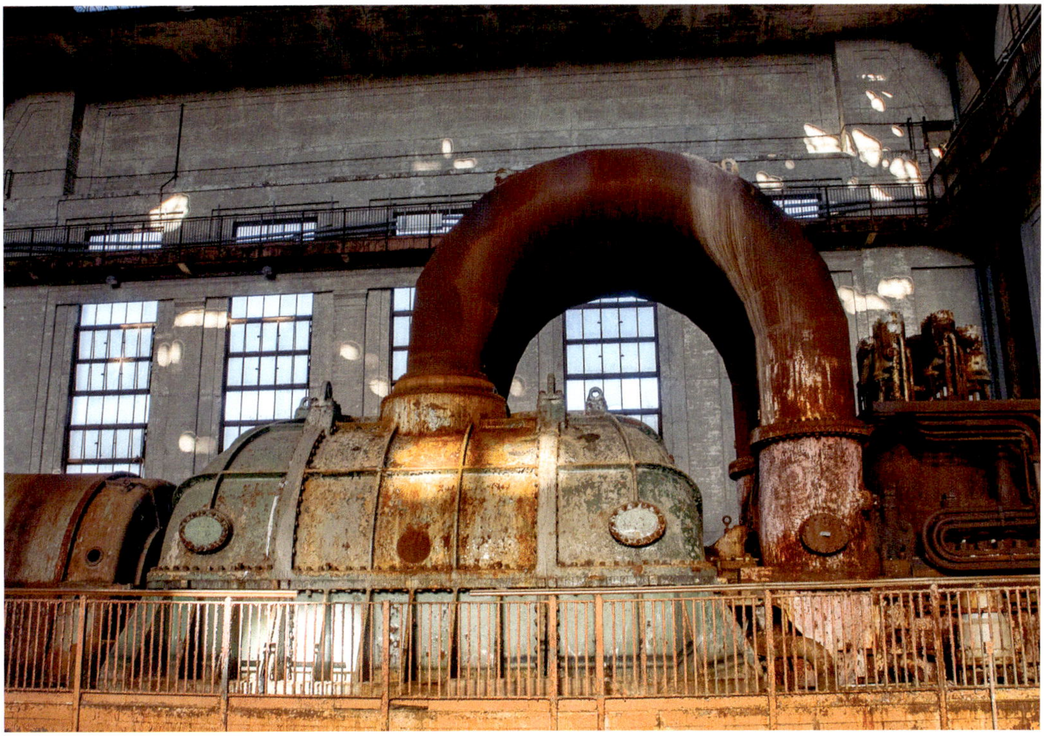

One of the turbines in turbine hall.

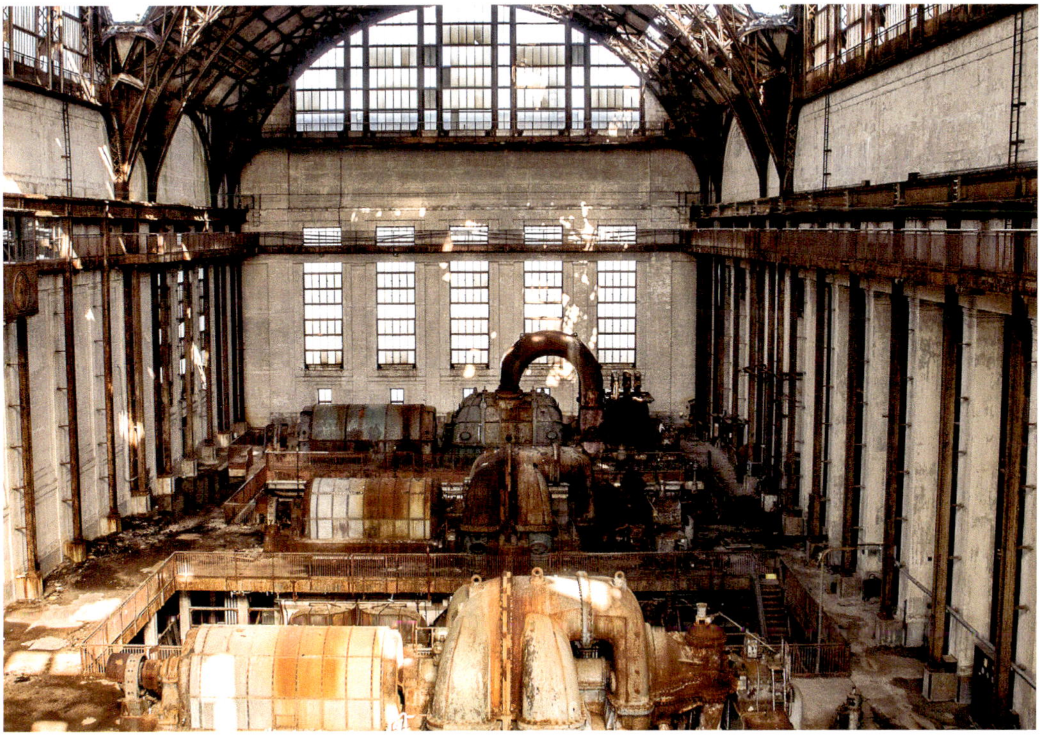

Sunlight streams into turbine hall.

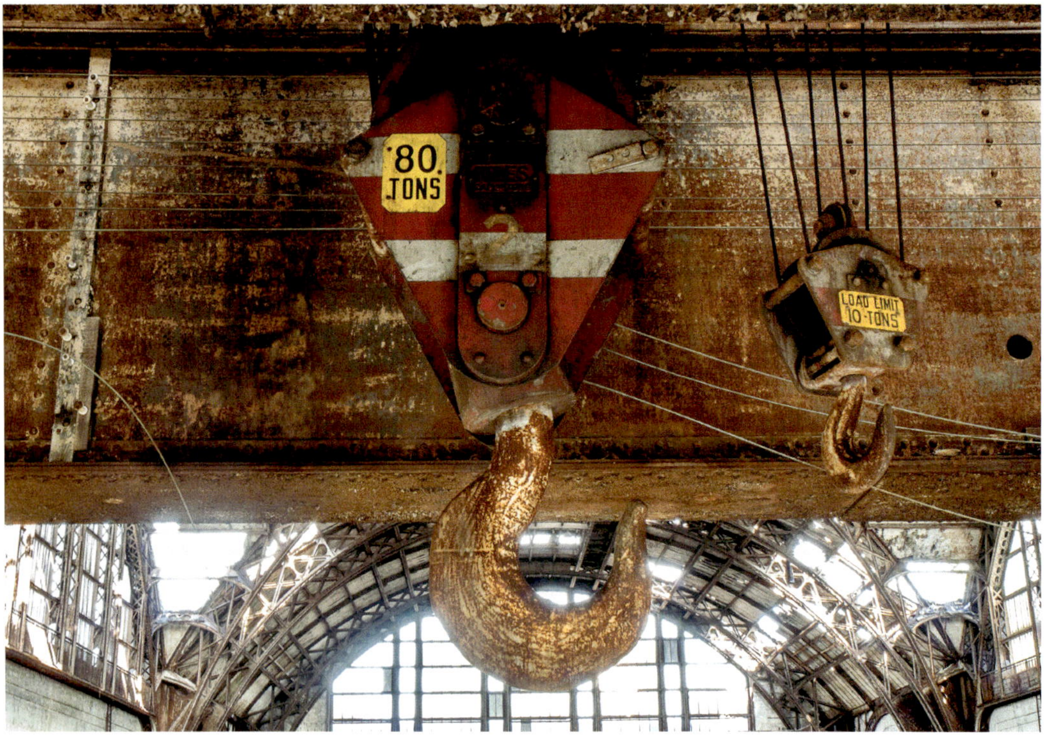

One of the large cranes located above turbine hall.

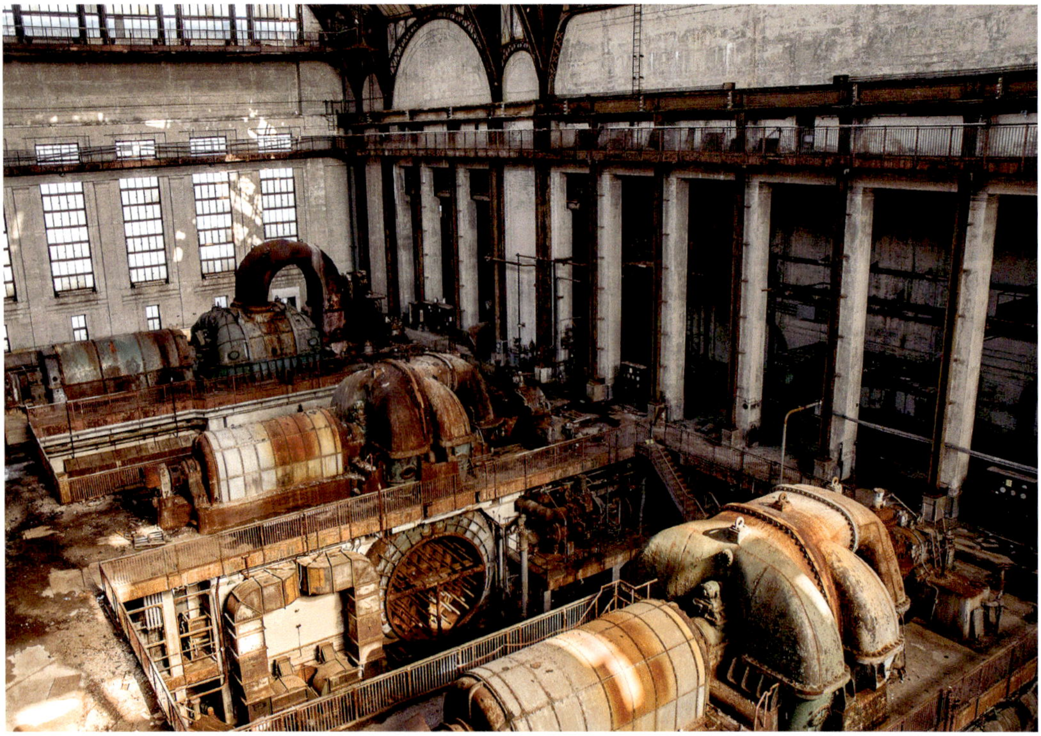

The hall that has inspired Hollywood producers.

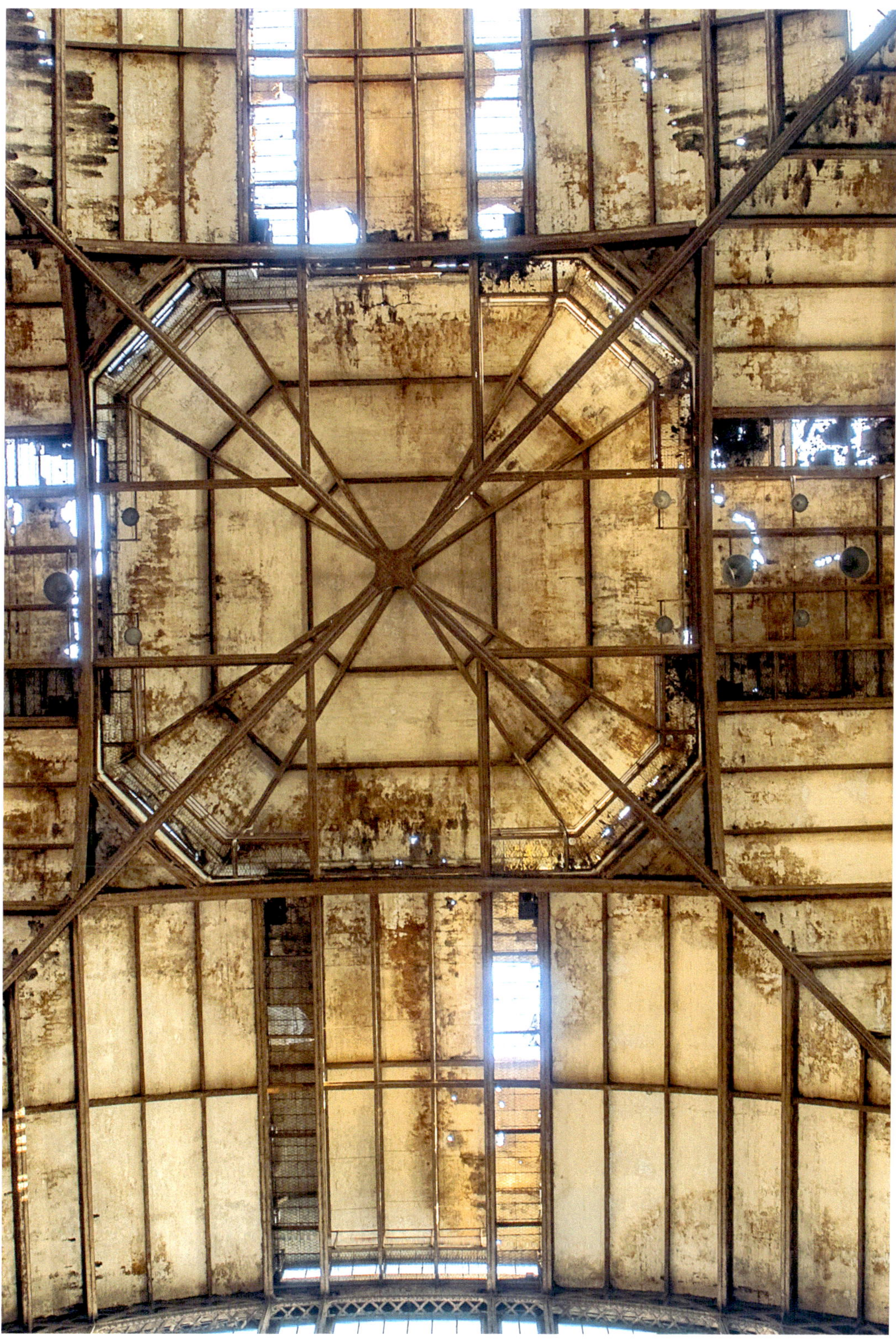

The intricate roof of the 125-foot-high structure.

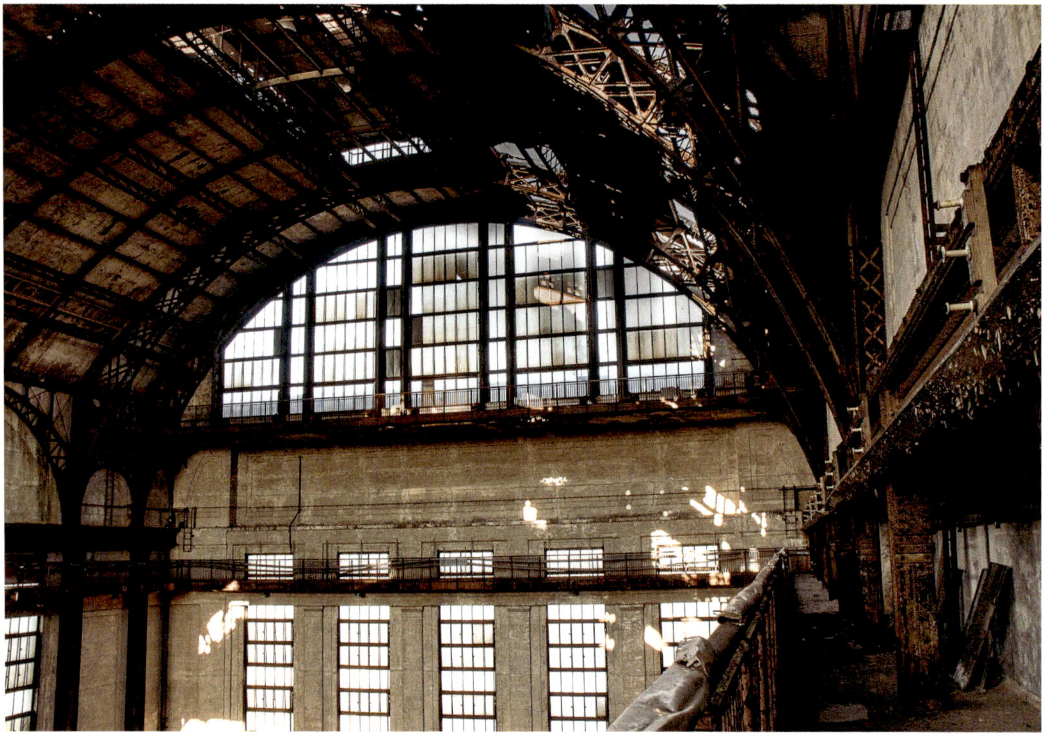

Constructed of reinforced concrete, steel, and glass, the sheer size of turbine hall is overwhelming.

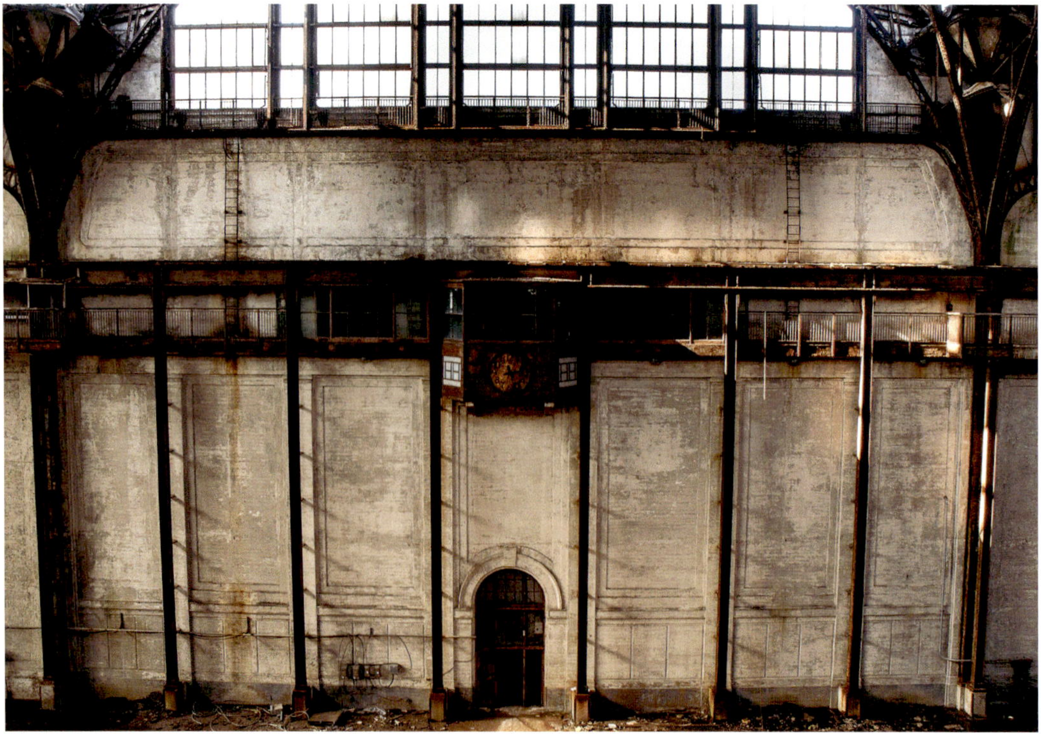

Looking toward the main control room where a long-ago stopped clock oversees the main hall.

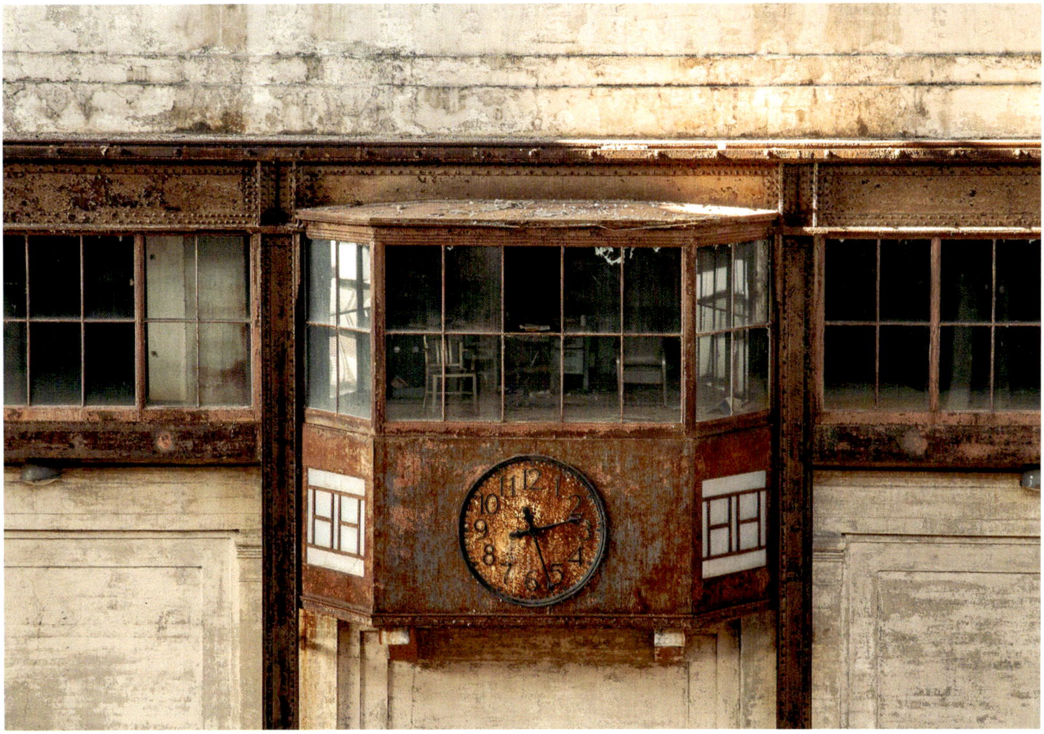

A closer view of the rusted clock.

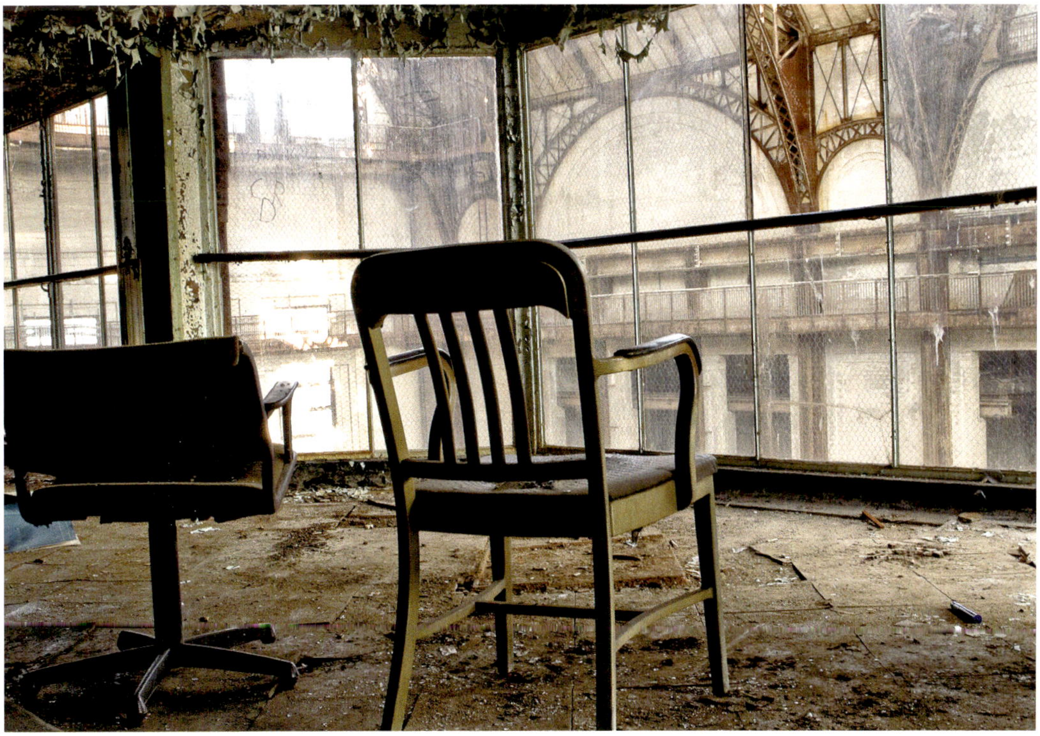

Chairs in the main control room where supervisors overlooked the turbines below.

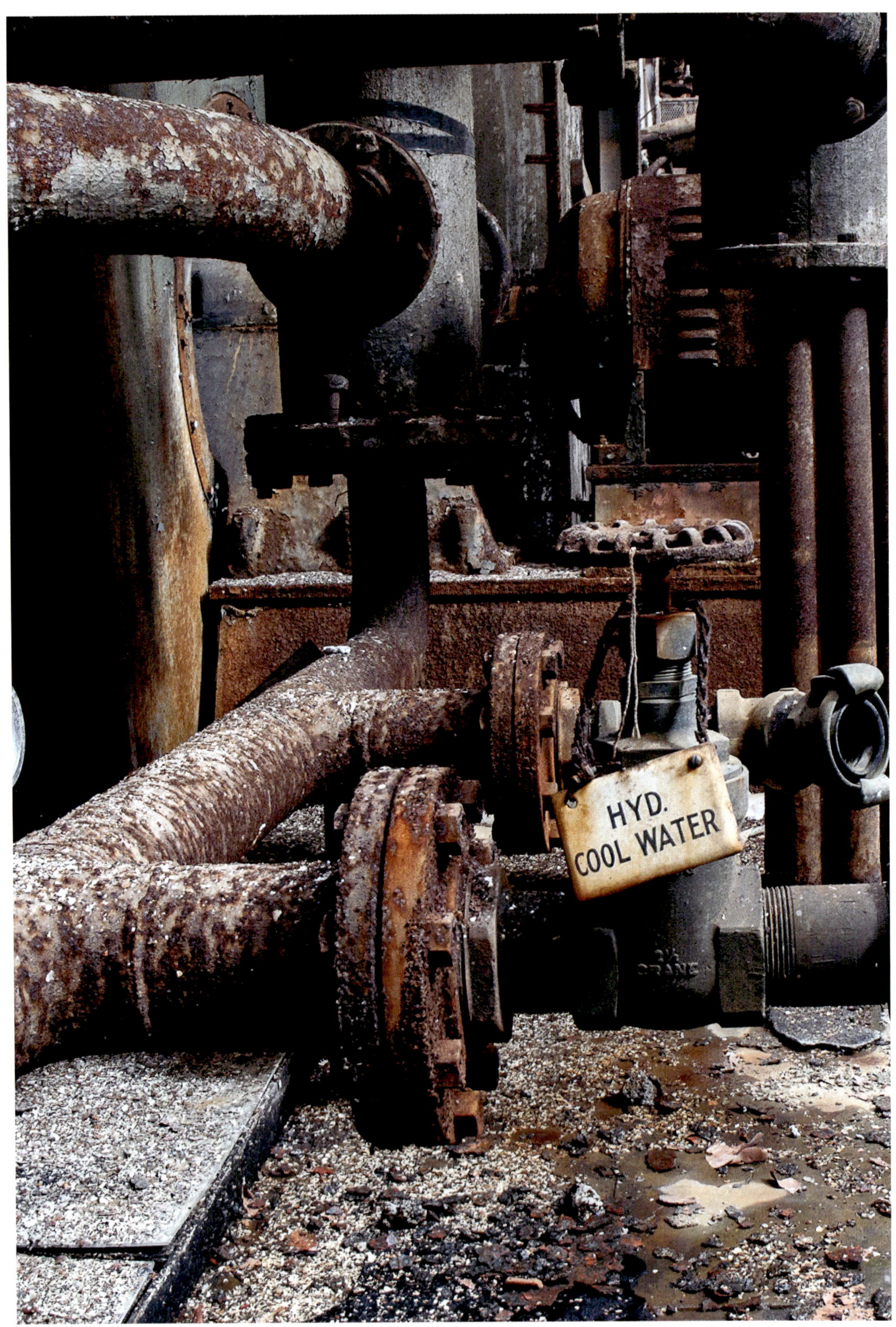

Detailed view of the machinery.

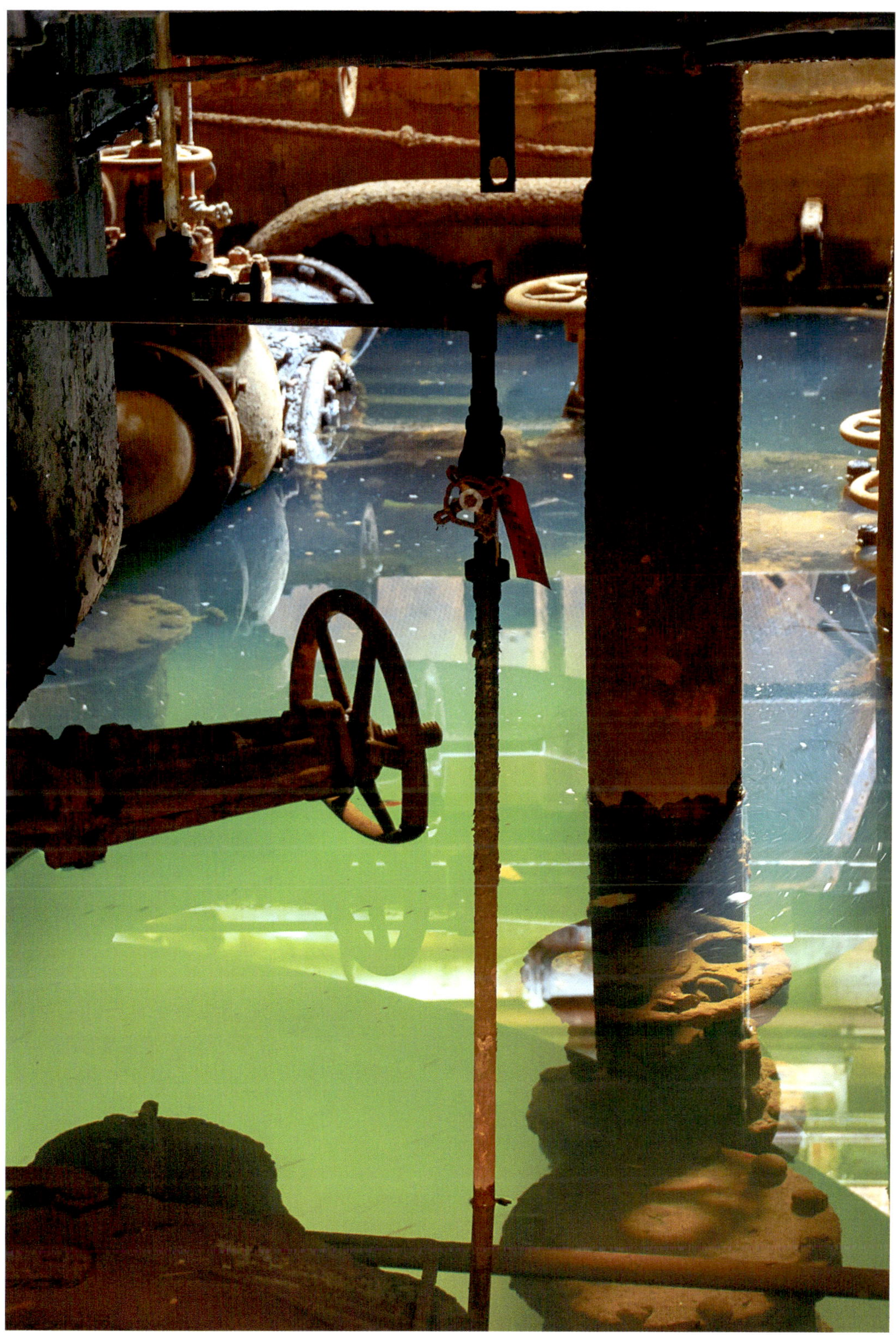

Much of the lower level is underwater.

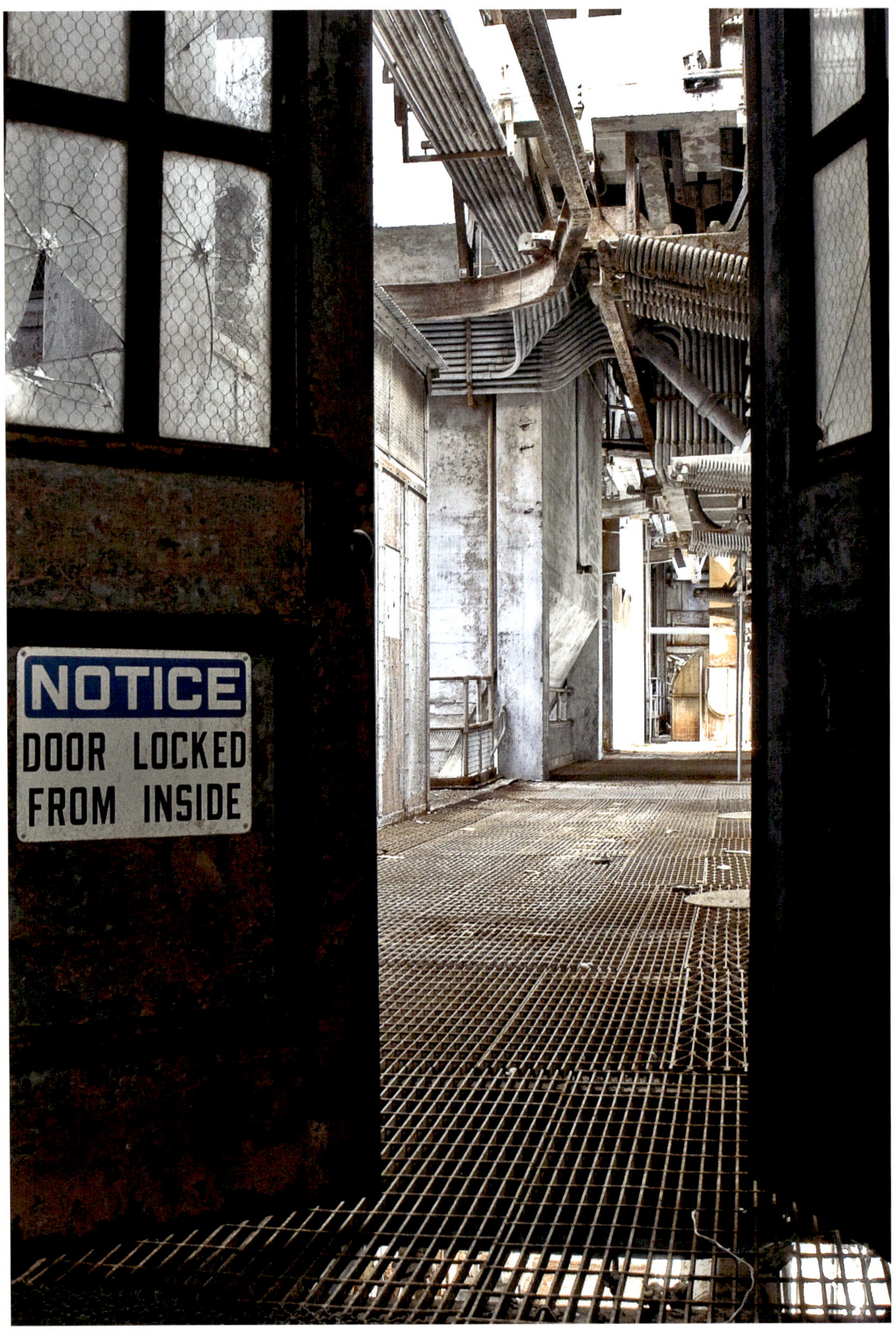

A less decayed area of the plant.

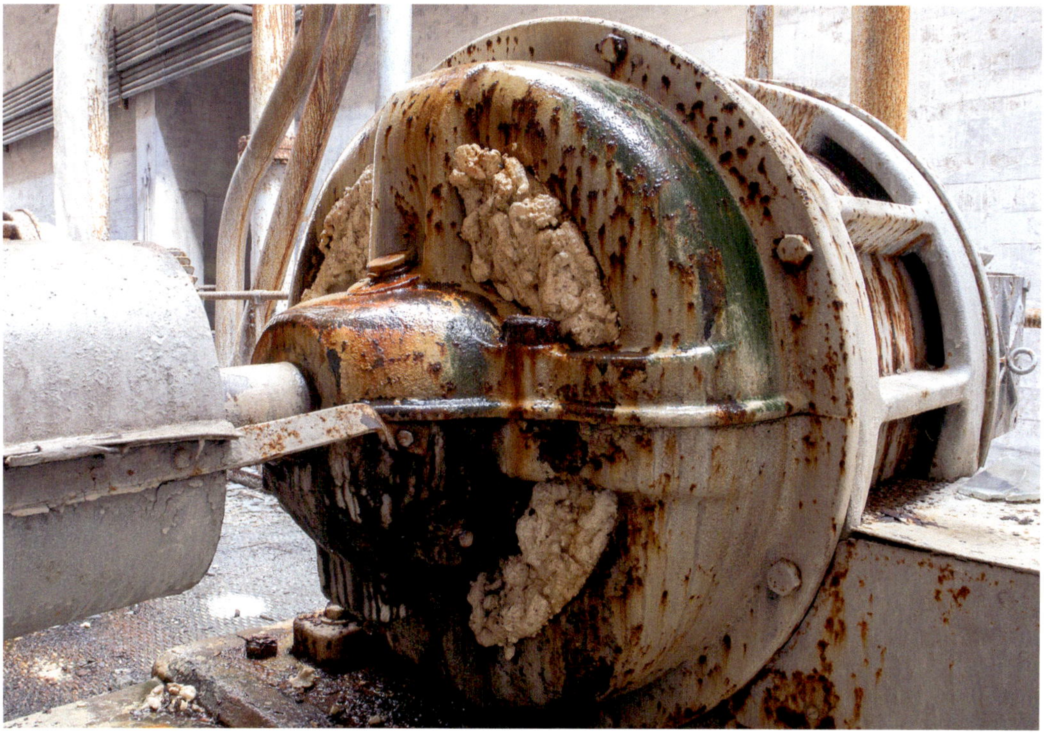

Disused equipment leaking chemicals.

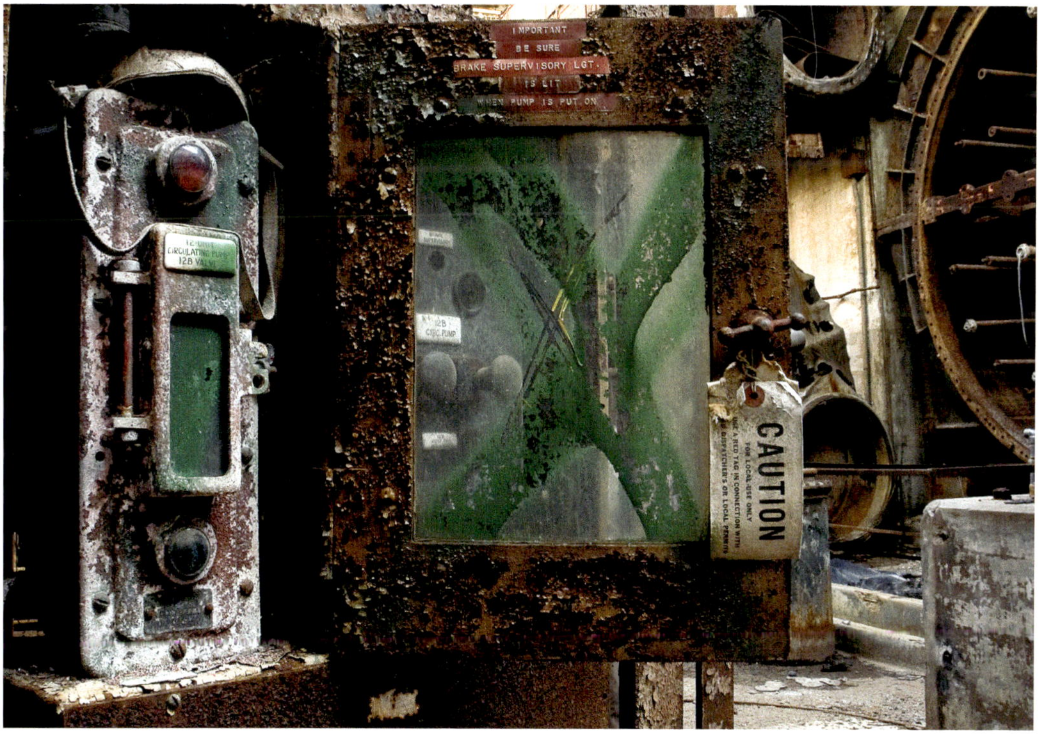

A section of a pump below turbine hall.

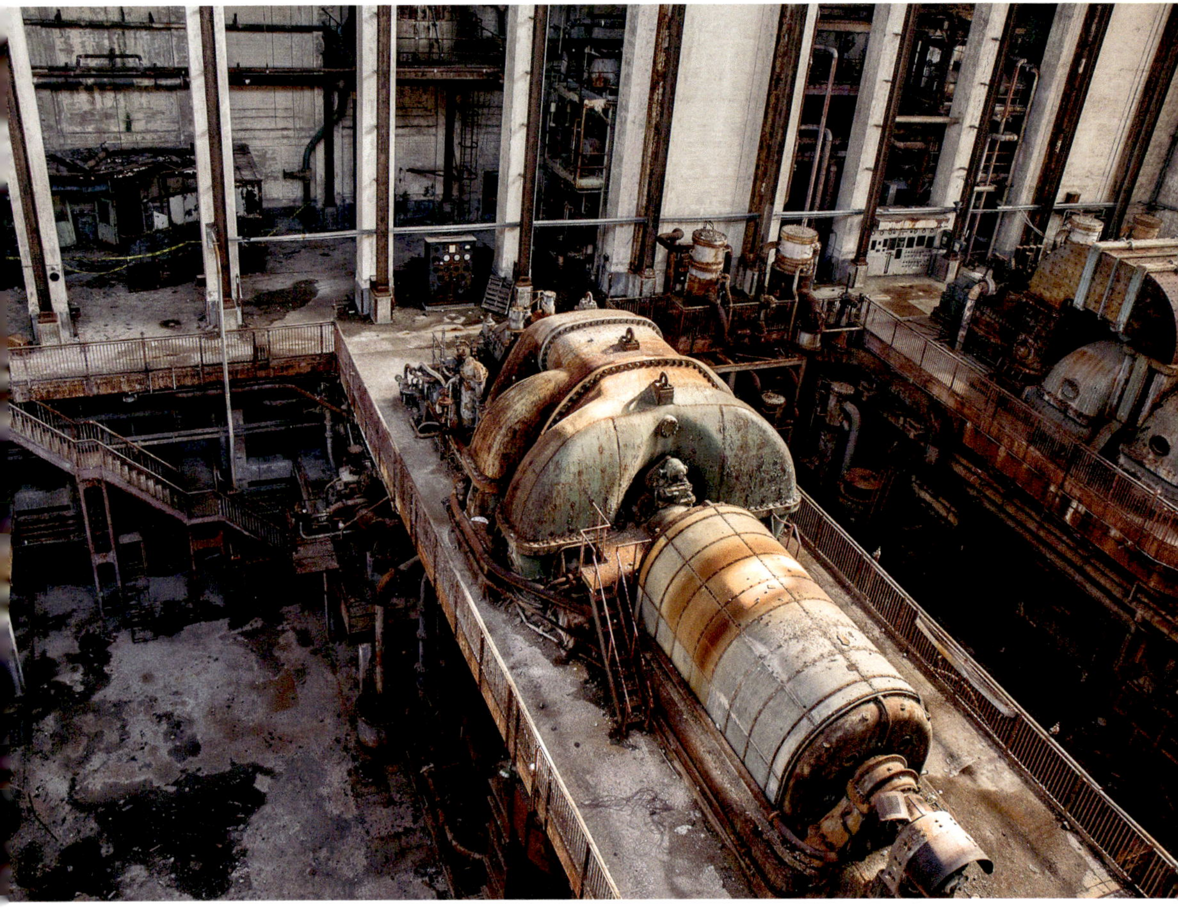

An aerial view of a decaying turbine.

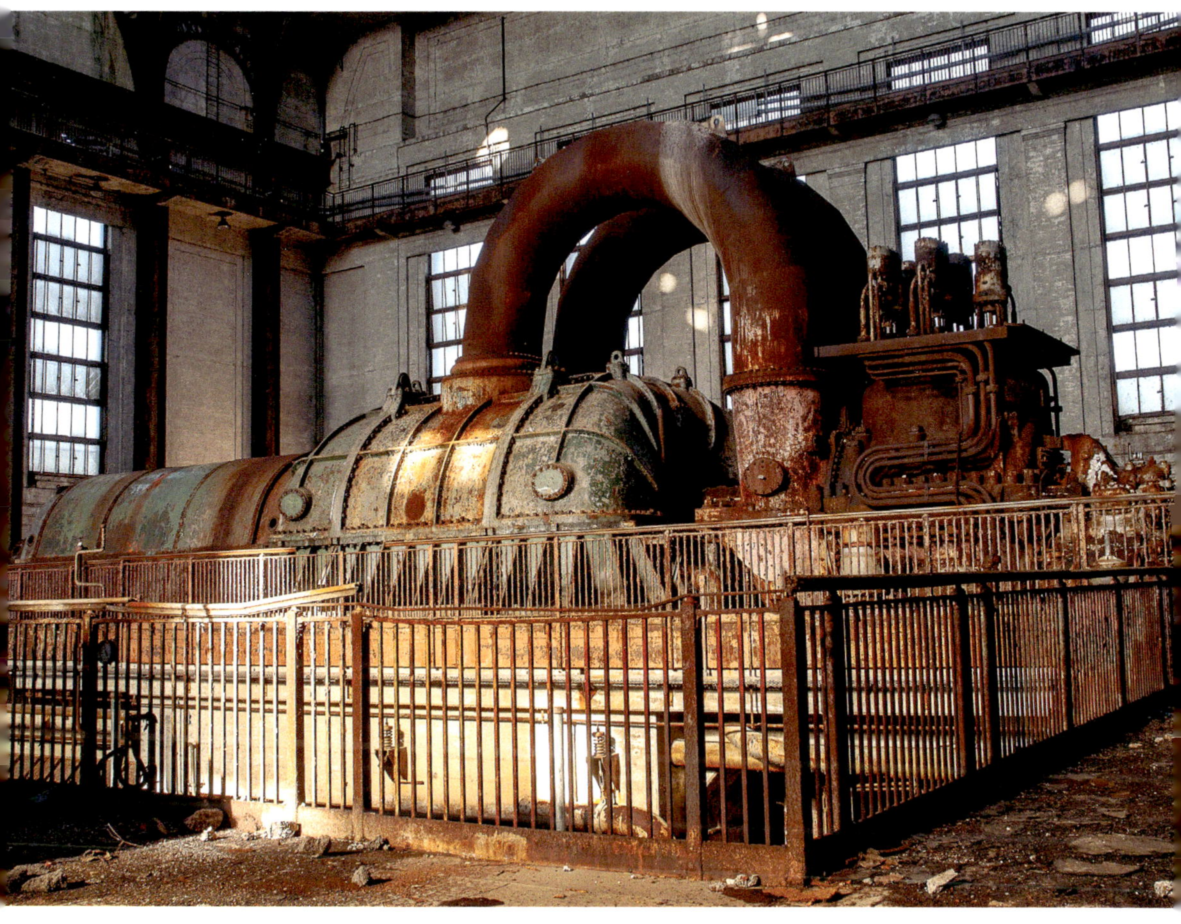

Sunlight bathes a corroded turbine.

SCRANTON LACE COMPANY

Bustling with industry and alive with the energy of more than 1,200 workers, Scranton Lace Company once set the standard for workplace amenities. More than a century before multi-billion-dollar Silicone Valley disrupters like Google and Apple started offering employees more than just a place to toil, Scranton Lace boasted a multi-lane bowling alley, a barber shop, a gymnasium, which also doubled as an auditorium, and a fully staffed infirmary. The stately clock tower grew to be a symbol of the town's prosperity.

A beacon of the industrial era, the lace factory was the first and largest producer of the famed Nottingham Lace in the United States. The colossal Nottingham looms weighed over 20 metric tons and stood over two and a half stories tall. The looms were developed and manufactured in Nottingham, England, in the mid-1800s when lace was a much-treasured commodity. The Scranton line boasted more than 3,000 intricate patterns, and these were not limited to curtains and table linens, but materials used for draperies, embroideries, cretonnes, and bedspreads. The 1940s saw the company partner with subsidiaries such as Victory Parachutes, Inc. and Sweeney Bros. to manufacture parachutes and camouflage netting. The war years saw the company thrive.

Mismanagement and diversification, fueled by greed, saw the company struggle during the late 1950s. Following the success of the previous decade, the demand for lace began to slow, and the company faced a steady decline in sales for much of the early to mid-1950s. It was during this time that outside investors seized a controlling interest. The takeover began in 1957.

Alexander Guterma, a Wall Street financier with questionable motives, saw the Scranton Company's cash-on-hand balance sheet as a way to diversify its holdings and to increase his personal wealth. A master manipulator, Guterma pushed the company to broaden its interests and manufacturing capabilities. His acquisitions saw the company take control of aerosol can manufacturing, a radio network, movie and television production, rugs, and engine rebuilding machinery.

In 1958, Scranton Lace Company was renamed Scranton Corporation to better reflect its growing interests. By 1959, Guterma was arrested for violating federal securities regulations and was later jailed. In that same year, Scranton Corporation declared Chapter 10 bankruptcy. The bankruptcy crushed the hopes of a community. In a 1958 article, the *Scranton Times* praised the diversification:

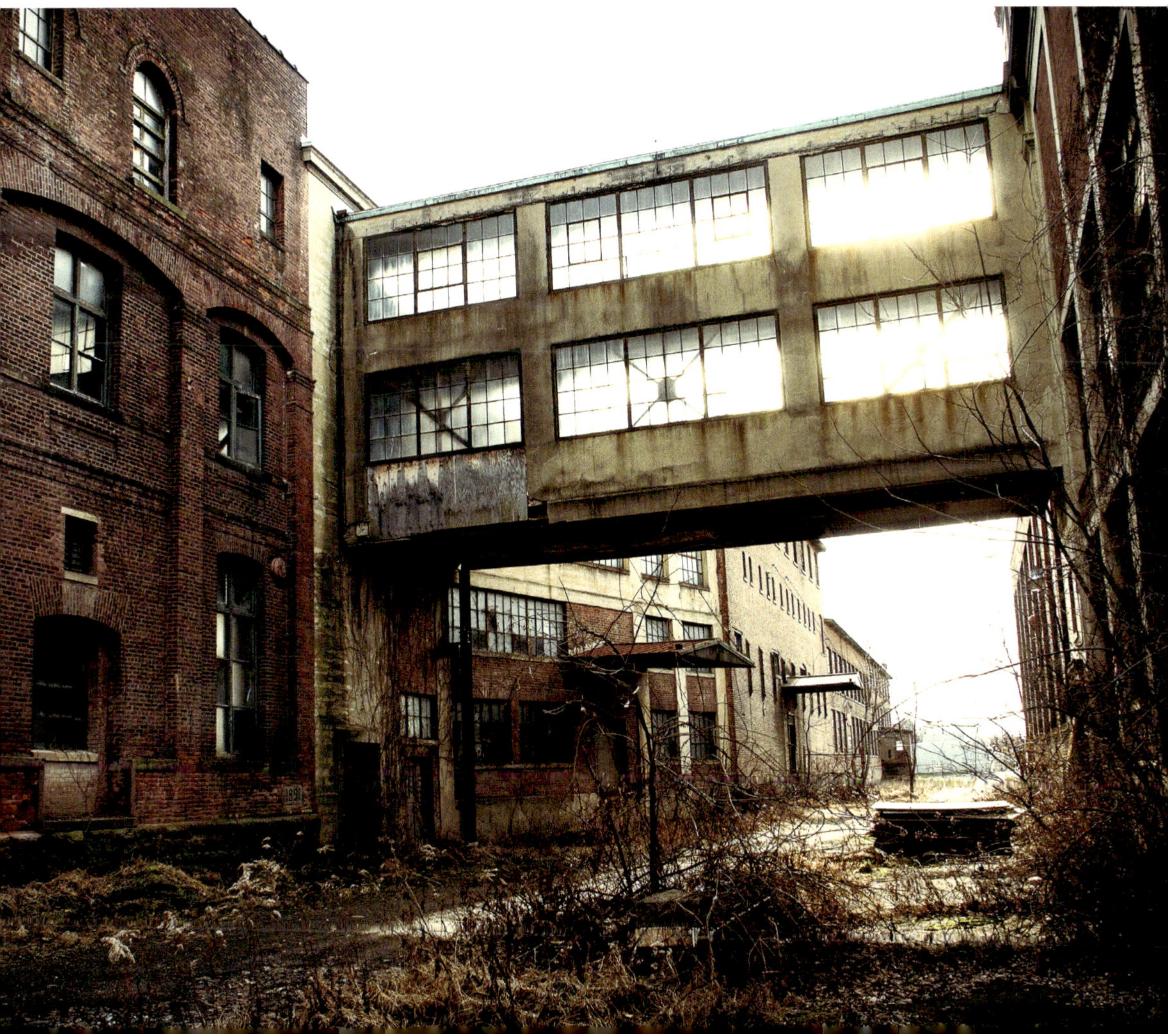

"The public hopes that the Scranton Corp.'s expansion will result in stabilized and increased employment at the local plant, long an important factor in our industrial family." Sadly, the reverse proved to be true.

Trustees of Scranton Corporation liquidated Guterma's empire, leaving only Scranton Lace and Storm Vulcan, which in 1964 was taken over and slowly rebuilt by Harry Weinberg. Scranton Lace would never again see the prosperity of its early years, but for the next four decades, it stood as an anchor in a struggling industrial town.

By the turn of the millennium, the number of employees filling the 288,000-square-foot facility had dwindled to fifty, and manufacturing in the United States became close to non-existent. On a Friday in May 2002, those fifty remaining employees were advised, mid-shift, the factory would be ceasing operations—immediately.

The demise of Scranton Lace is so indicative of the current state of American deindustrialization that Pulitzer Prize-winning journalist Chris Hedges, in his 2018 book *America: The Farewell Tour*, states that the lace factory "was America." In his opening chapter, "Decay," he poignantly describes his 2012 visit to the long-abandoned and now decaying complex of buildings. Hedges paints a picture of another age and offers a stark parallel of what Scranton Lace Company represented then and now:

> ...the company gave more than a wage to the thousands of men and women who worked here. It gave them dignity, purpose, pride, a sense of place, hope and self-esteem. All of that was gone. It had been replaced in Scranton and across America by desperation, poverty, drift, a loss of identity, and a deep crippling despair.

Demolition of the Scranton Lace site by the current owners, Lace Building Affiliates, began in 2018 and was completed in 2019. For more than a decade, there had been discussions surrounding the repurposing of the buildings and incorporating them into Lace Affiliates' grand plan for new housing and community development. The cost proved to be too high.

The clock tower remains, and one of the thirty colossal Nottingham looms was not sold for scrap. I wonder if the remaining loom still contains the lace from that fateful May day in 2002 as it did when I visited a decade later in 2012. The lace that was abandoned on its journey. Stuck. Never to attain completion and reach its destiny. Never to be removed from the incredible Nottingham Loom.

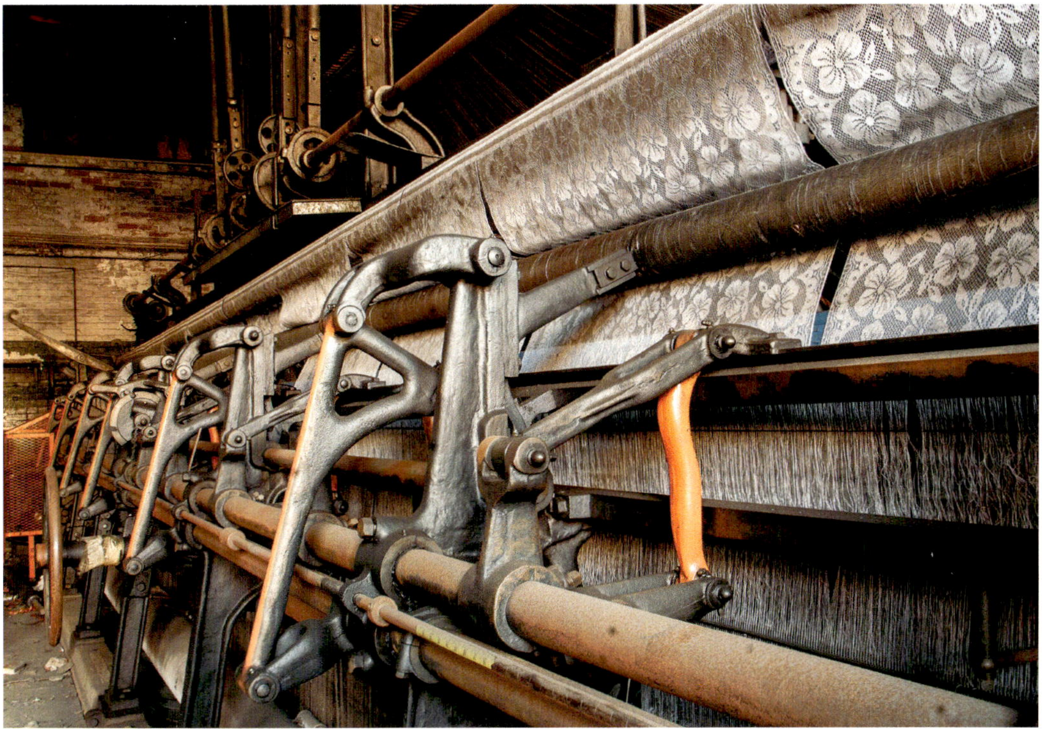

A loom with unfinished lace.

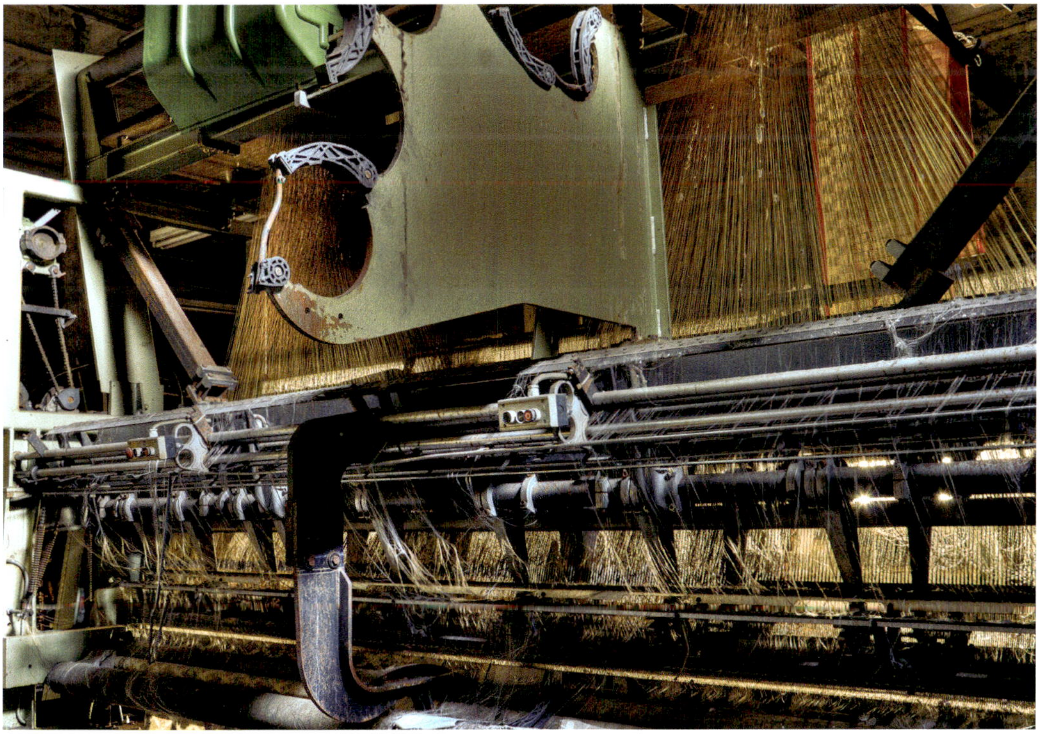

Layers of thread stuck in time.

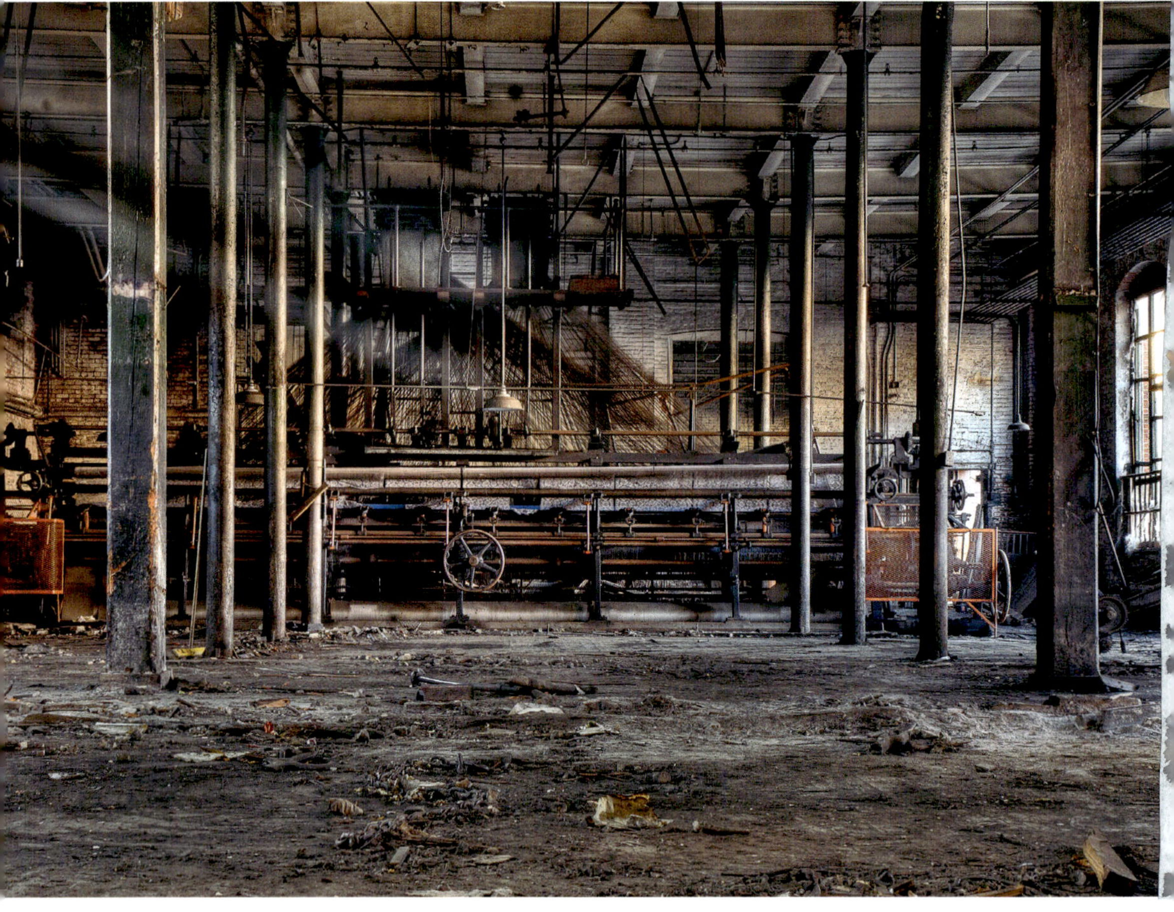

A famous Nottingham Loom stands among dust and debris.

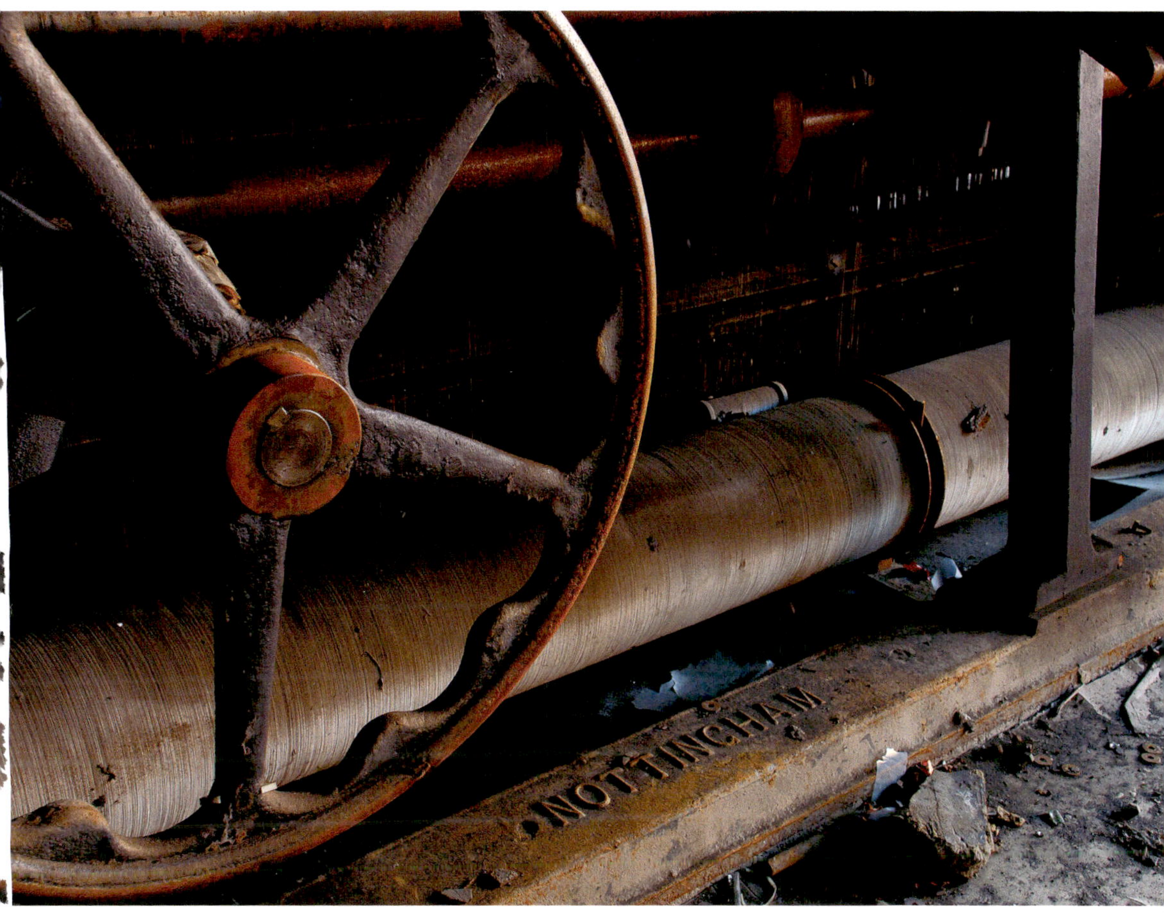

A detail of the Nottingham Loom.

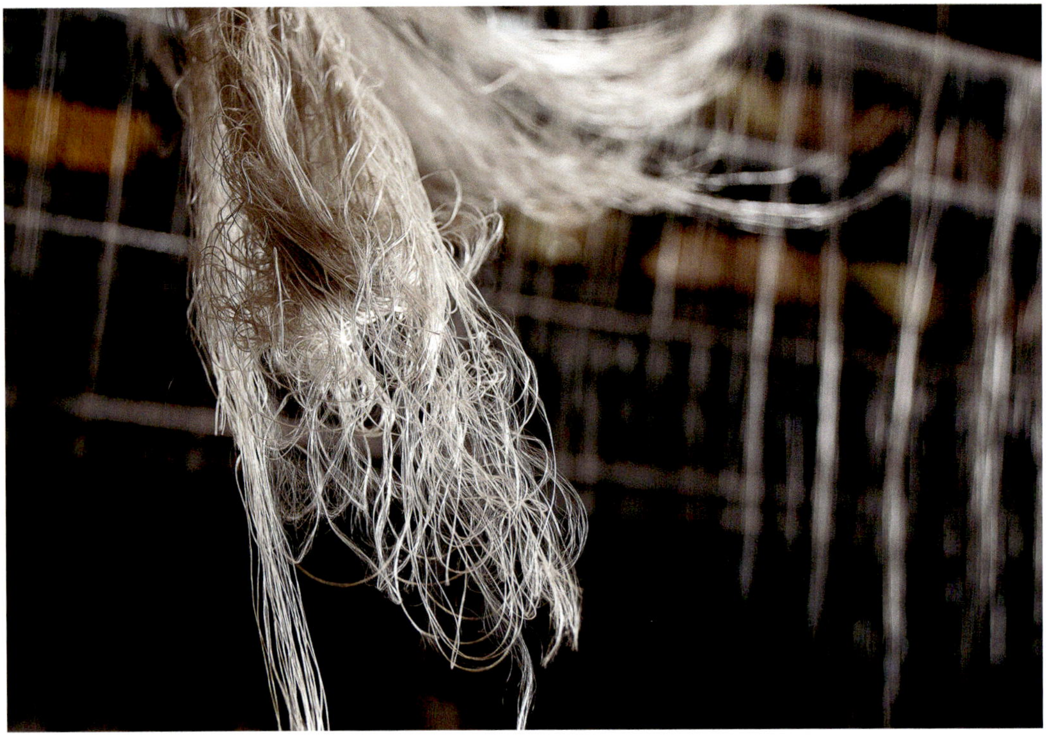

Tangled cotton hangs from a loom.

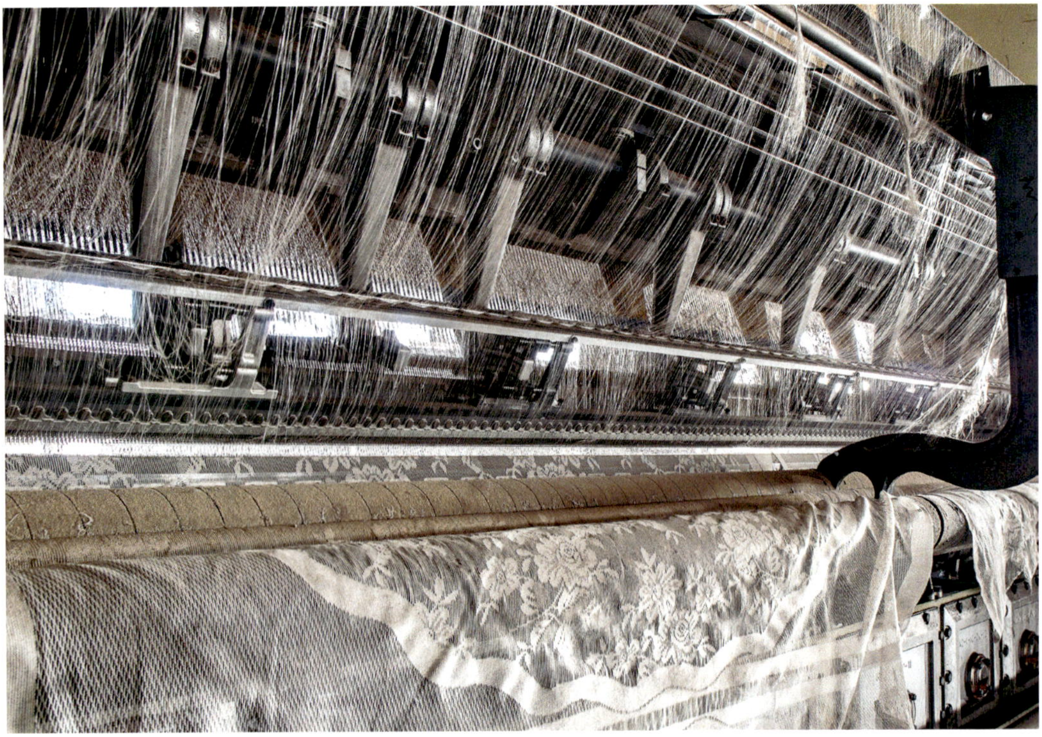

Unfinished lace curtains.

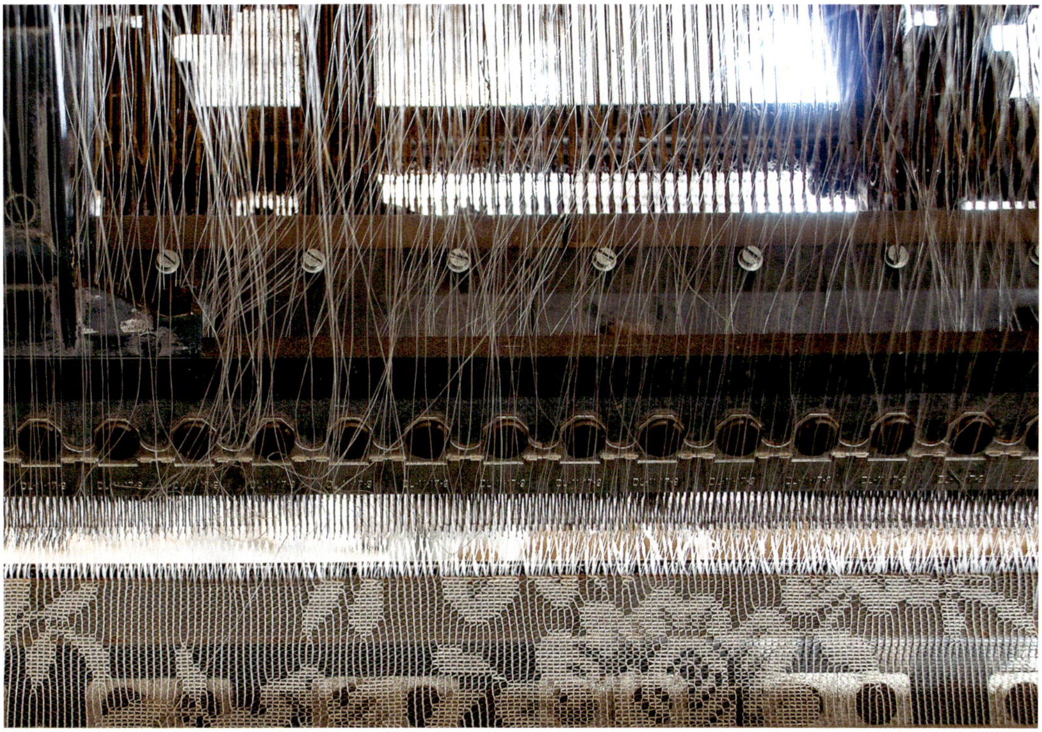

The intricacy of lace is cleary evident.

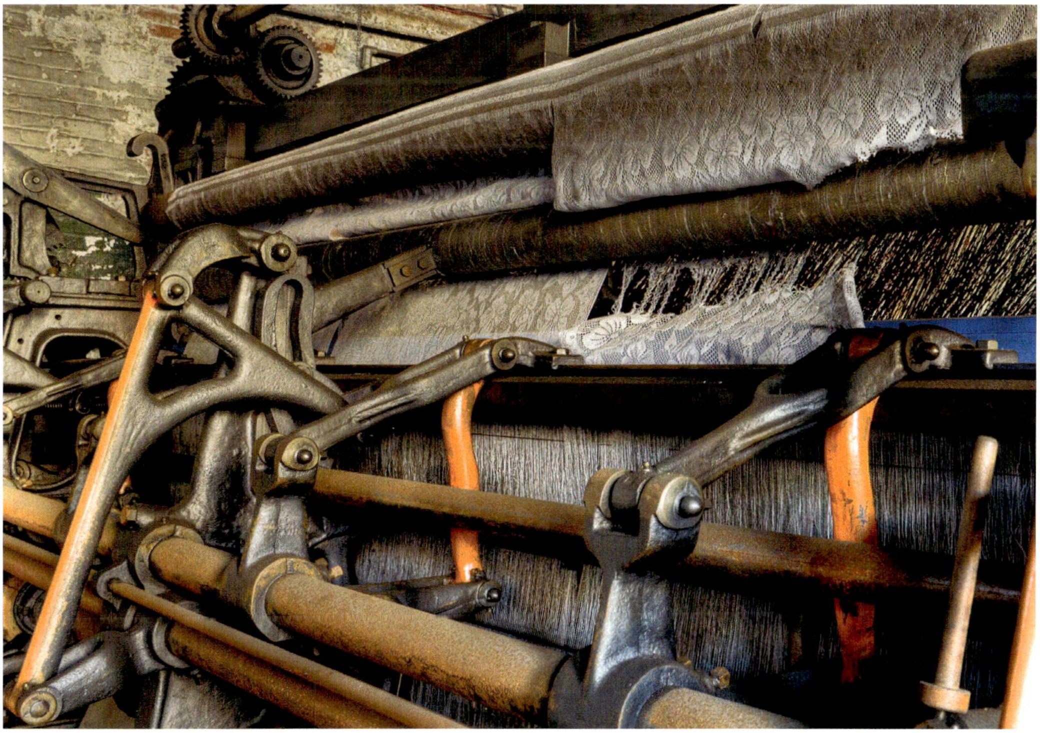

Another loom embracing unfinished lace products.

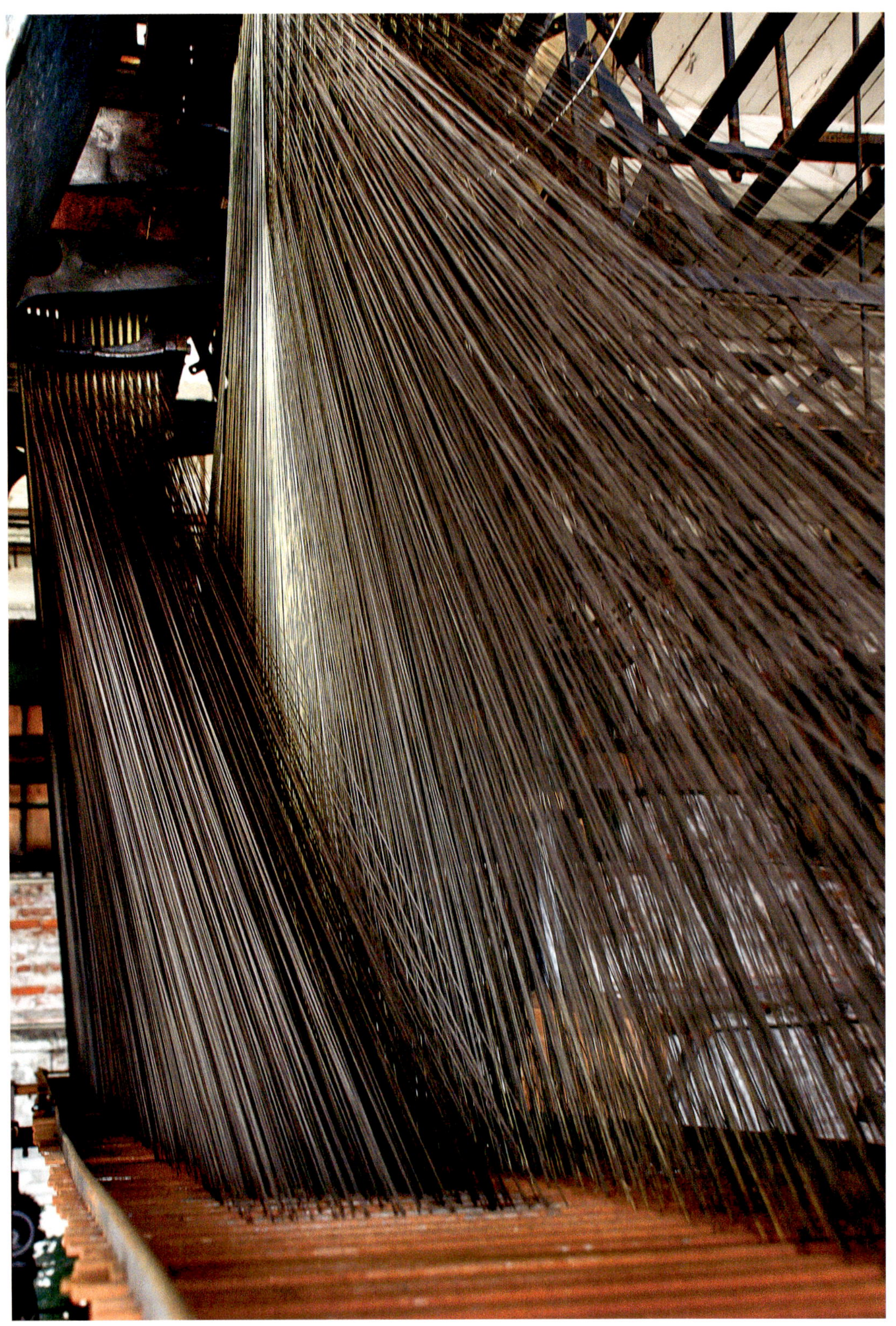

Thousands of strands create a compelling pattern.

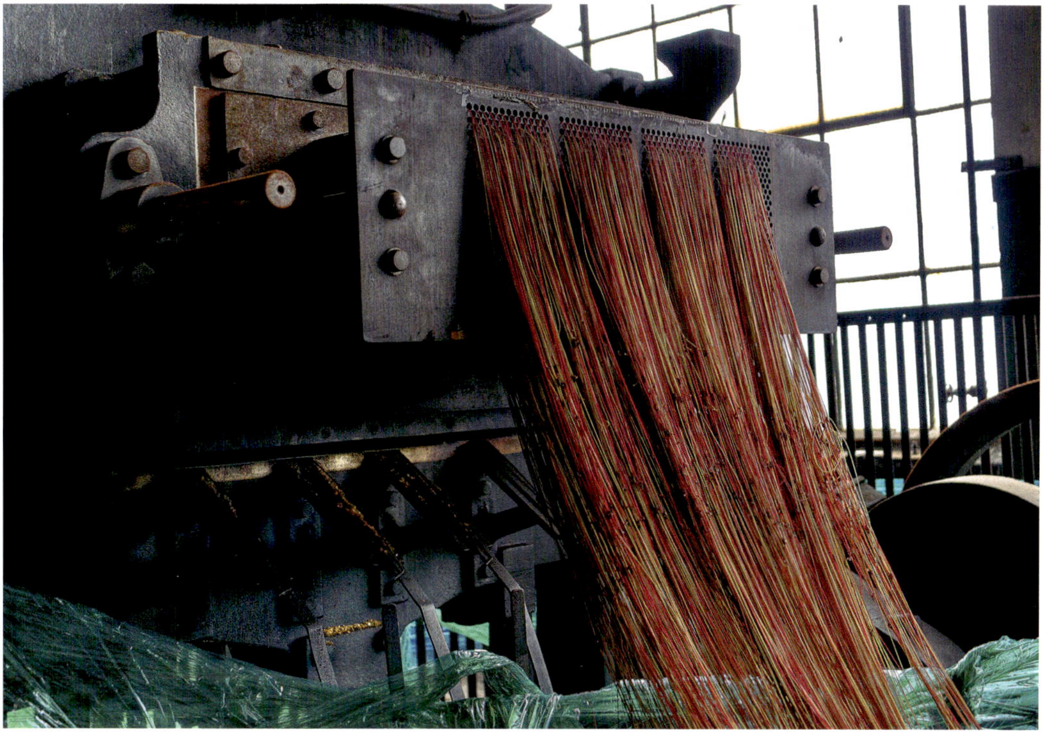

Gold and red filaments stuck in time.

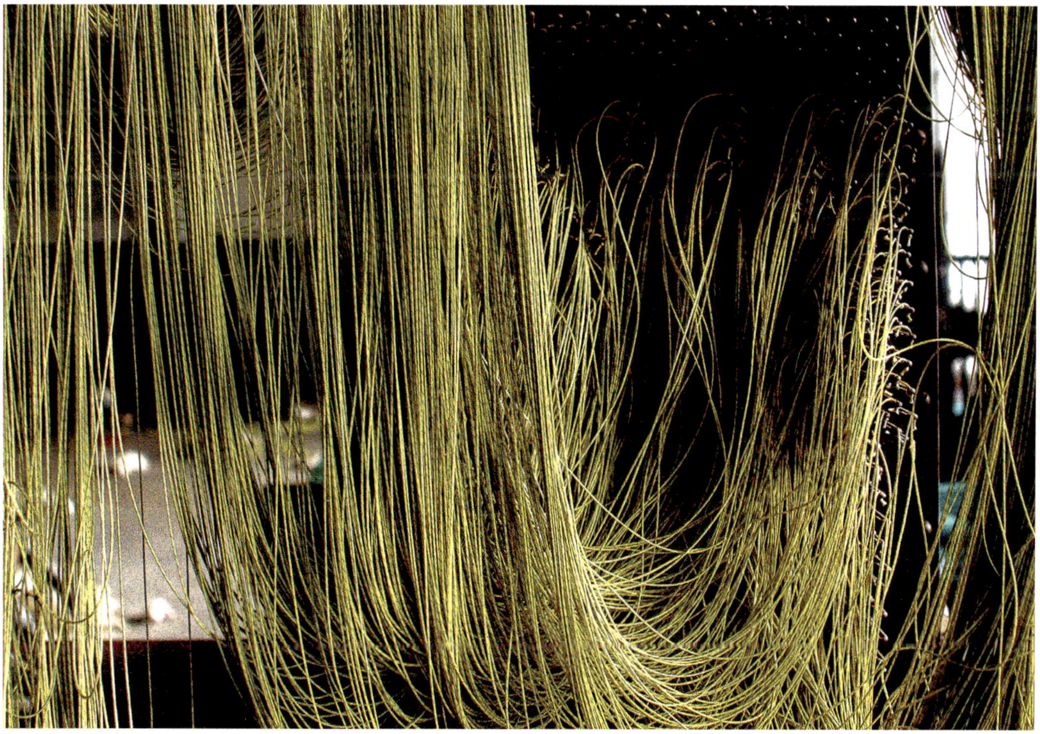

A tangled mass of thread.

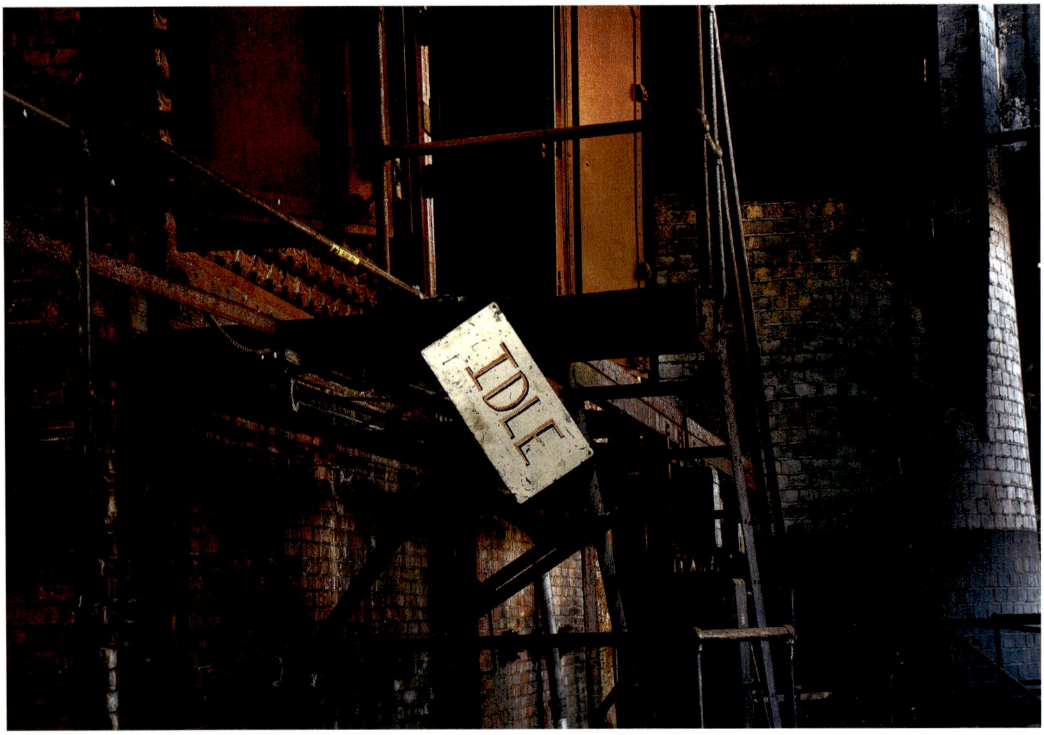

An ironic idle sign.

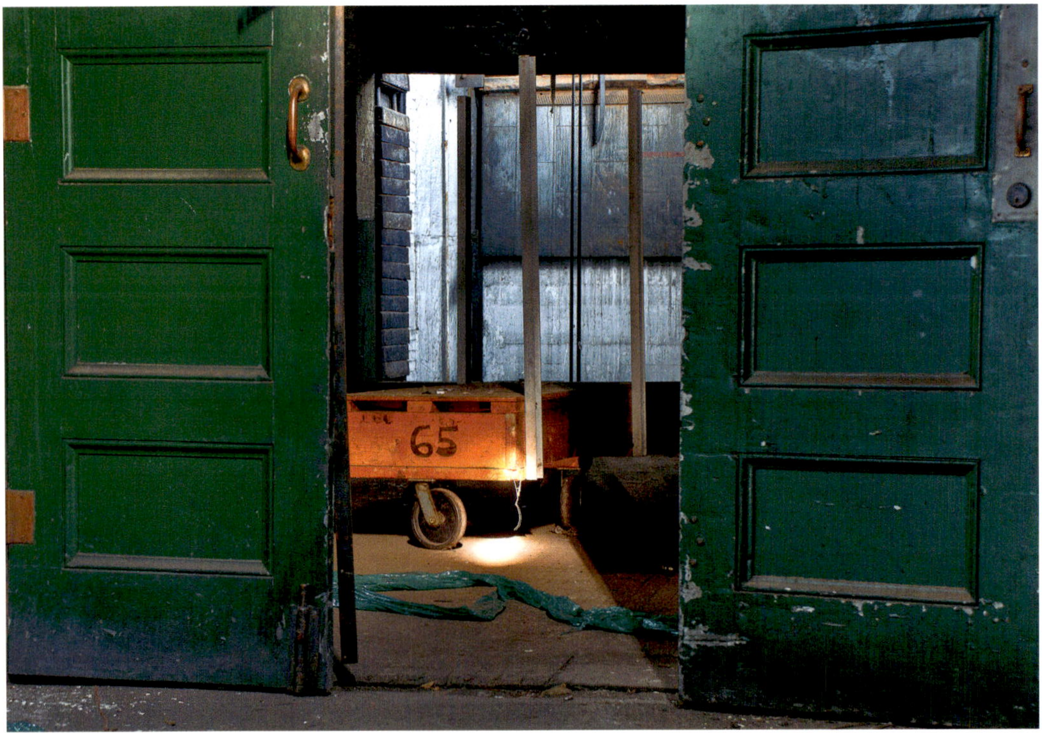

Sunlight gives life to an otherwise desolate scene.

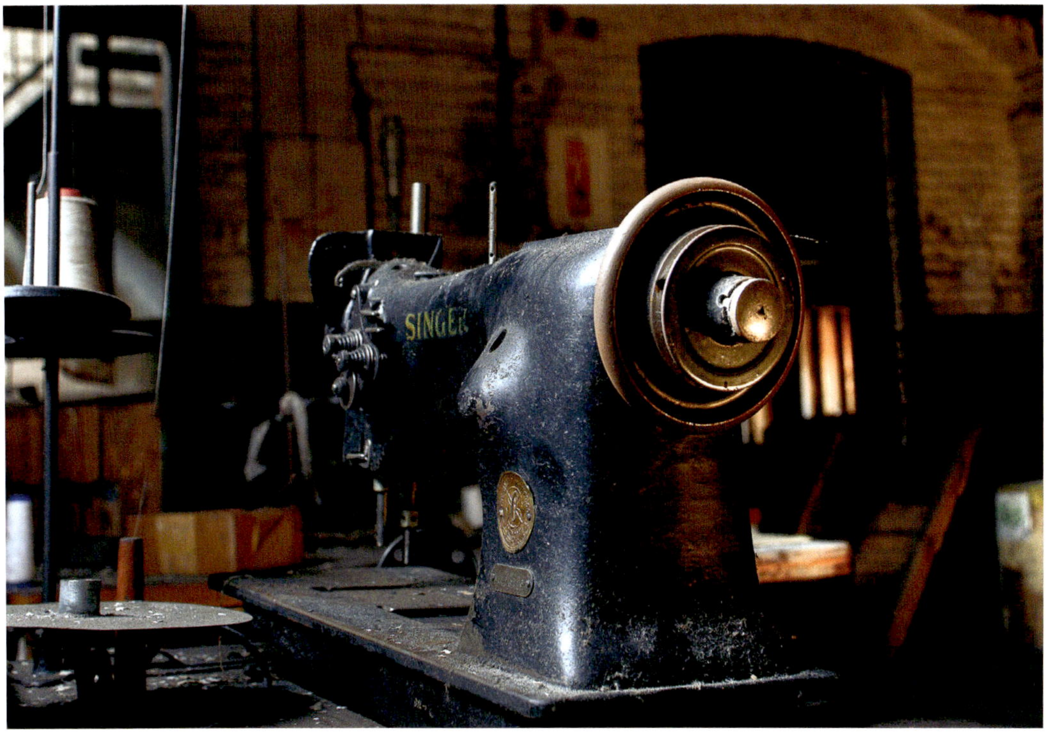

An inactive Singer sewing machine.

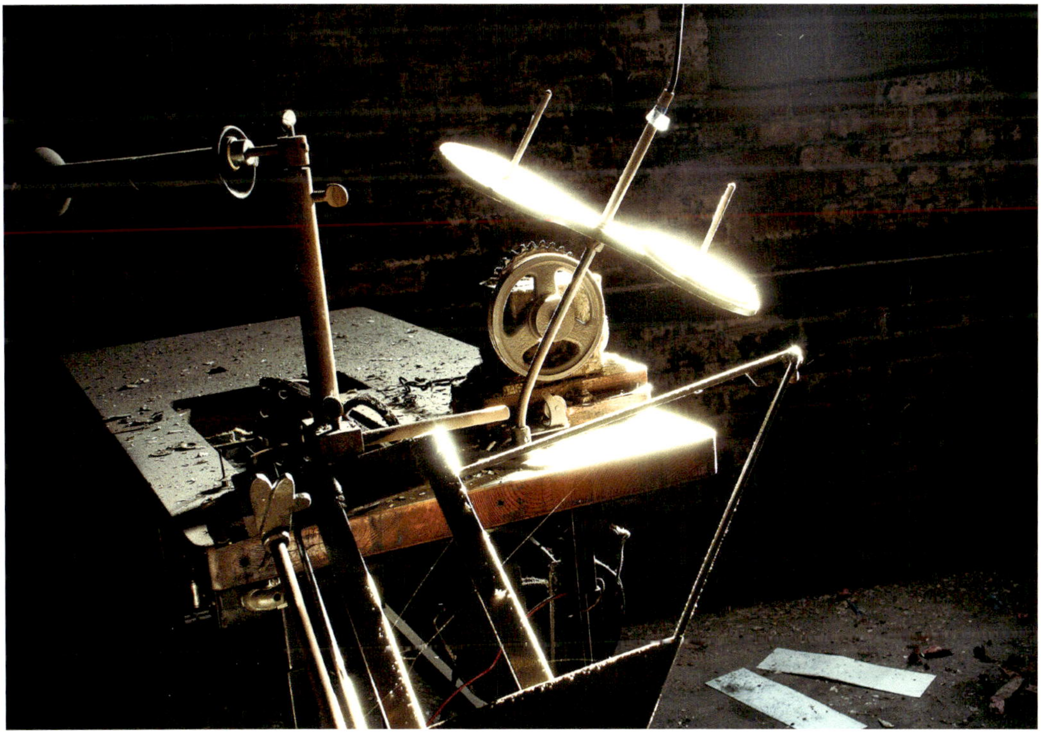

Light through a window provides an otherworldly glow to a spool holder.

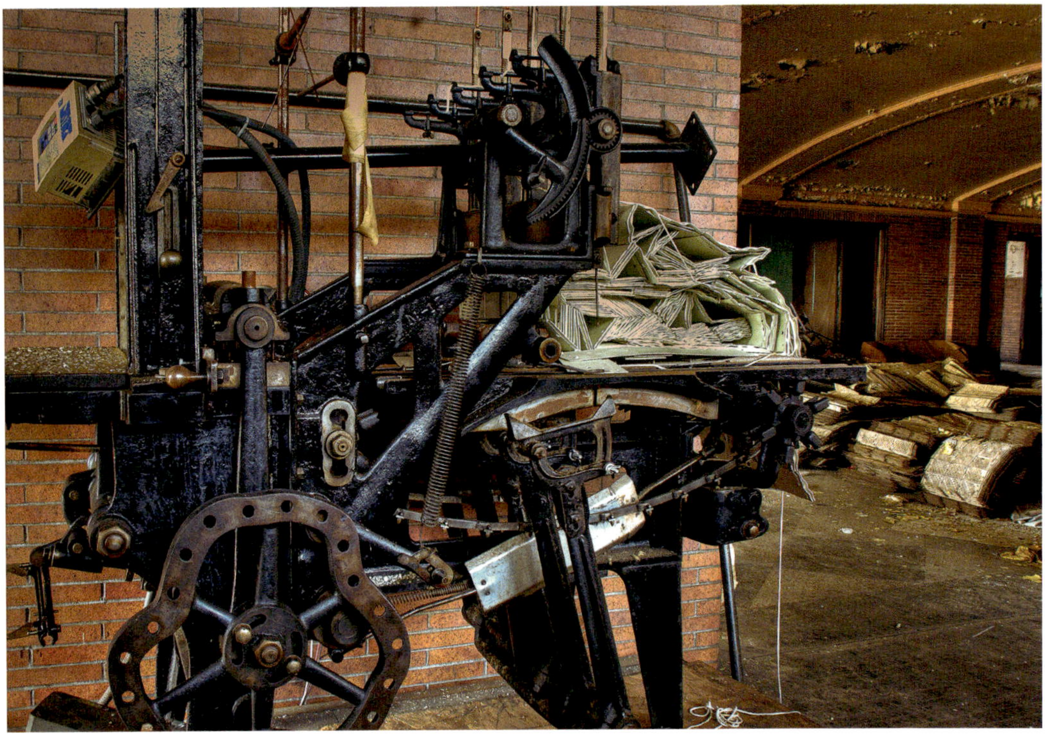

A stamping machine.

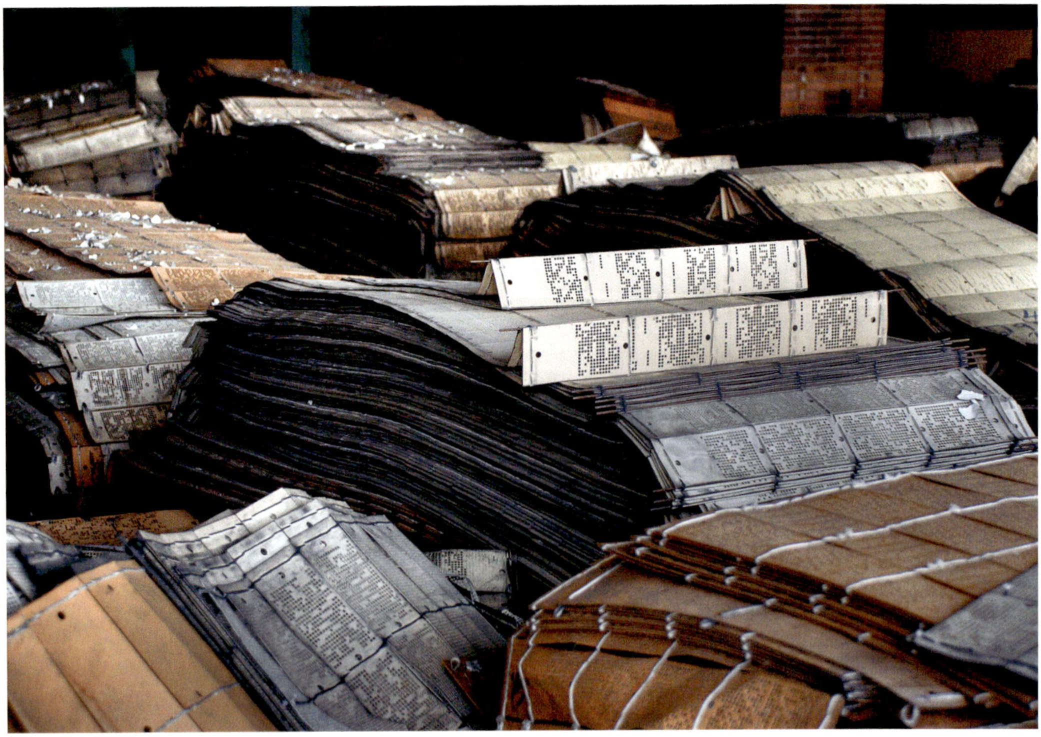

Piles of discarded lace patterns.

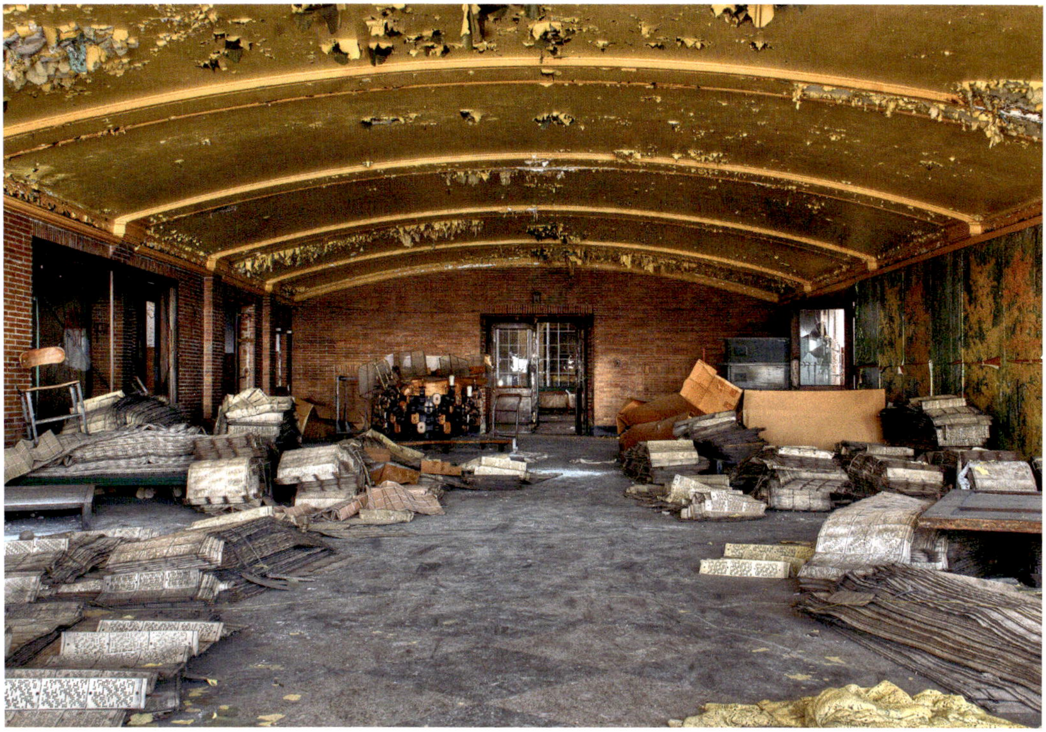

A storeroom filled with lace patterns.

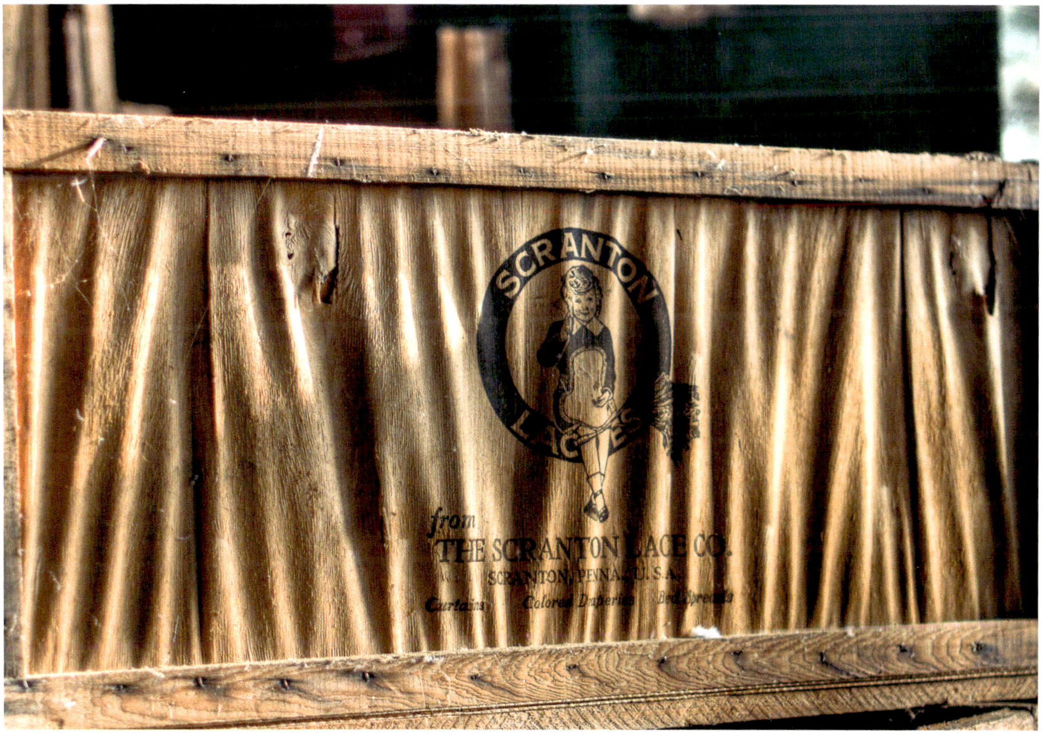

A packing crate bearing the Scranton Lace logo.

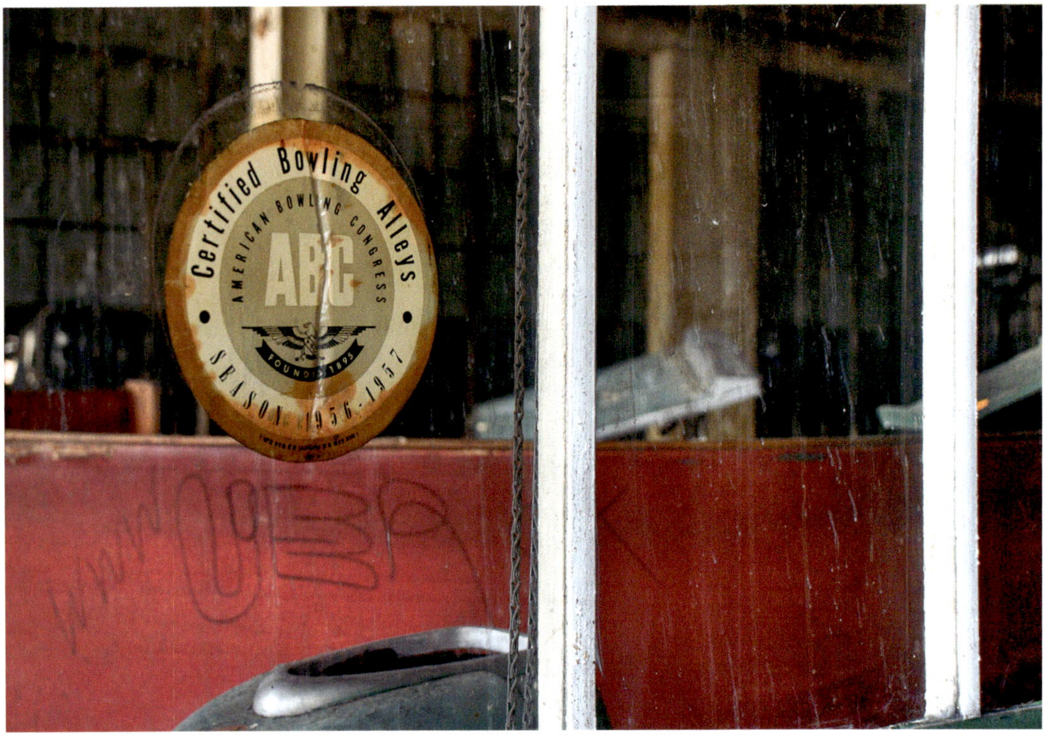

The entrance to the staff bowling alley.

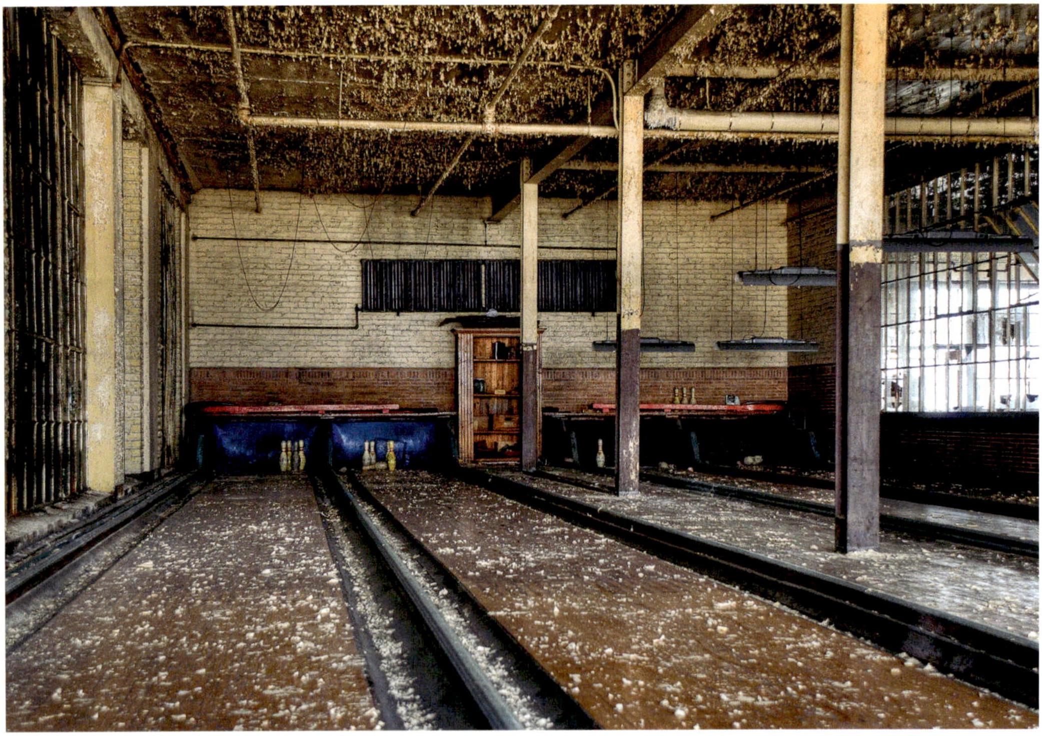

Decaying bowling lanes.

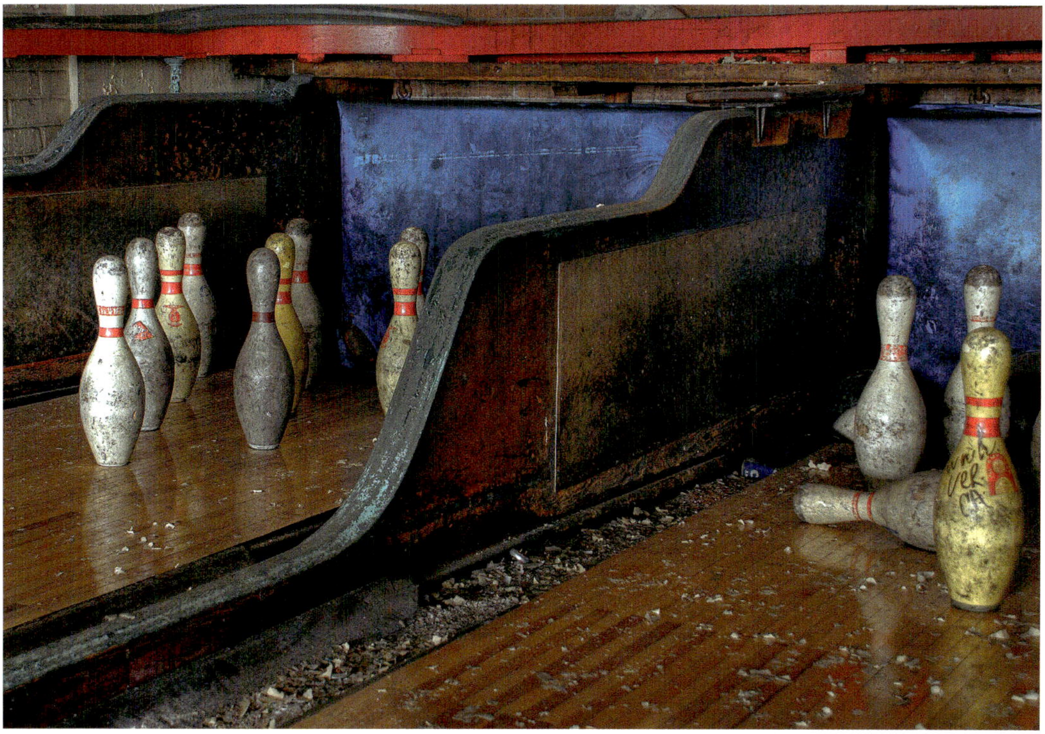

Bowling pins still standing.

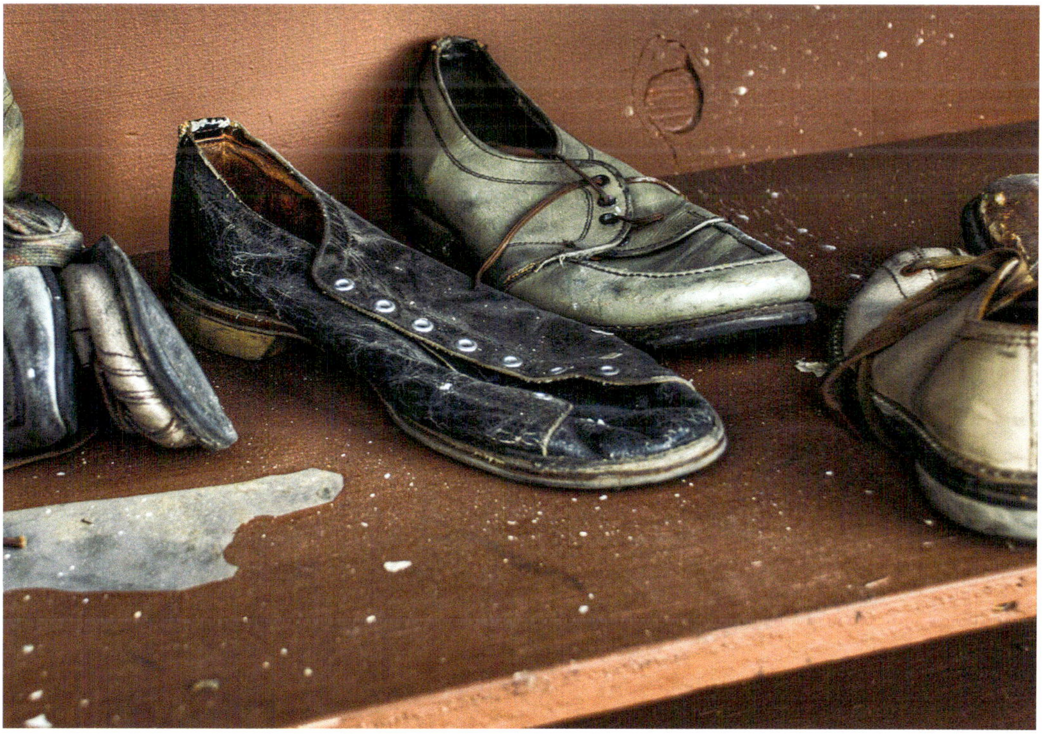

Well-worn bowling shoes.

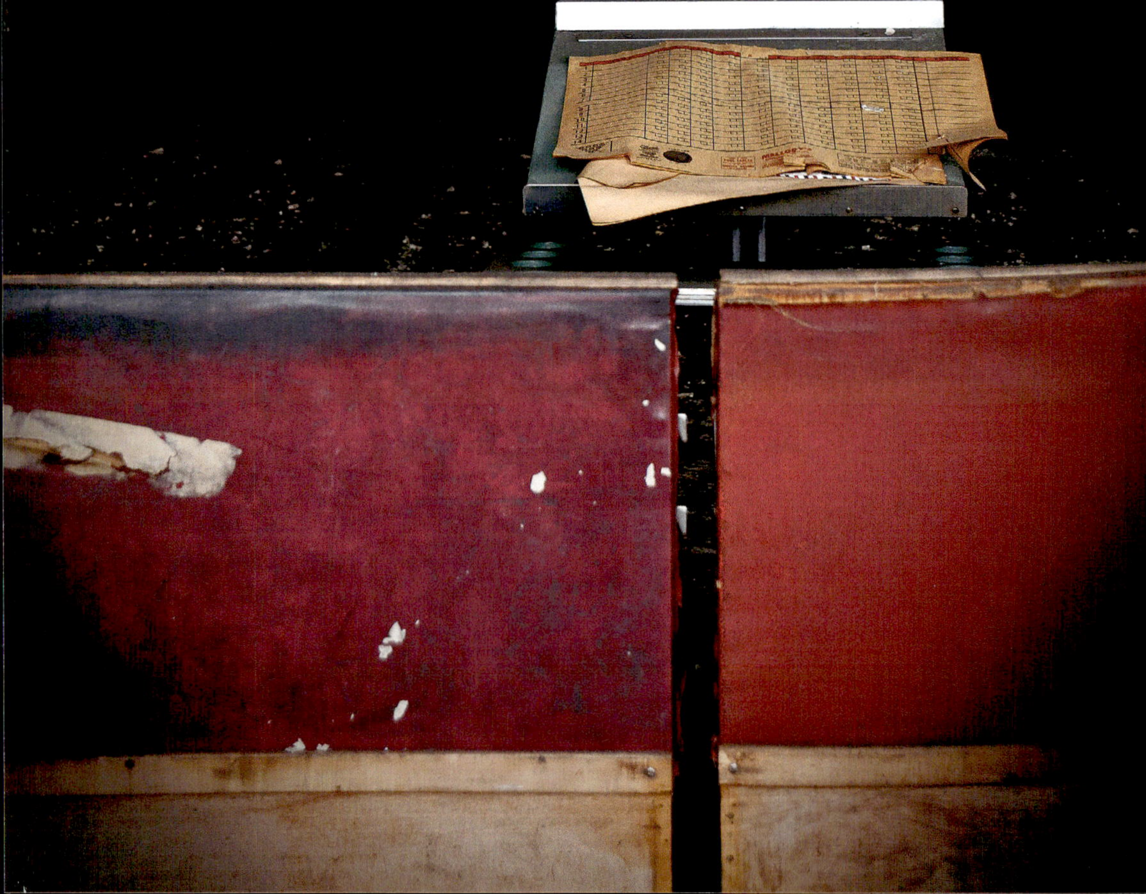

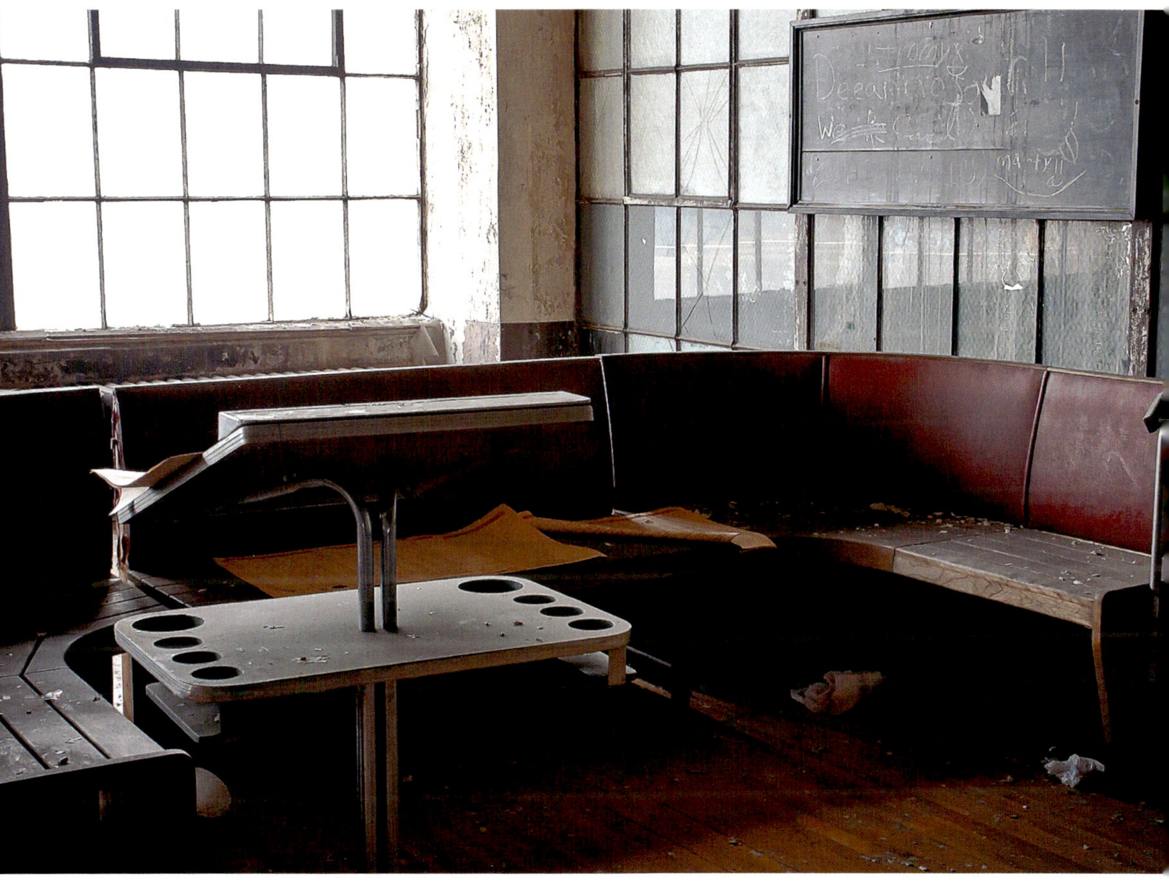

Above: A booth in the bowling alley.

Opposite page: A decades-old score card.

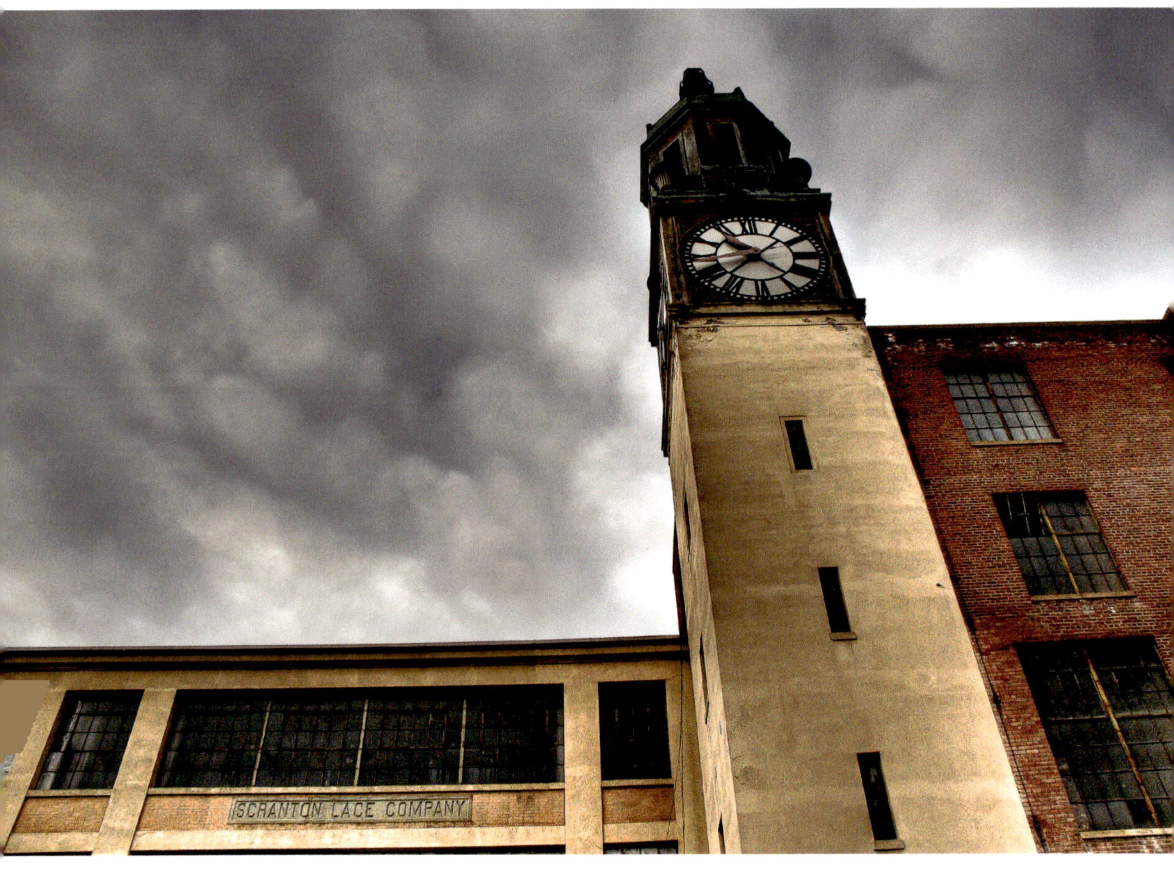

Above: An exterior view of the Scranton Lace factory.

Opposite page: The iconic clock tower overlooks the town of Scranton.

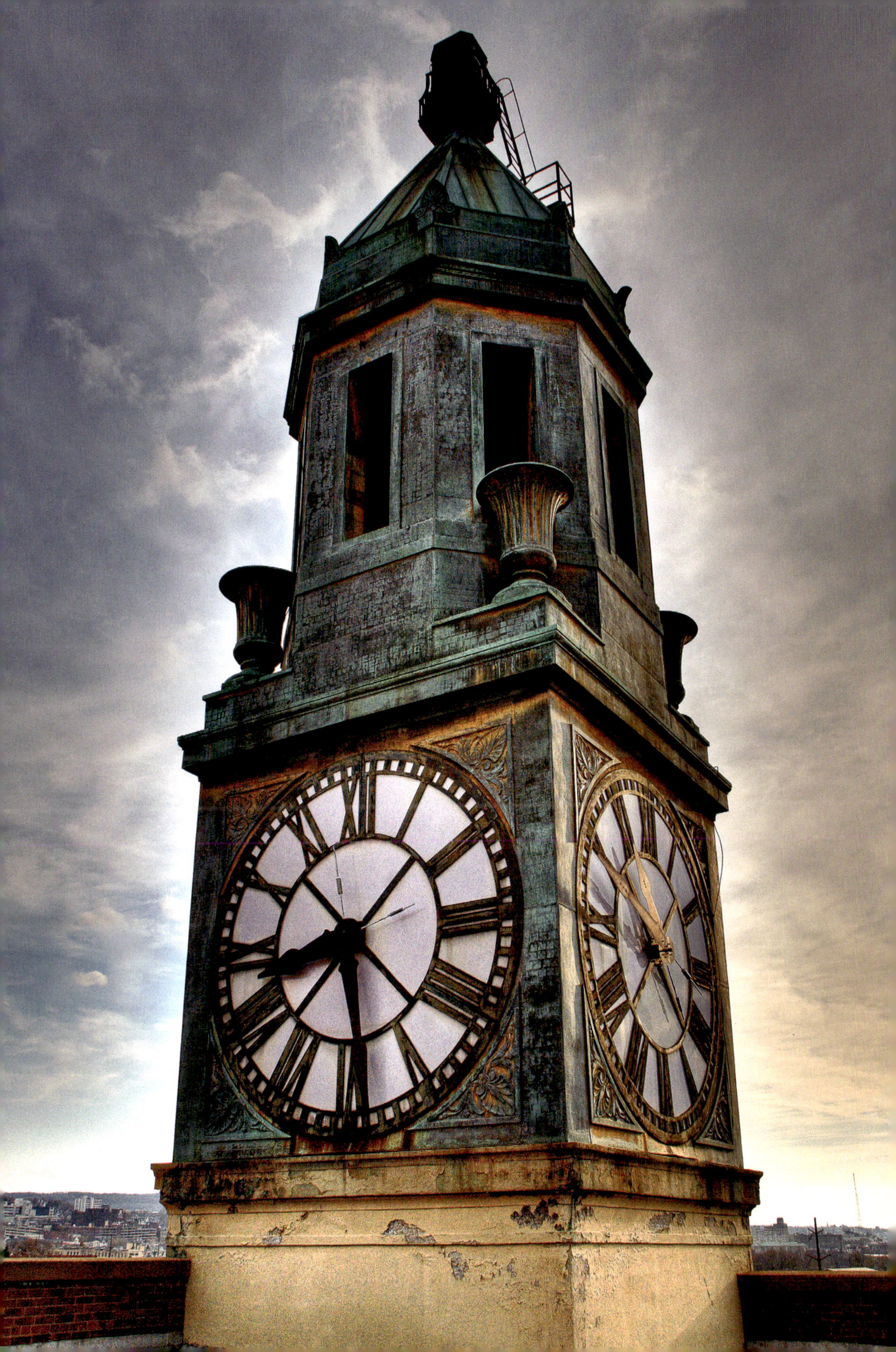

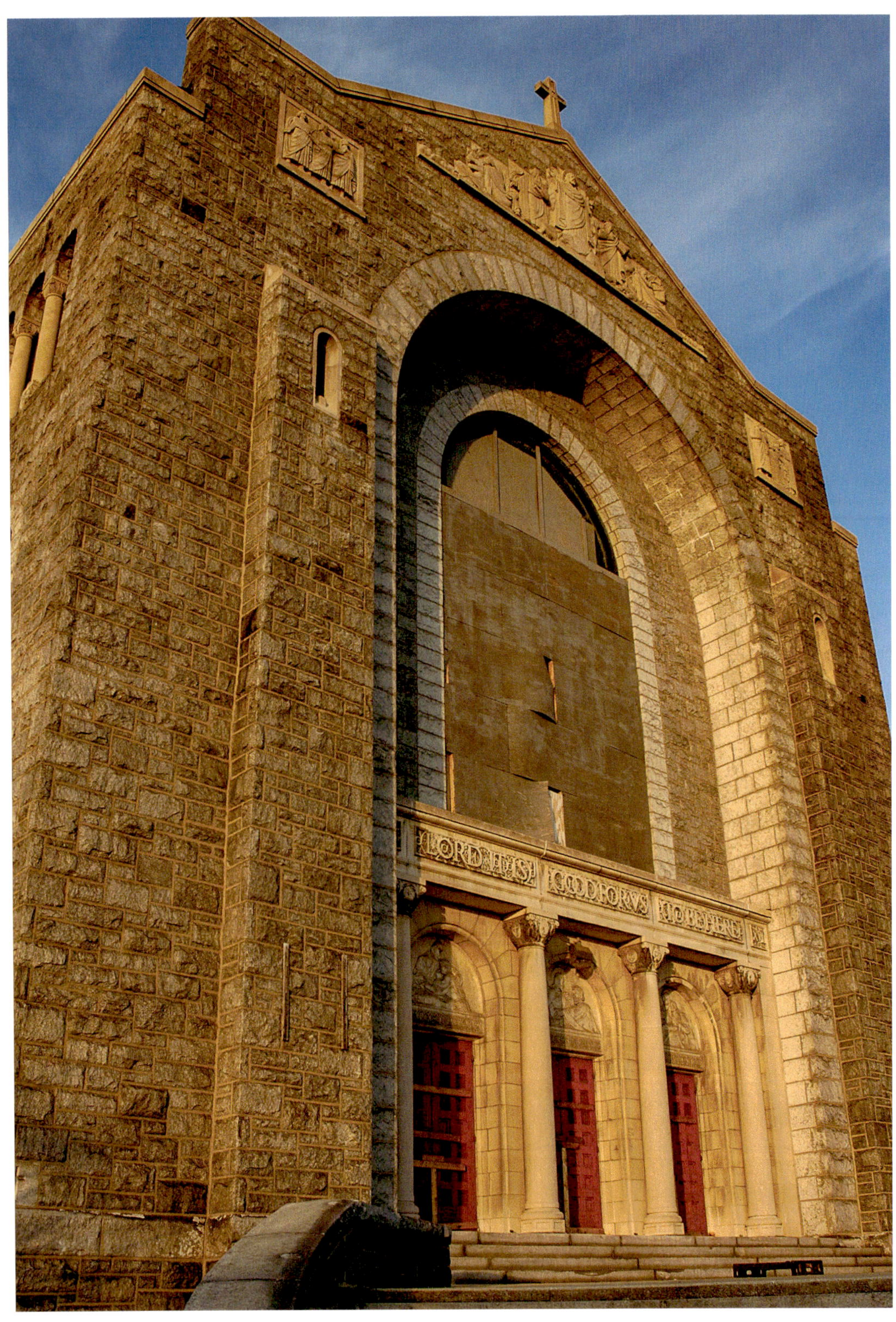

Transfiguration of Our Lord Church.

TRANSFIGURATION OF OUR LORD CHURCH

As citadels of worship, churches are often repositories of our greatest joys and sorrows. Baptisms, weddings, funerals: the theatre of human dramedy plays out before their elaborate altars. Even for those with no religious denomination, the magnificent architecture and intricate attention to detail inside Catholic churches is often awe-inspiring. Breathtaking stained-glass scenes of saints and biblical passages are often combined with soaring pillars and detailed mosaics of ecclesiastical figures. There is an unspoken expectation that such beauty be revered and the intent with which it was built be respected—if not by outsiders then at the very least by those who are entrusted with its care.

Demise by demolishment for these soaring architectural masterpieces seems abhorrent yet has become a common fate as archdioceses across America claim to be facing severe budget shortfalls. Schools are being shuttered, parishes are being merged, and churches are being closed and then sold to the highest bidder. Many parishes across Philadelphia have succumbed to the same fate. As churches were abandoned, their displaced parishioners watched in dismay as the once-stately beacons of their communities fell victim to neglect.

The Transfiguration of Our Lord Church, situated in a working-class area of West Philadelphia, occupied the corner of Cedar Avenue and 56th Street for almost a century. The two-acre parcel of land was also home to the Transfiguration school and rectory. Sadly, this once-beautiful example of parochial architecture fell to the wrecking ball in 2009.

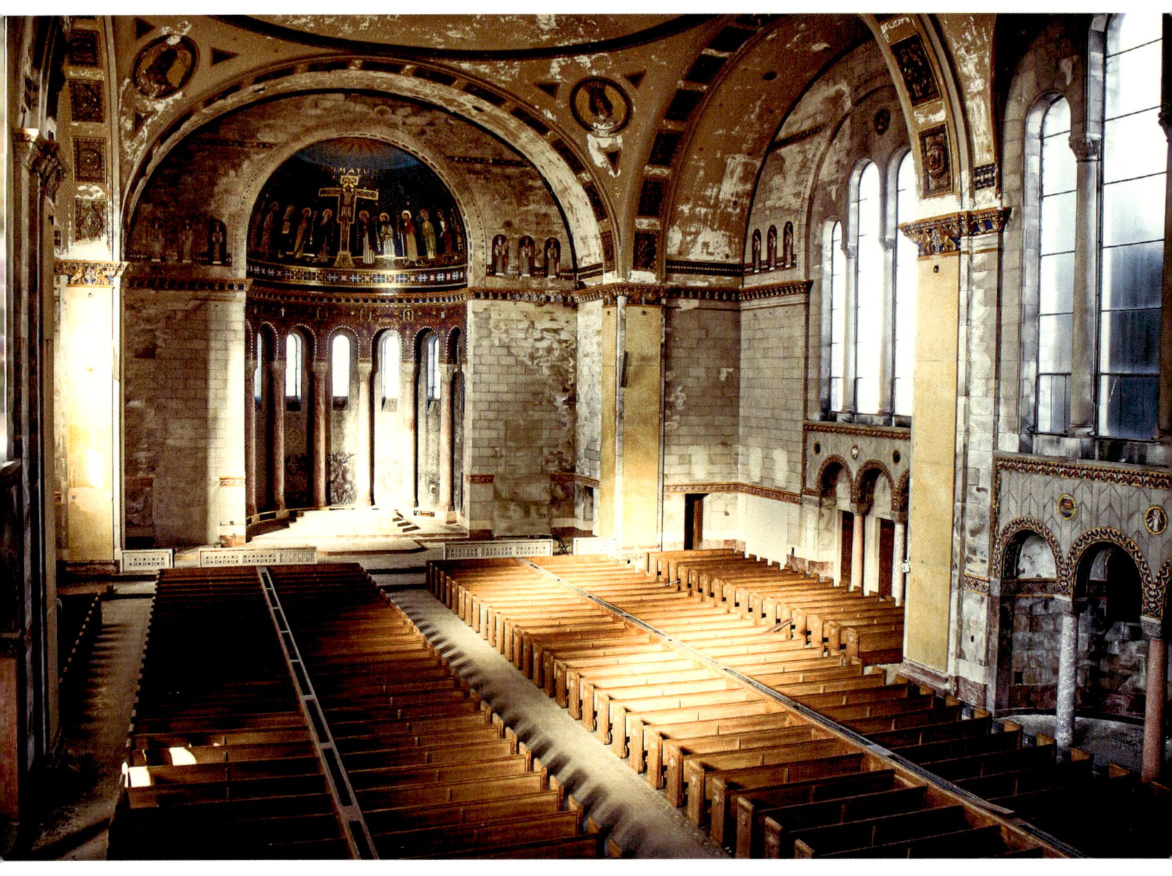

The still-beautiful interior of the upper church.

Established as an unassuming wooden building for worshippers in 1905, the church grew to include an upper and lower level, which, combined, seated more than 2,000 people. The lower level was completed in 1924 and the stunning upper level in 1928.

The attention to detail, both interior and exterior, was astonishing. No expense was spared for the Henry D. Dagit-designed church. Elaborate mosaics, which comprised of faience tiles, adorned much of the interior. A 1,200-square-foot glass tile depiction of the Crucifixion, which was created by hand, surrounded the altar. Twelve different types of marble, imported from Italy and France, clad the pillars, altar, and steps. The stained-glass windows originated from the celebrated Zettler stained-glass studio in Munich. It is unimaginable that when the wrecking ball struck in 2009, none of these treasures were salvaged.

After the church's closure in 2000, the archdiocese of Philadelphia made cosmetic attempts at upkeep; nuns kept the gardens manicured, but the more expensive structural maintenance was neglected. In 2005, they offloaded the decaying house of worship for $1.1 million to the soon to be disgraced Follieri group.

An Italian real estate group, led by entrepreneur Raphael Follieri, who was later jailed for his part in "Vati-Con," planned to turn the church property into affordable housing. A strong community backlash resulted in delays to the abatement and it was during this time period that Follieri was charged with five counts of money-laundering, six counts of wire fraud, and one count of conspiracy to commit wire fraud. The house of cards Follieri was building, with the purchase of Catholic Church-owned properties, collapsed. After he was sentenced and jailed, ownership of the church was quickly transferred to Boys' Latin of Philadelphia Charter School. The exact date of the sale to Boys' Latin is difficult to ascertain from online sources.

Founding CEO of Boys' Latin, David Hardy, wasted no time in ordering the demolition of the church. His only interest had been in the former school building; the rectory and church were of no use to Boys' Latin. The destruction was swift. The beauty that was the Transfiguration of Our Lord Church is now an athletic field.

The importance of education cannot be argued, and the achievements of Hardy's charter school cannot be denied. Young African American men who would otherwise have little to no educational opportunities are thriving at Boys' Latin and continuing on to universities and colleges at a heartening rate. Yet community members are questioning the ethics of the throwaway culture the demolition of sacred buildings is promoting to the young students.

In July 2021, Boys' Latin was in the news once again as they prepared to demolish another hallowed site. This time an even more historically significant church was under attack. Our Lady of the Blessed Sacrament was built in 1890 in the Romanesque style by architect Frank Rushmore Watson. Preservationists strove for historic certification and locals banded together, picketing the fenced-in site and trying desperately to prevent another demolition. They failed.

After the demolition, a local teacher was quoted in a newspaper article as saying, "I'm a teacher myself, and Boys' Latin is showing their students an ugly lesson. That

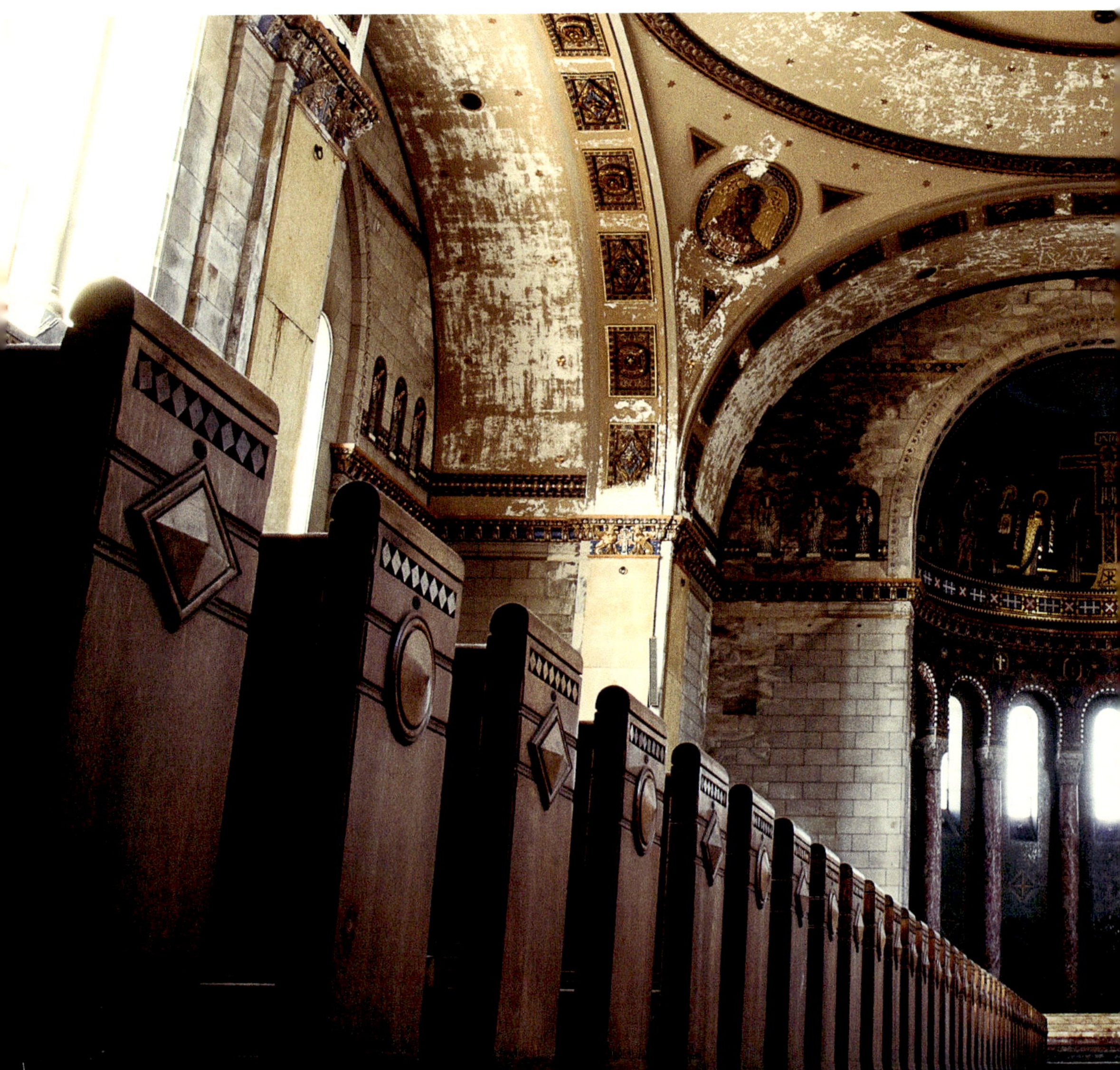

it's OK to demo historic buildings, that it's OK to disregard your community." His words are hard to ignore when all that stands in place of Our Lady of the Blessed Sacrament is another Boys' Latin athletic field.

More than a decade separates the demise of these two architectural masterpieces, yet the memory of the Transfiguration lives on. An online group of former parishioners are dedicated to keeping their memories of the church alive. They share wedding photos from decades ago and historical documents from the Archdiocese Archives. The group is optimistic, but there is also an underlying anger directed at the Catholic Church by some. The Roman Catholic Church has much to answer for in its inability to care for such sacred spaces.

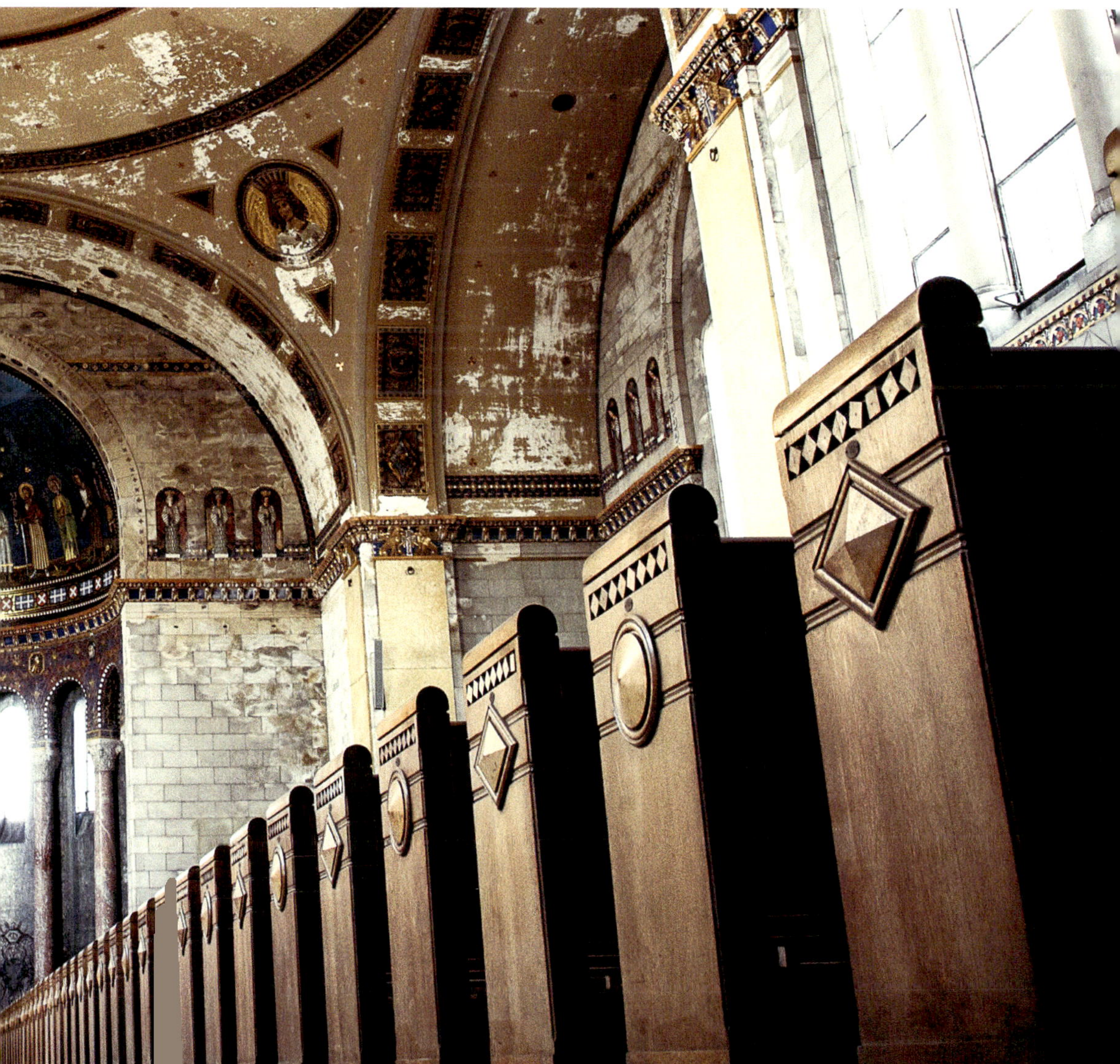

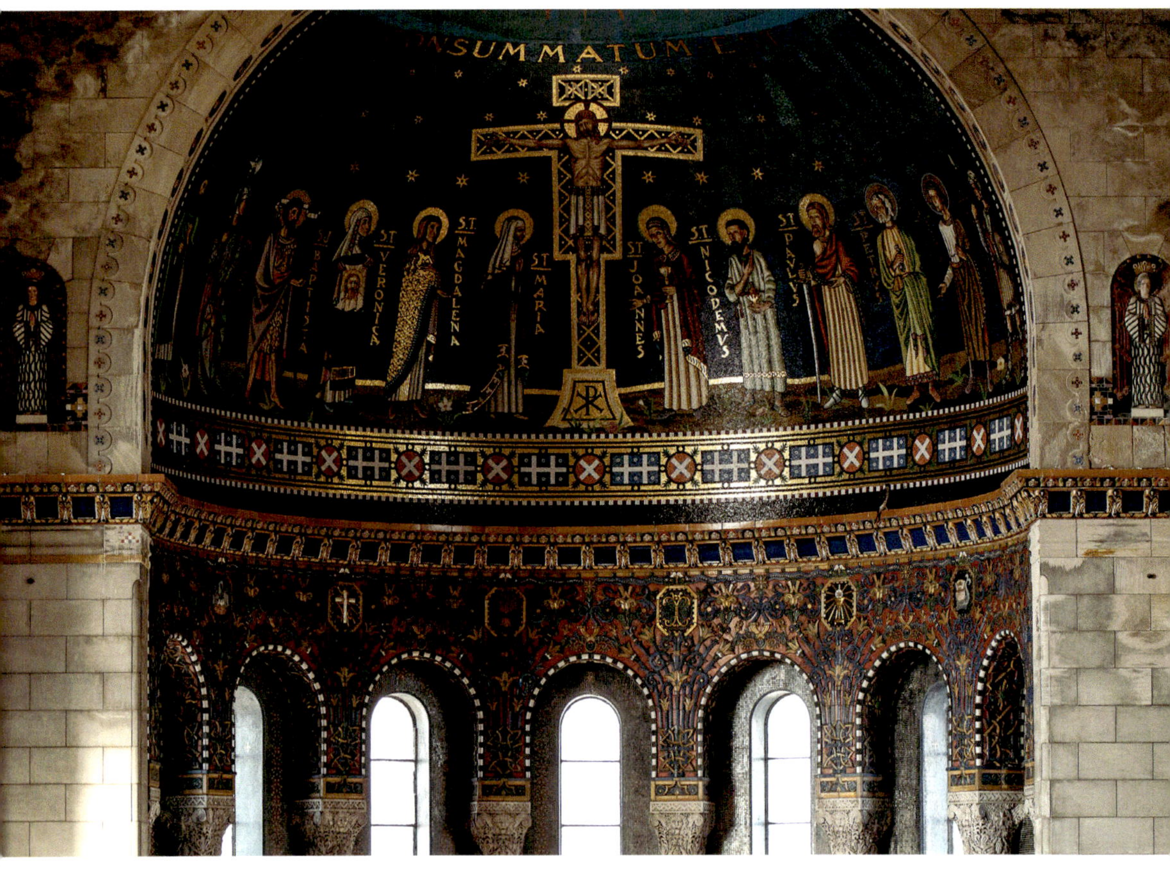

Above: The intricately detailed mosaic tiles above the altar.

Opposite page: Soaring arches were a striking feature.

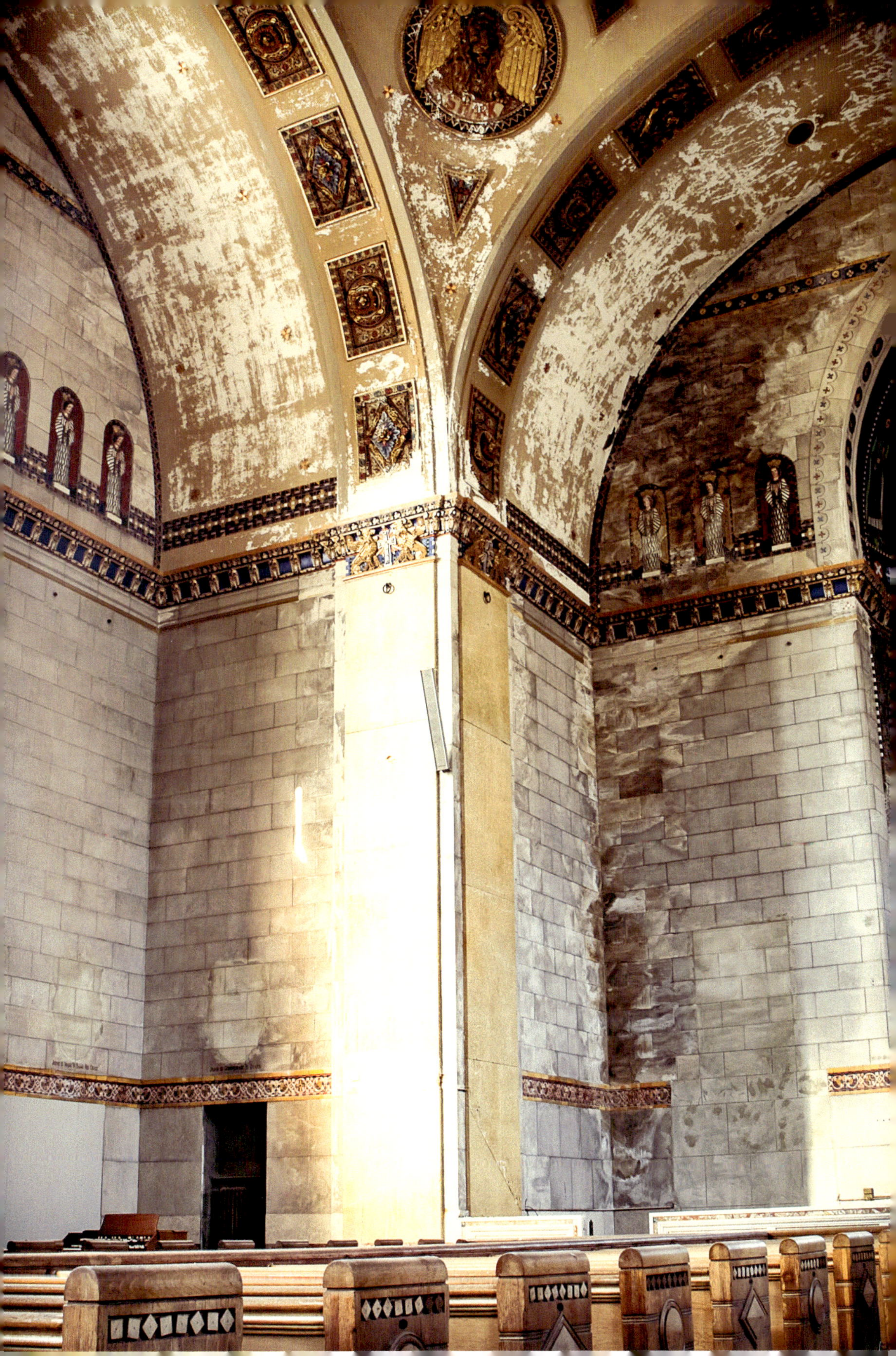

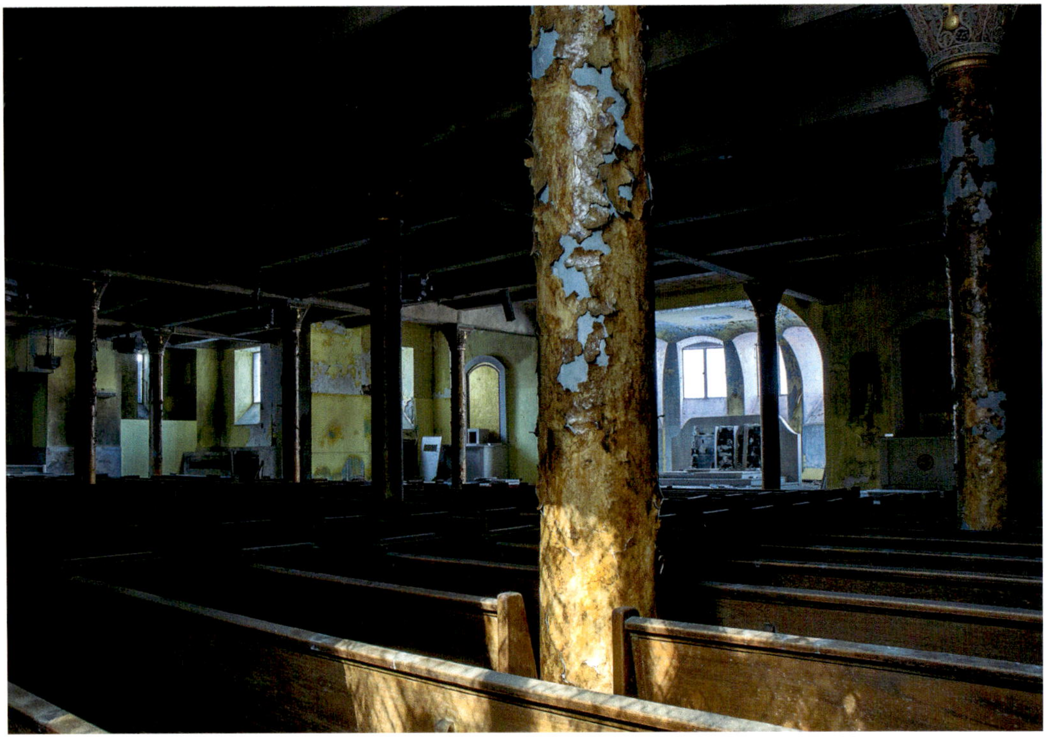

The lower church.

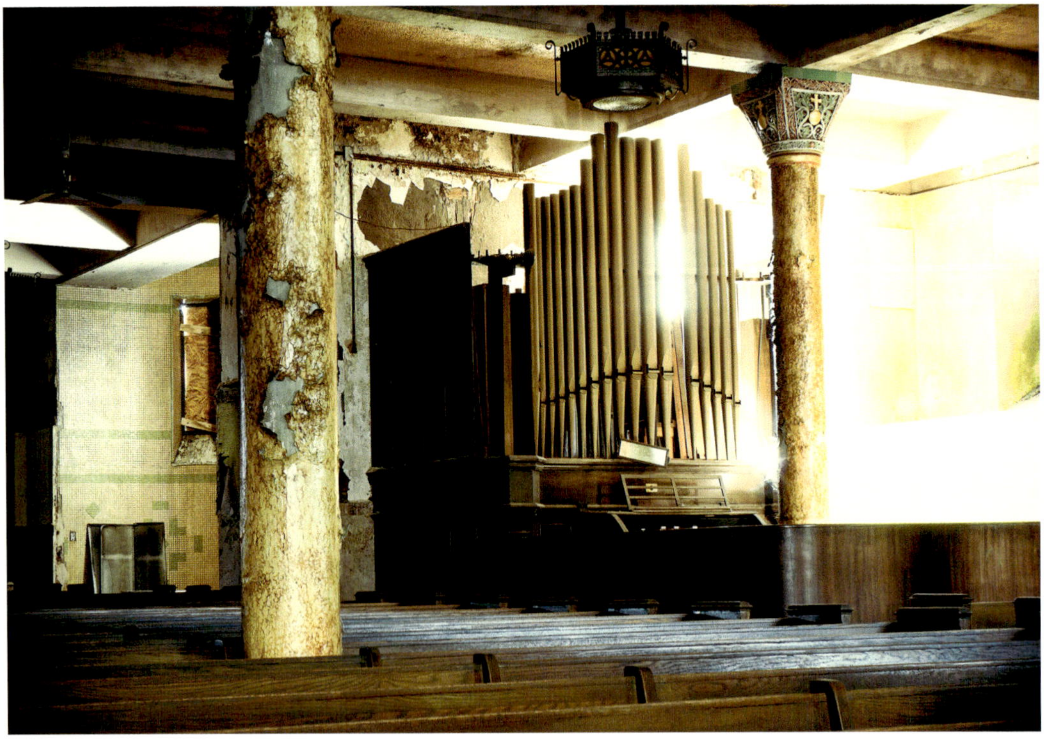

A sunlit organ in the lower church.

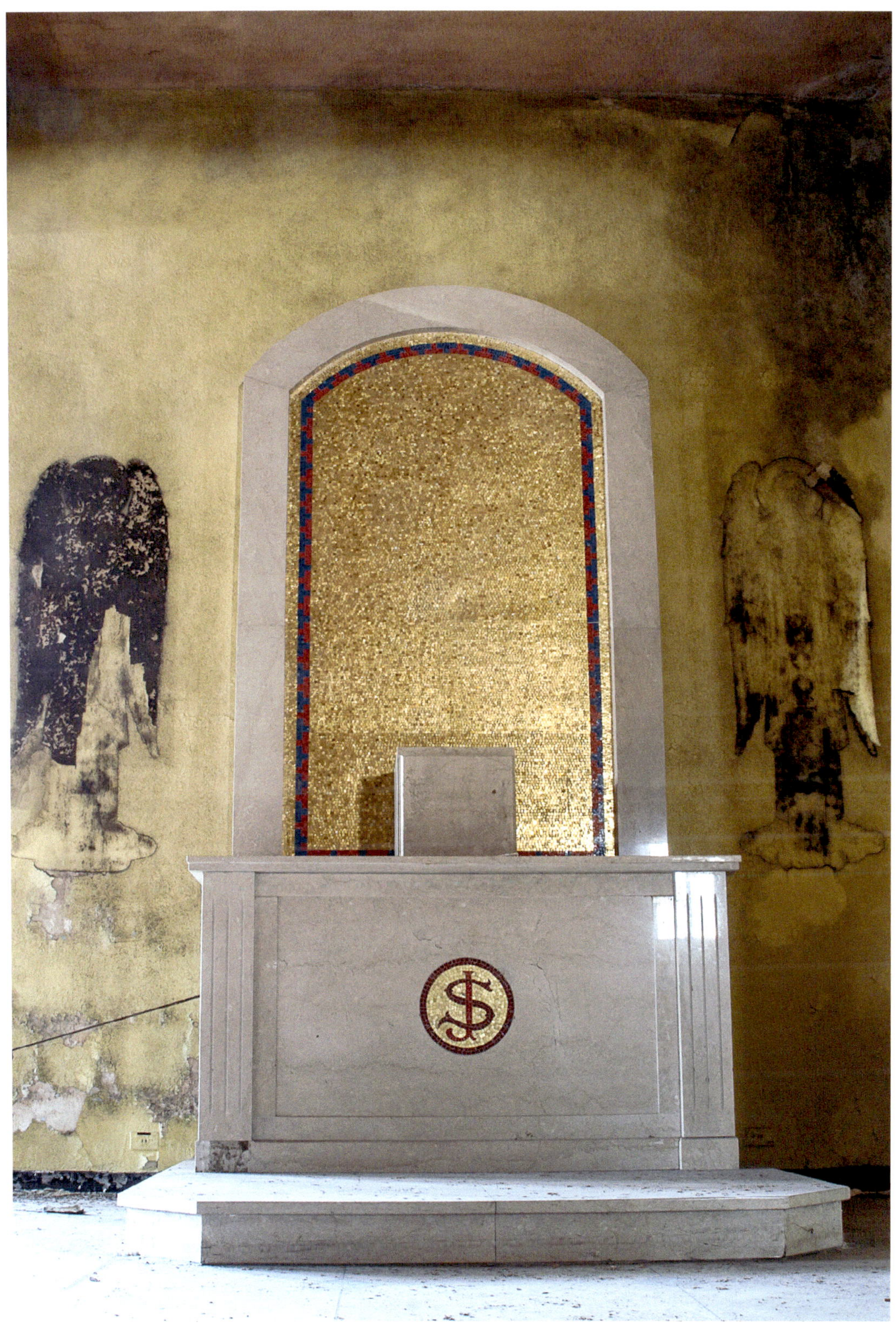

The lower church altar framed by interesting outlines of removed statues.

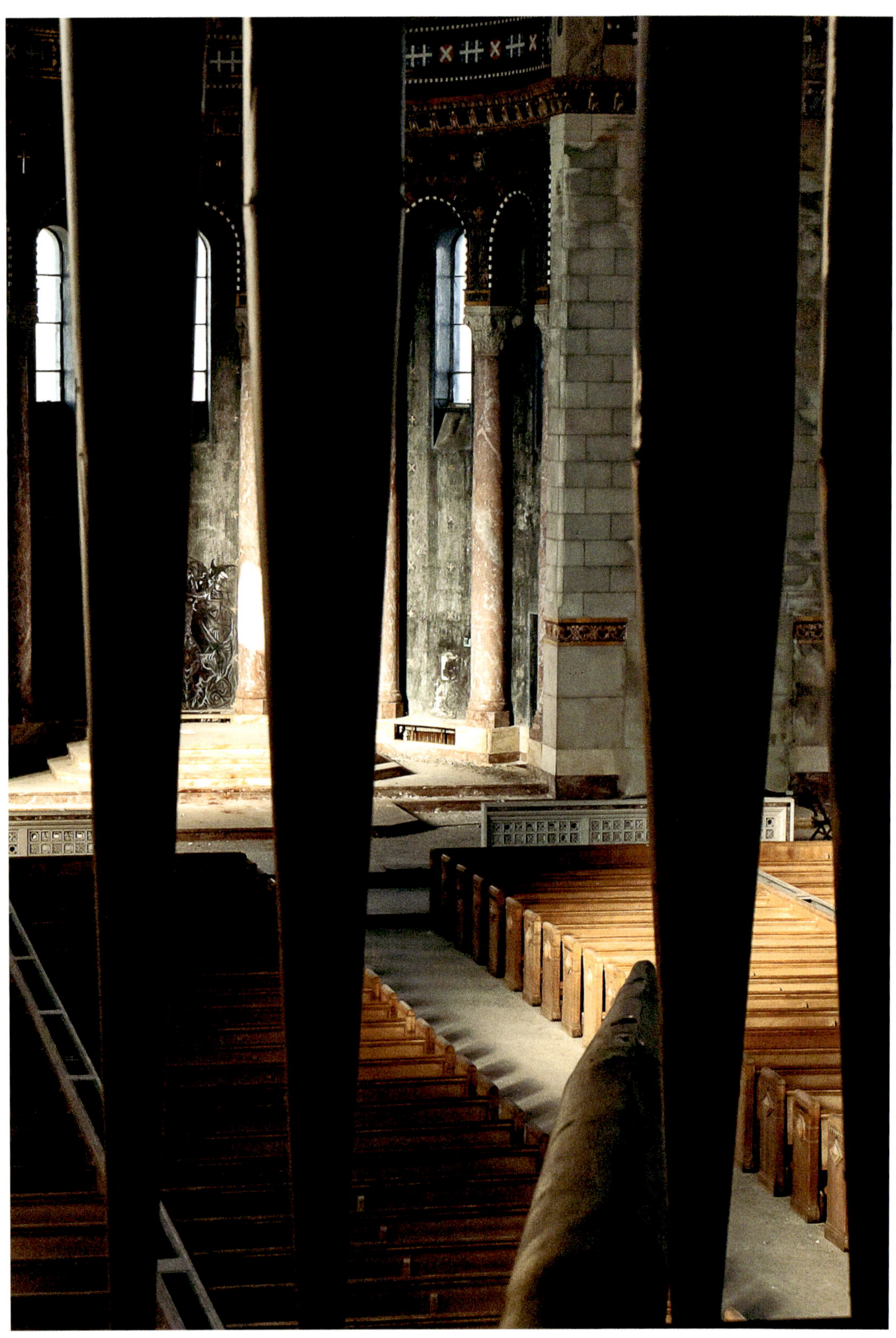

Looking through the main church organ pipes toward the altar.

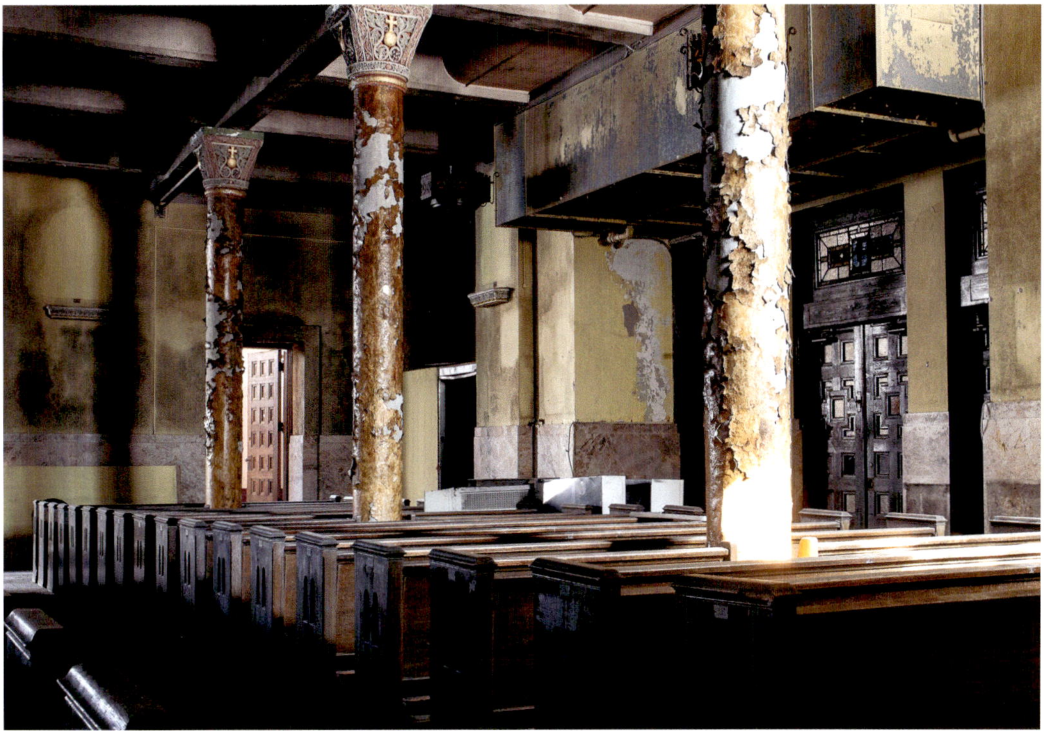

Paint peels from pillars in the lower church.

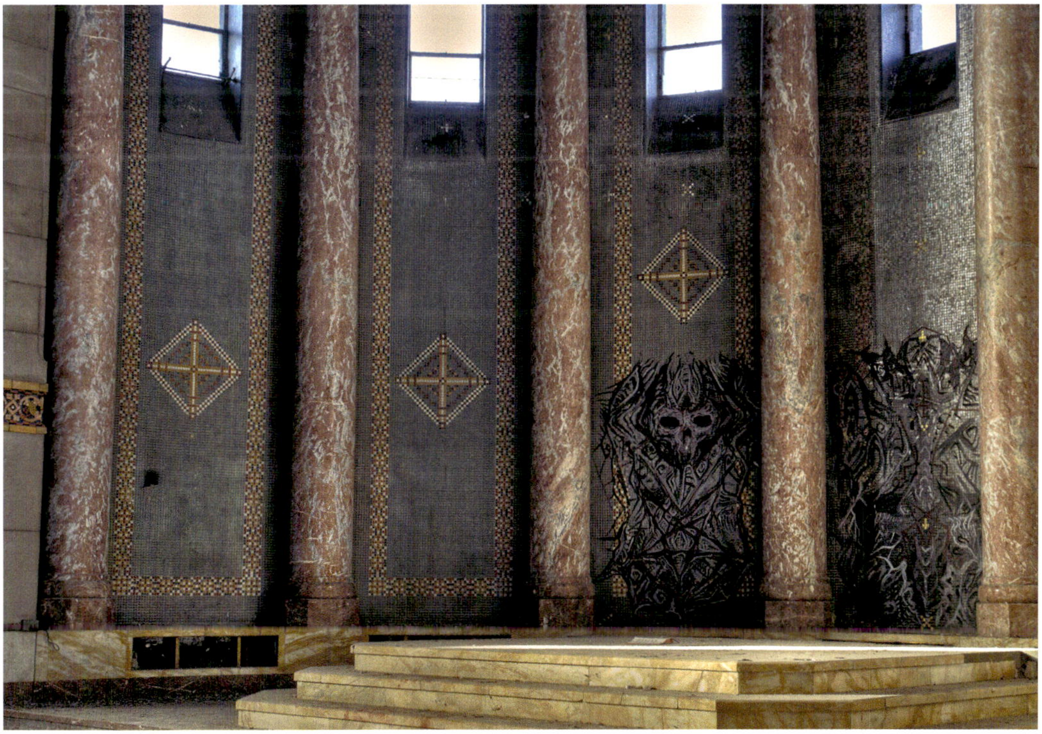

Satanic graffiti defaces the main altar.

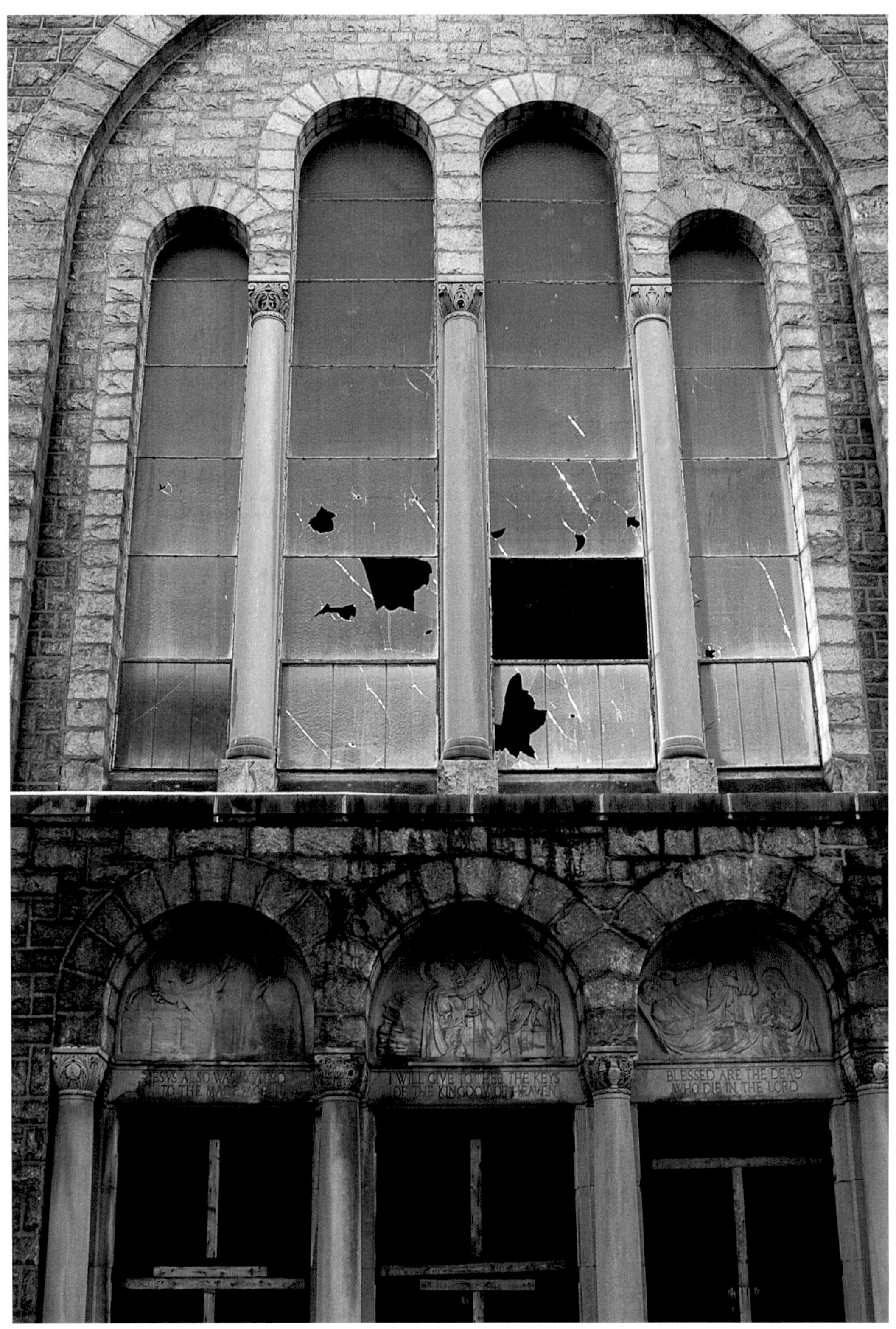

Broken windows and boarded-up doors at the main entrance.

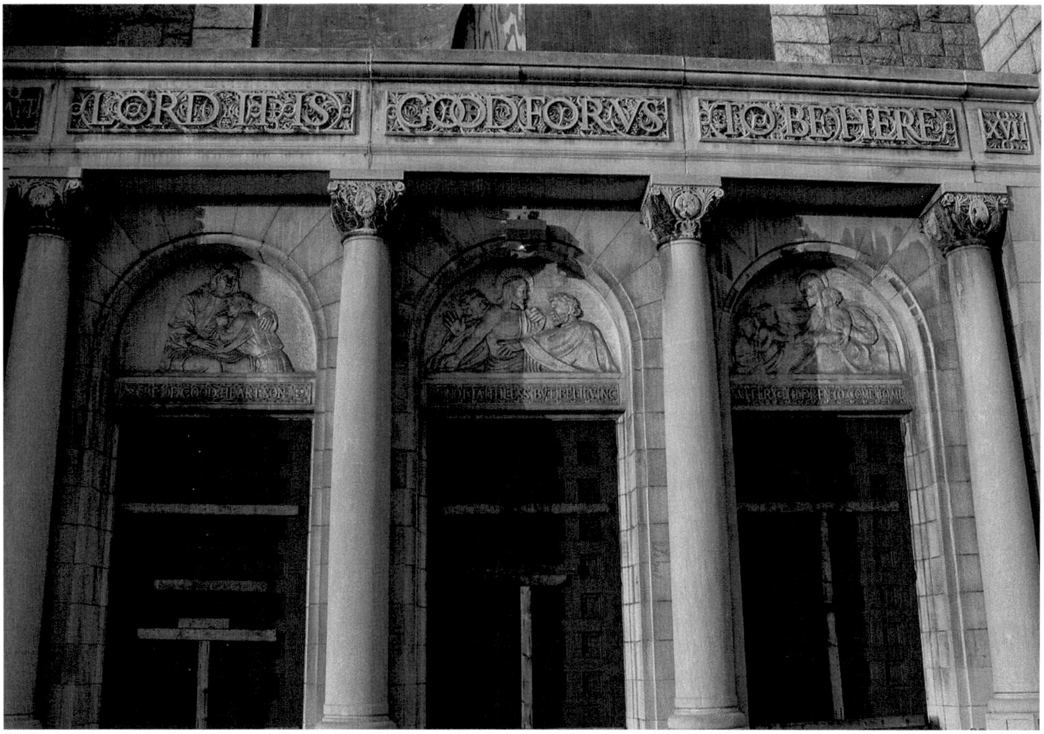

Exterior stone relief sculptures above the entrance.

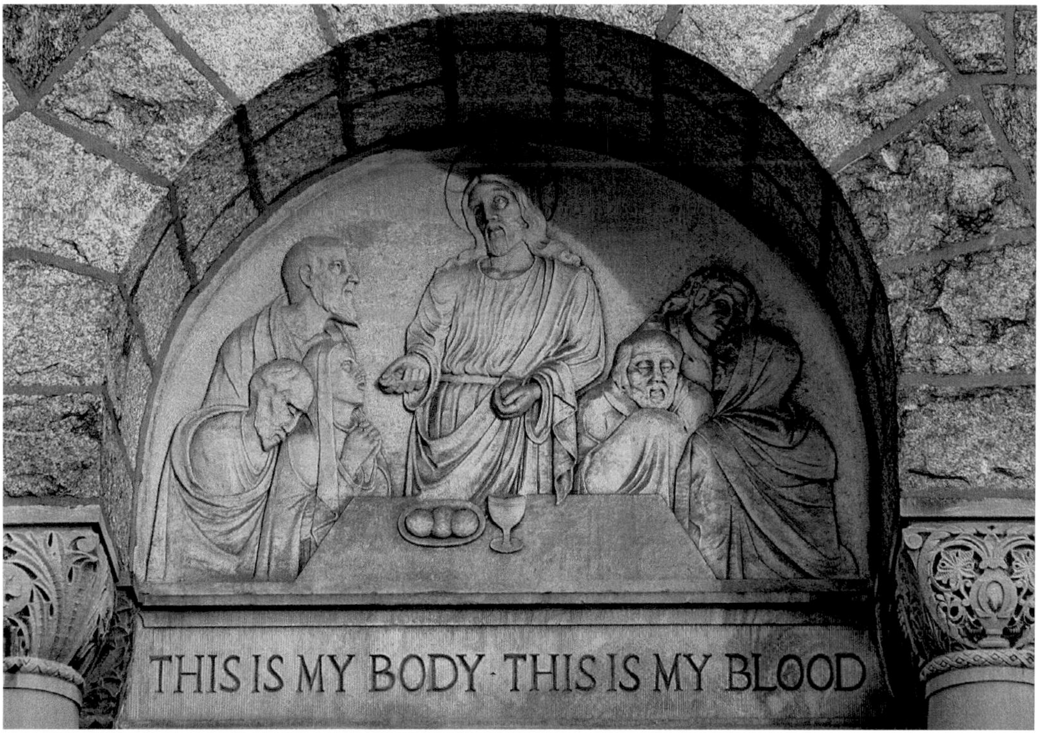

Detail of a stone relief sculpture.

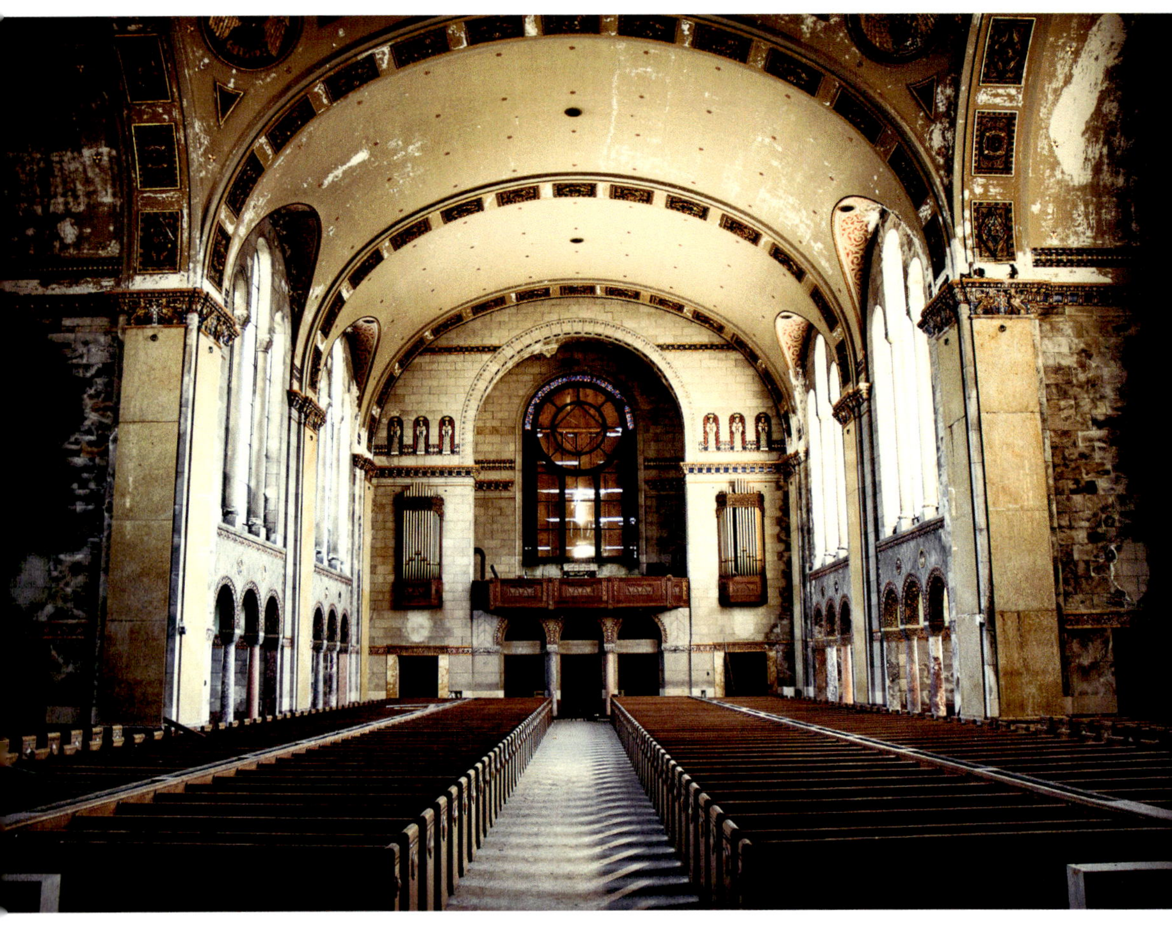

The view to the rear of the main church.

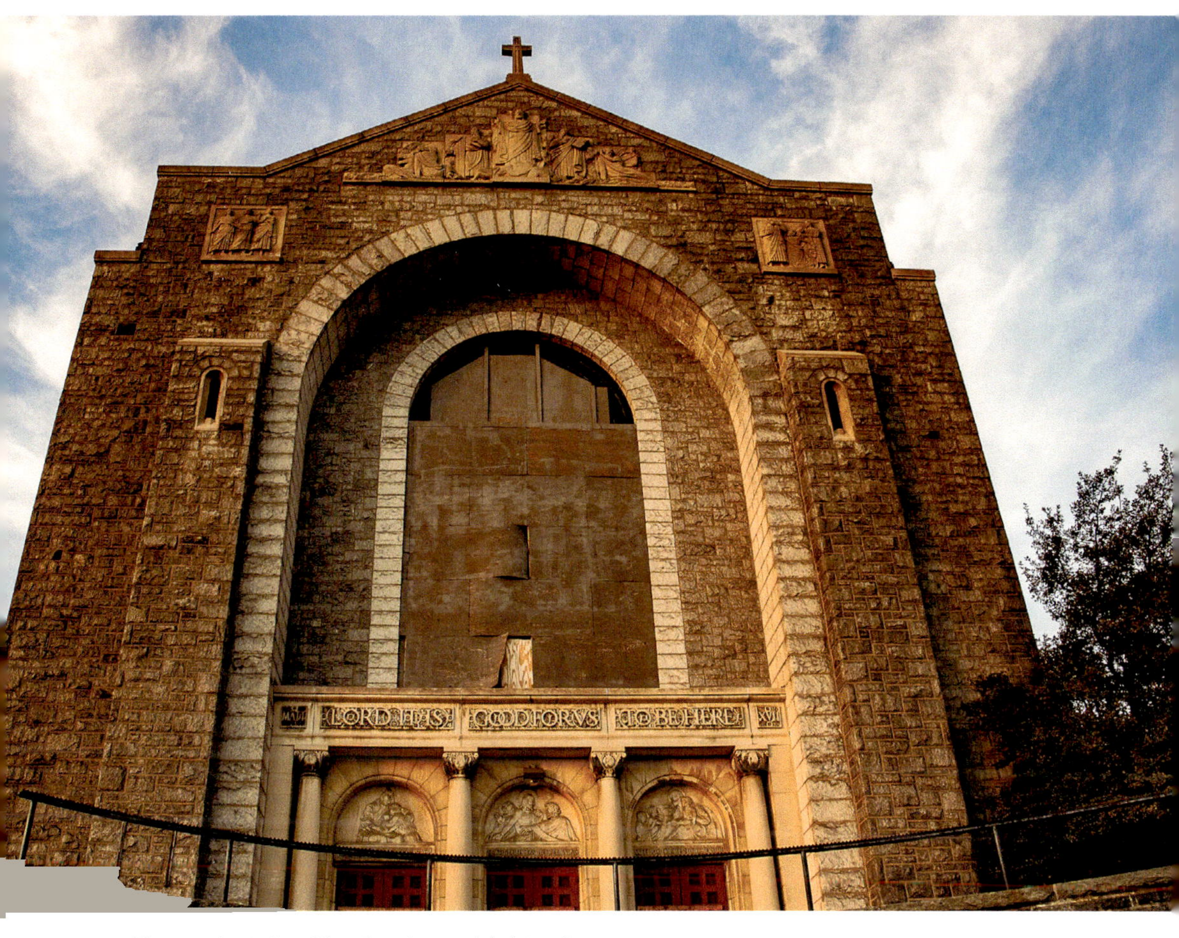

The grand exterior of the church, awash in late afternoon sun.

YORK COUNTY PRISON

As fortresses of despair with foreboding facades, prisons inspire fear; enclosed within their walls are living conditions no one would ever want to experience. Their seemingly impenetrable exteriors and razor-wired perimeters conceal from public view all that goes on within. All have their secrets, and many reportedly, especially abandoned ones, have their ghosts. The old York County Prison is no exception.

The six-story, 30,000-square-foot facility was erected in 1906, and replaced the original castle-like complex—built in 1853—and which also housed the county courthouse and hospital. The York County prison closed in 1979 after years of prisoner unrest and rumors of appalling conditions. While the walls can't talk, as per the old adage, they can give us a glimpse into the minds of the prisoners. Many cells contain artwork or personal artifacts, and one cell in particular contained a sketch of a makeshift calendar that marked the passing of time and included the date of an upcoming court hearing. One can only imagine the desperation of counting days until possible release from unbearable confinement.

At the turn of the century, America's justice system was barbaric. According to a former warden, who was interviewed for a *York Daily Record* article, executions took place at the prison in the early 1900s. A trapdoor in the floor at the back of prison opened up to the basement and was used for hangings. The last execution of a prisoner took place in 1908. Damning reports appeared during the 1950s, including complaints of overcrowding, racial segregation, and horrifyingly unhygienic

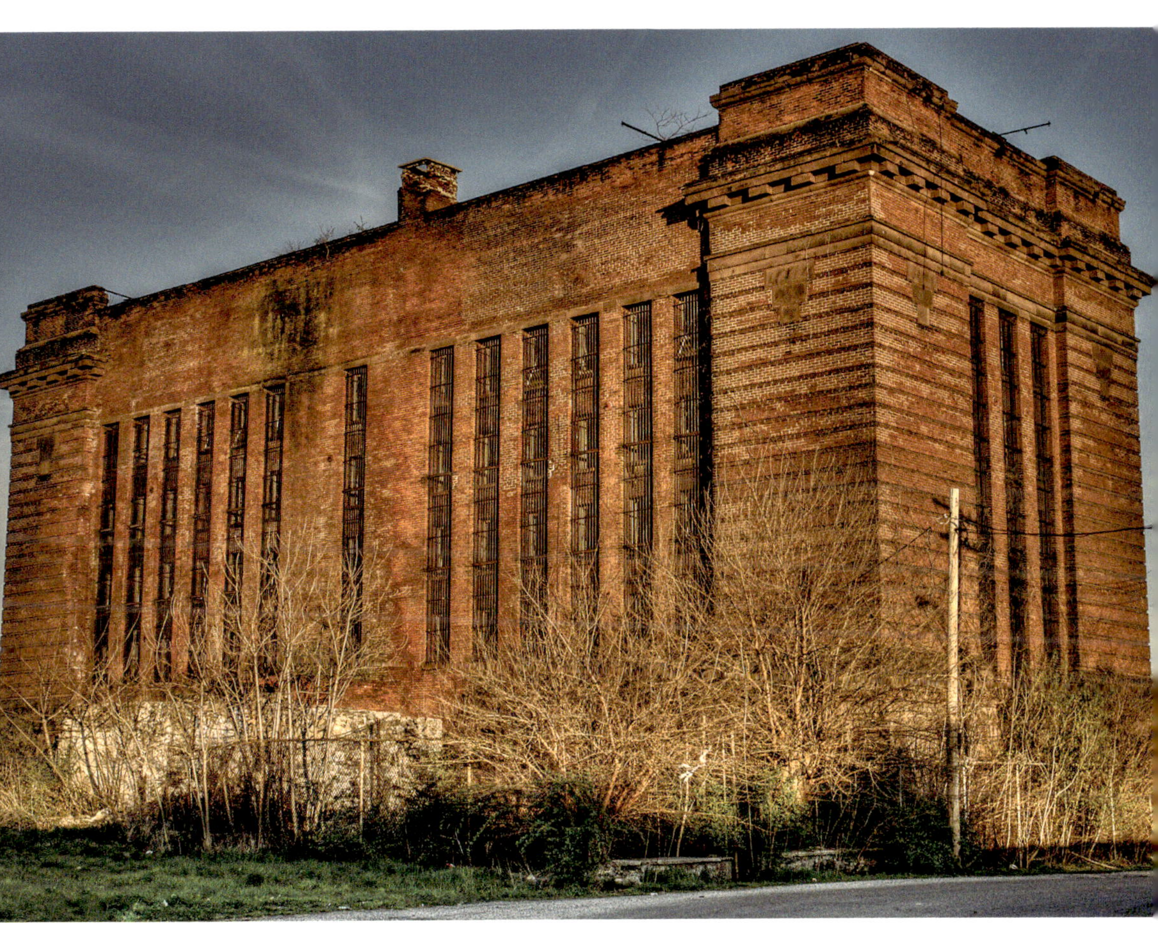

The foreboding York County Prison.

food practices. Prisoners lamented about being served venison that was roadkill, and intolerable conditions continued to plague the prison until its closure in 1979.

It is no wonder then that stories of the ghosts of angry prisoners, roaming the empty cell blocks, abound. The unsettled spirits are said to follow visitors through the deserted floors and the smell of lit cigarettes sometimes fills the stale prison air, although there is not a smoker present.

As is the case with so many long-abandoned structures, the prison is now privately owned but has had a tumultuous history since its closure. The prison was purchased by John and Joyce Gearhart in 1982. John was in real estate and had dreams of one day redeveloping the prison. The dreams never became a reality and the prison continued to rot for decades. In 2003, the Gearharts tried, unsuccessfully, to find a purchaser. Fast forward to 2014 when the Redevelopment Authority of the City of York (RDA) suddenly decided to seize the Gearhart's property using eminent domain. The RDA had moved in 2013 to successfully have the property designated as blighted, which aided the eminent domain claim.

A soap opera, lasting several years, ensued. The Gearharts sued the RDA and won. The settlement awarded to the Gearharts of $1.25 million sent the RDA administration reeling and an appeal soon followed. The evidence revealed during the 2018 appeal trial did little to assist the RDA's case and the judge found, once again, in favor of the Gearharts.

A complicated tale of corruption was uncovered, and its telling is beyond the scope of a chapter concerning the history of a forlorn, abandoned prison, deteriorating in a Rust Belt town. In summary, though, ownership of the prison was eventually transferred to Unified Fiber and Data (UFD), a telecommunications company. The intent was to convert the prison to a data center. UFD was a tech start-up owned by 120 York, which also owned Think Loud Developments. Think Loud Developments had been in private talks, prior to the 2013 blight designation and the 2014 eminent domain seizure, with the RDA concerning the possible purchase of the prison for use by UFD.

The ghosts that roam York County Prison can rest easy; their century-long abode will not be filled with the constant hum of a data center anytime soon. In April 2021, 120 York declared Chapter 11 bankruptcy. UFD is embroiled in a lawsuit against its former CEO, William Hynes, who founded 120 York and Think Loud Developments. The Pennsylvania Public Utility Commission has moved to cancel UFD's certificate to provide services in the commonwealth. The York County Prison will continue to stand as a solemn reminder of both a troubled past, and now, more recently, of the inability by city officials to move beyond greed and corruption.

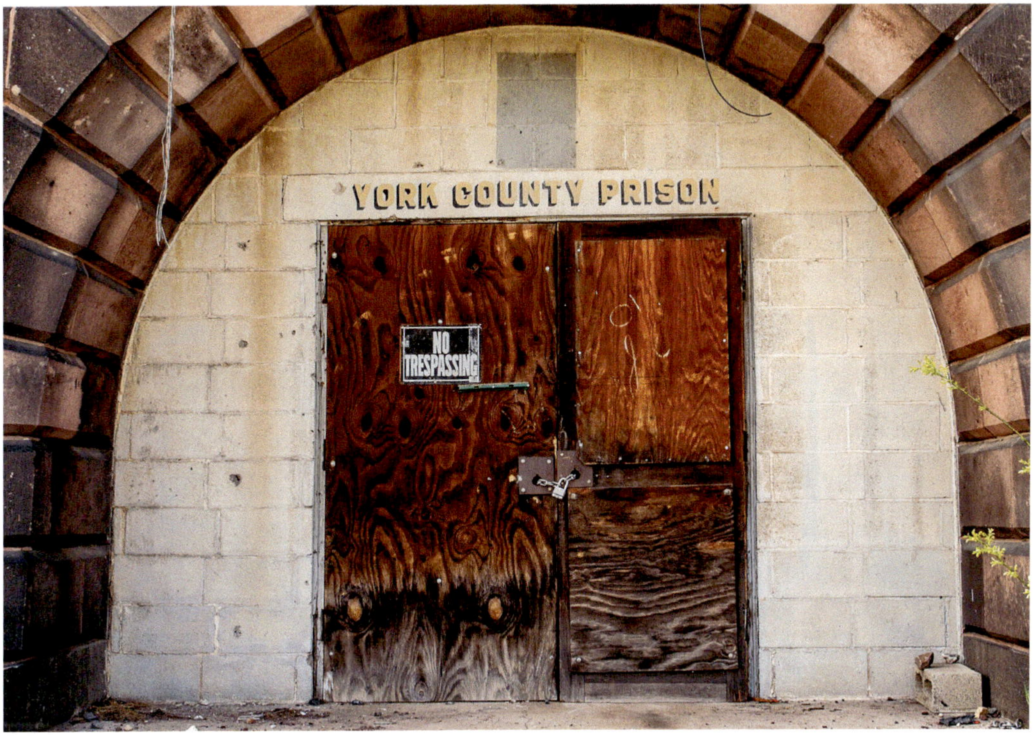

The boarded-up and locked entrance to the prison.

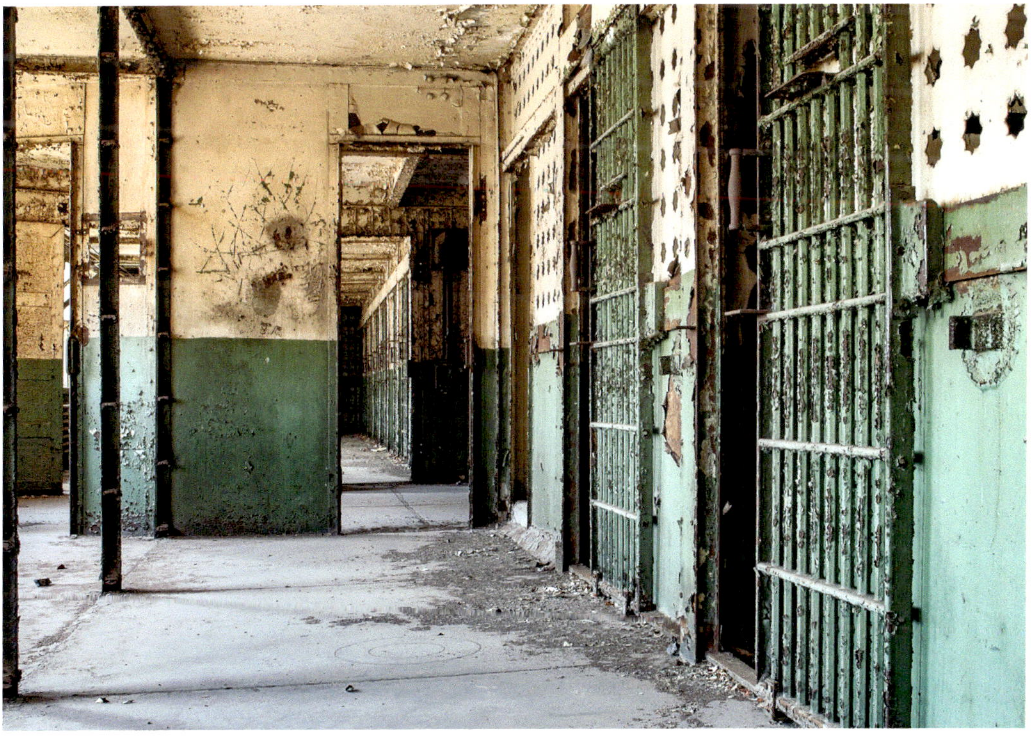

A deteriorating cell block.

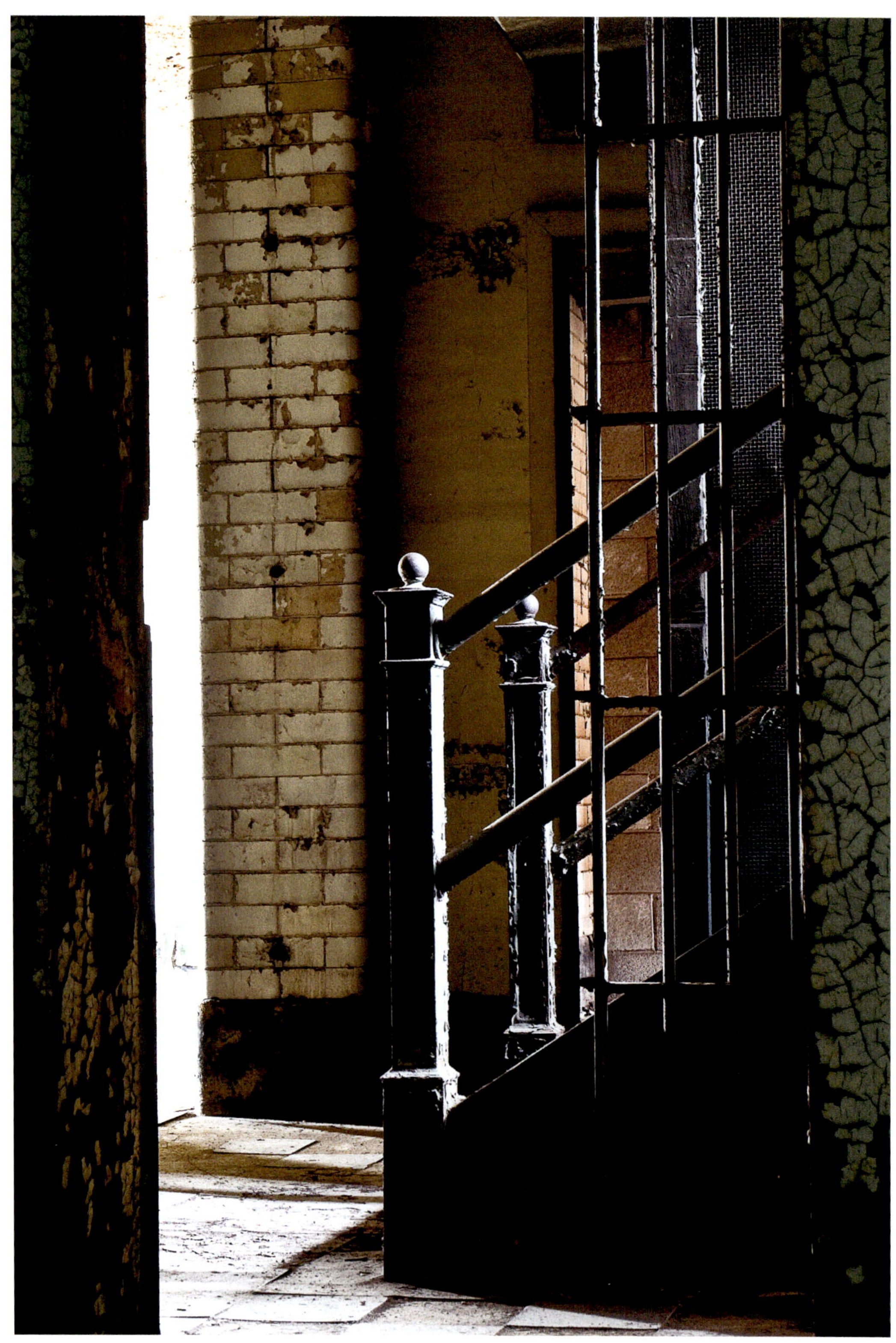

Stairs leading to the second-floor cell block.

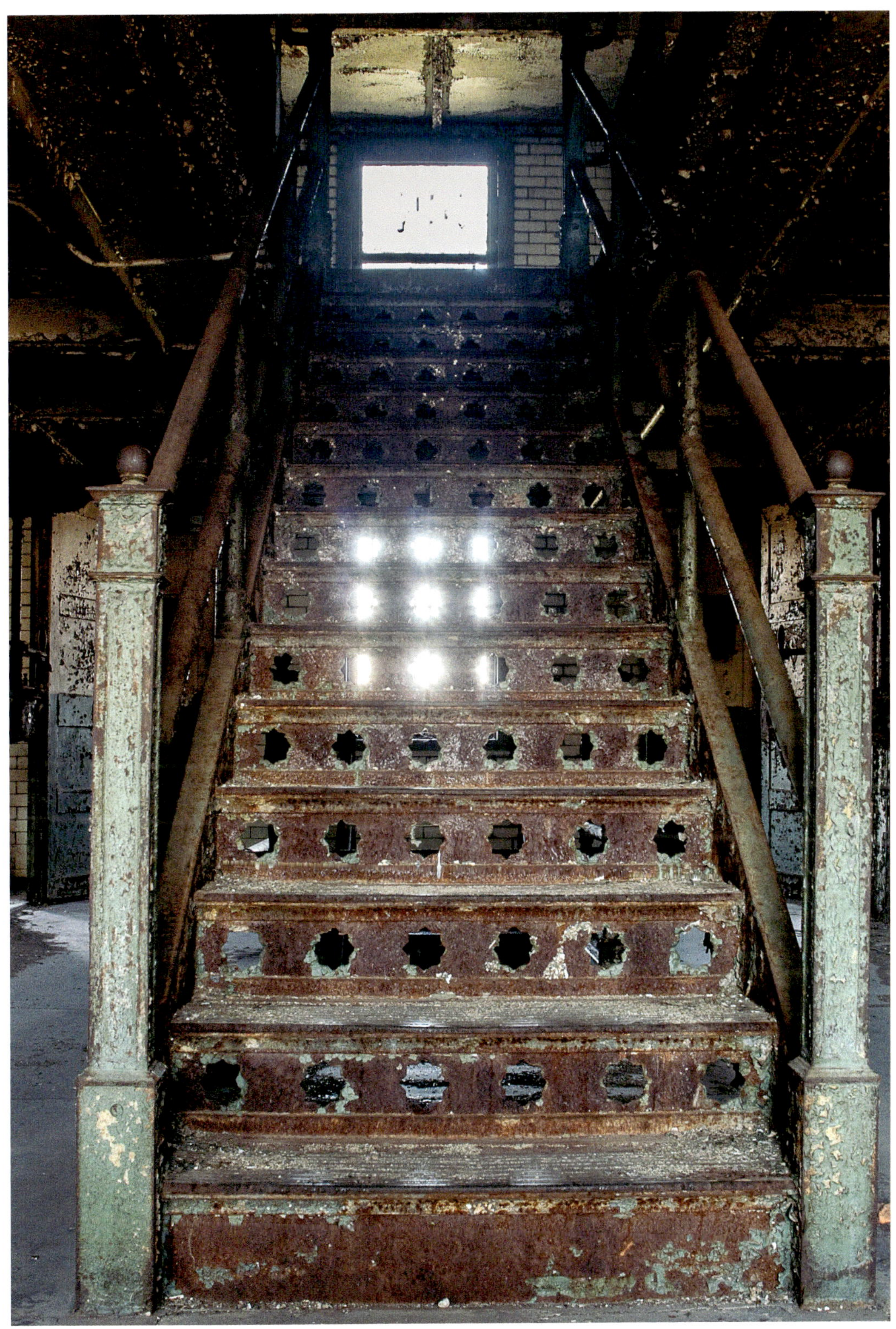

Light shining through the star like patterns in the stairs.

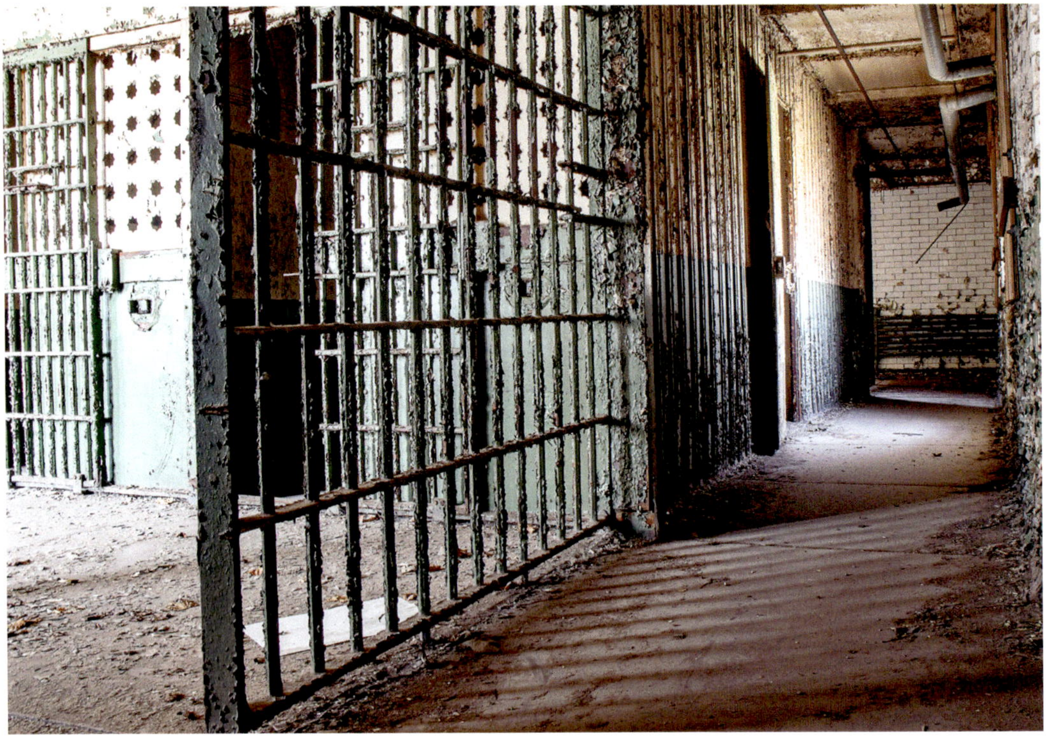

An outer hallway of the second-floor cell block.

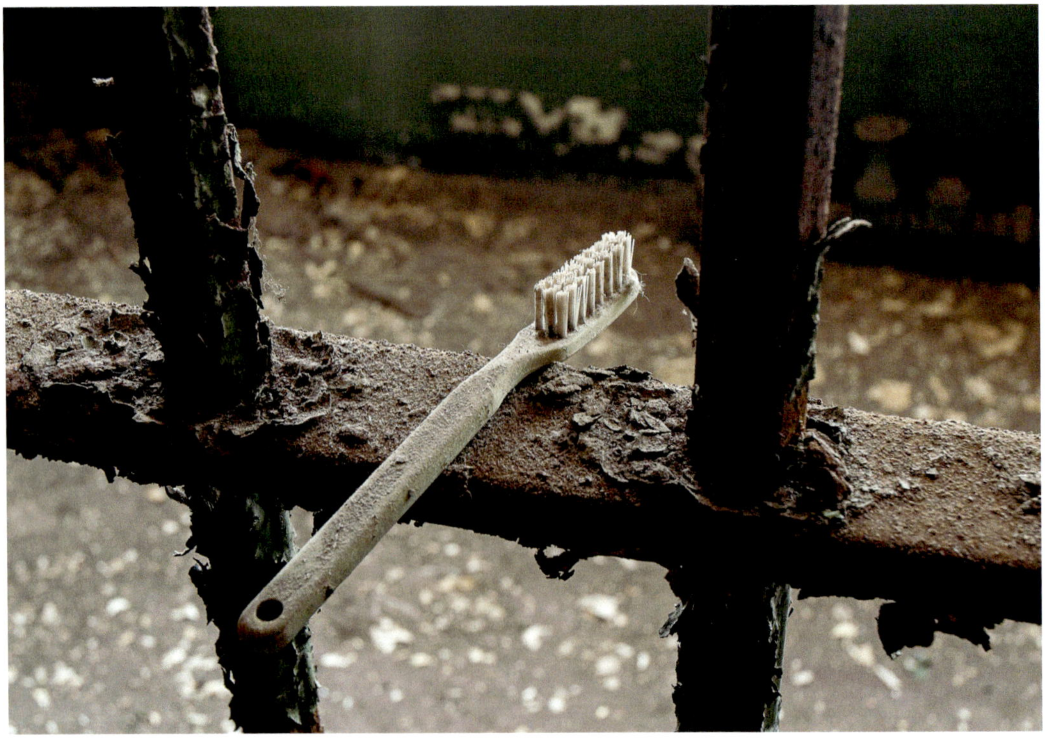

A former prisoner's toothbrush is one of few personal items that remain.

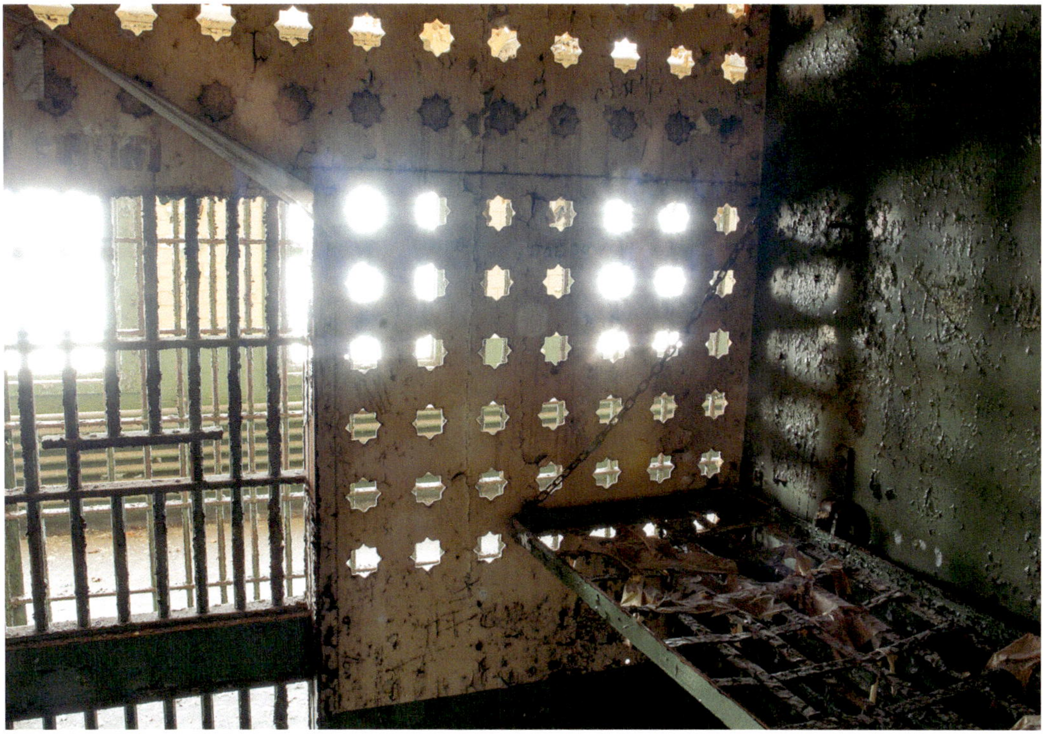

Looking outward from a cell.

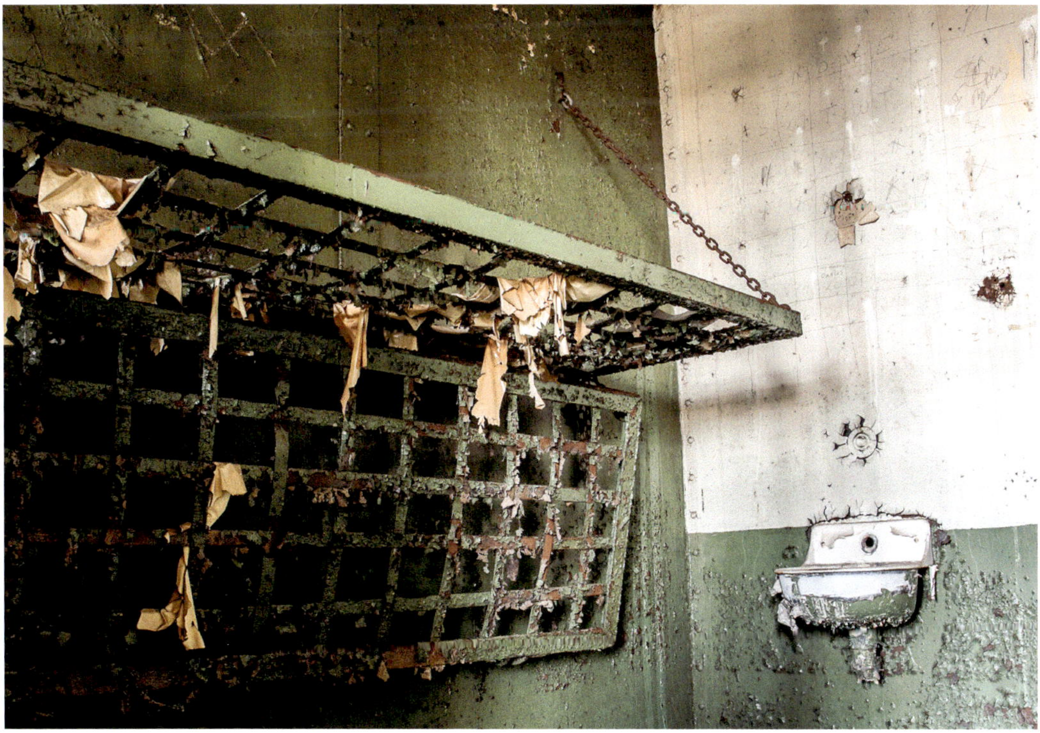

A bed and sink inside a cell.

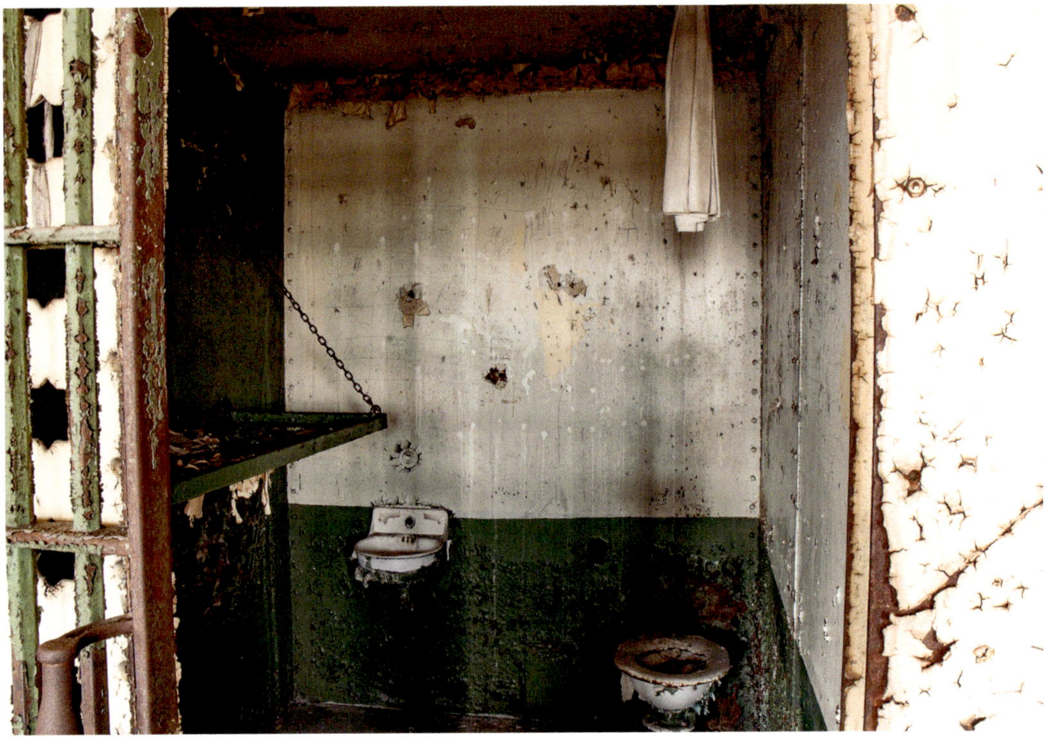

A haunting picture of a corroding cell.

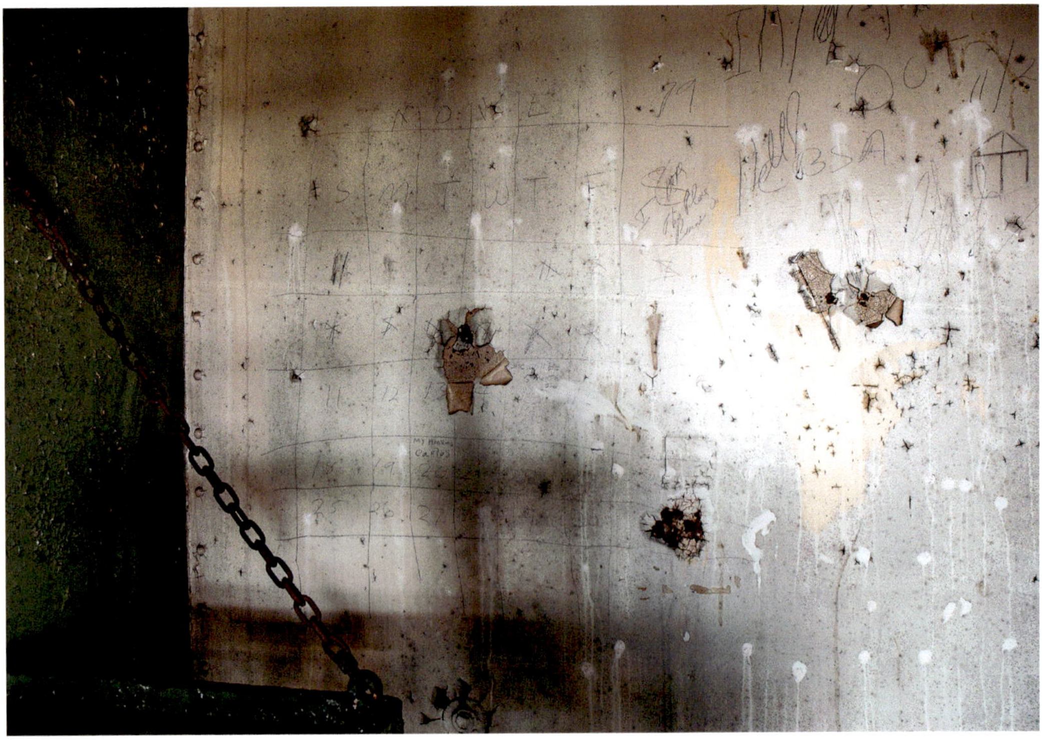

A crudely sketched calendar used by a prisoner to mark off days.

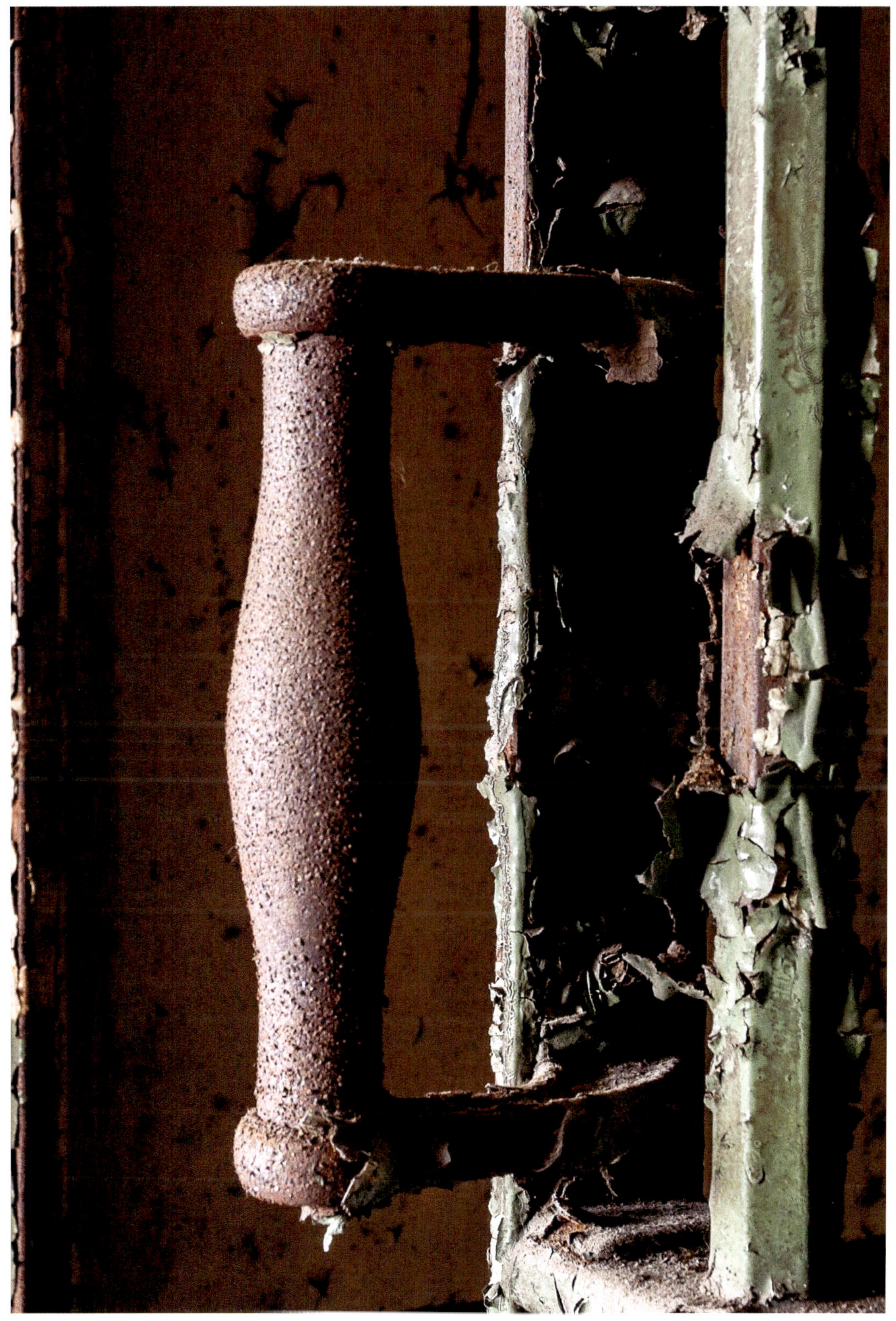

A cell door handle.

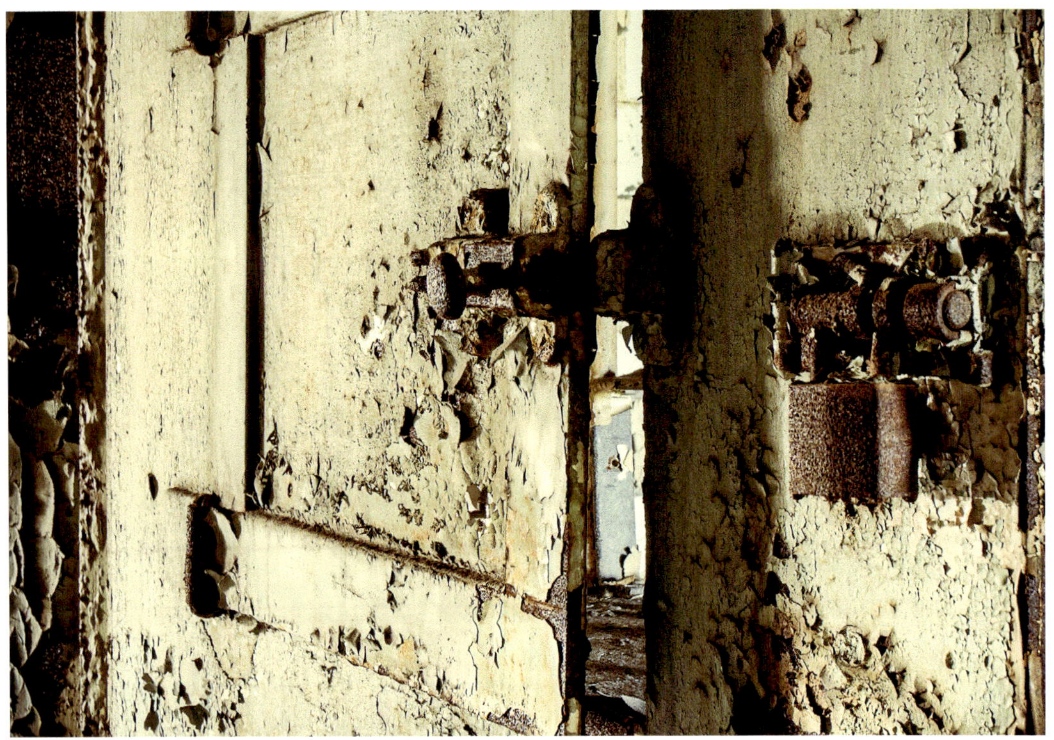

Large bolts covered in peeling lead paint.

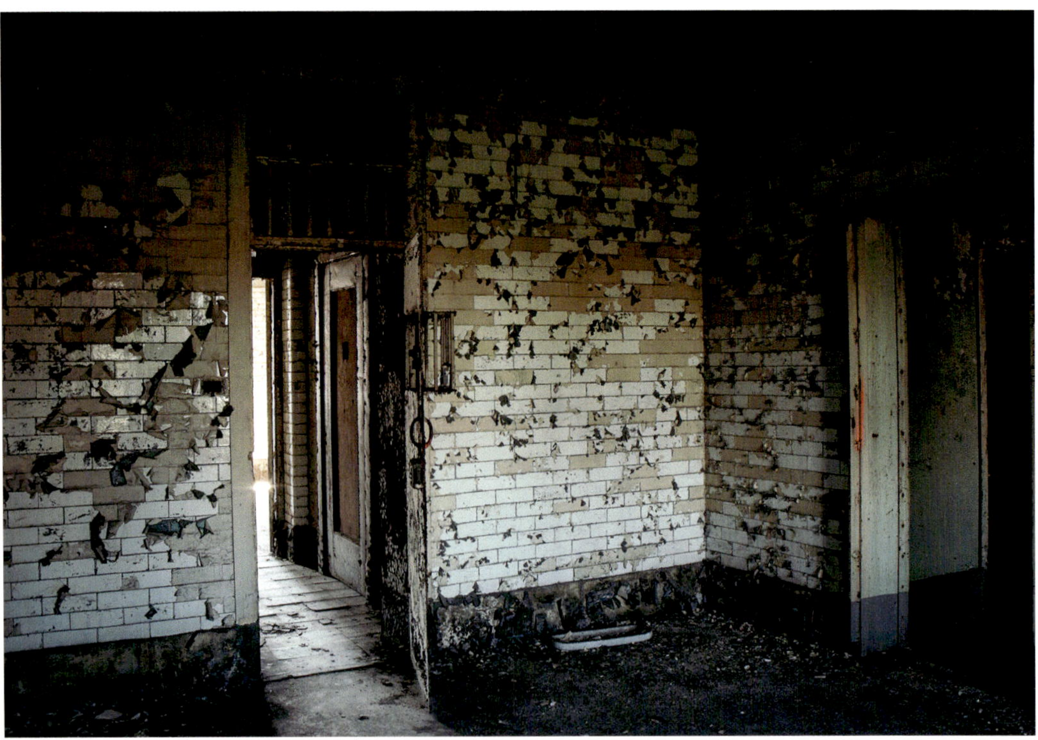

The door to the bathroom area.

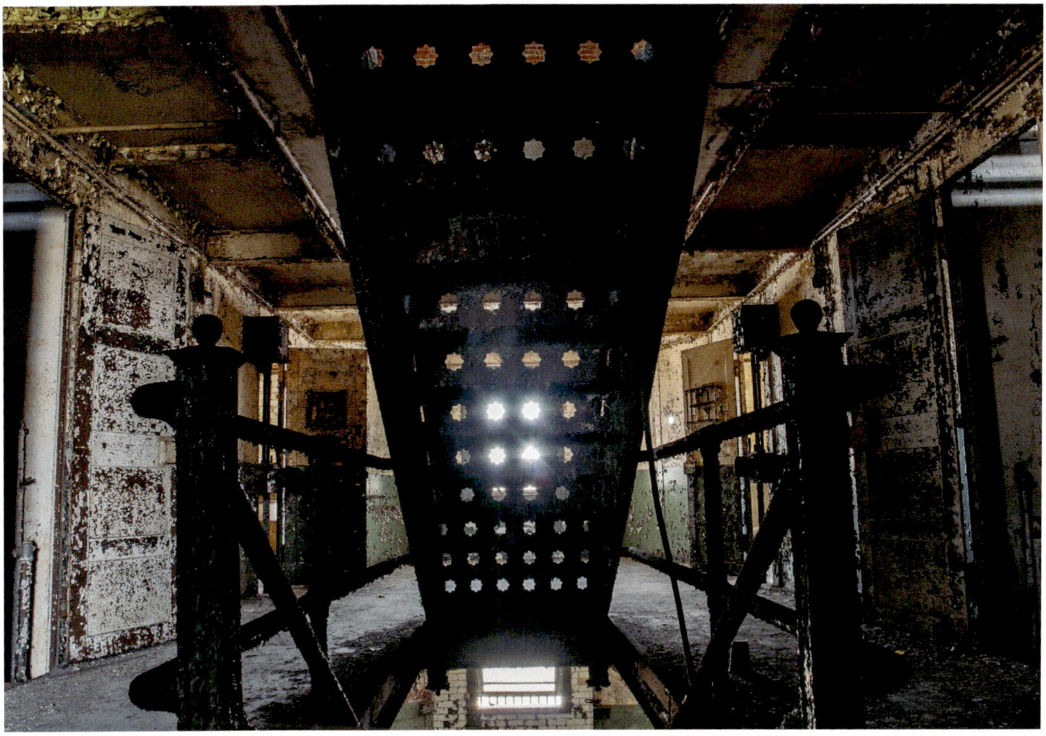

A view of underneath the main stairwell.

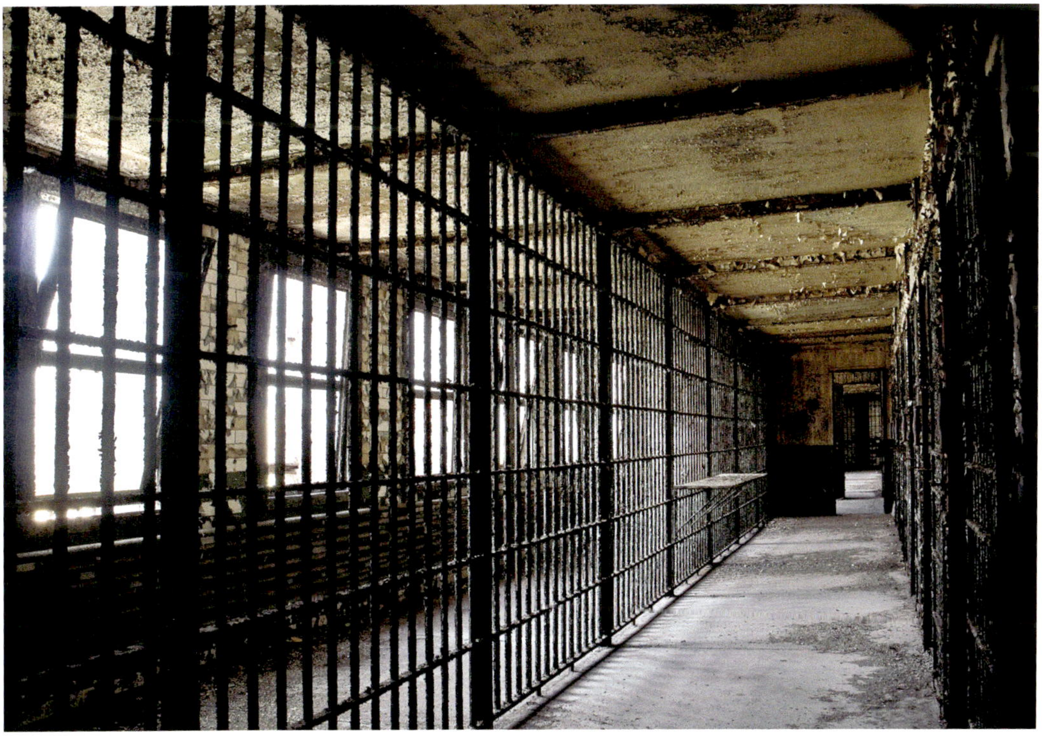

A wide shot of the cell block.

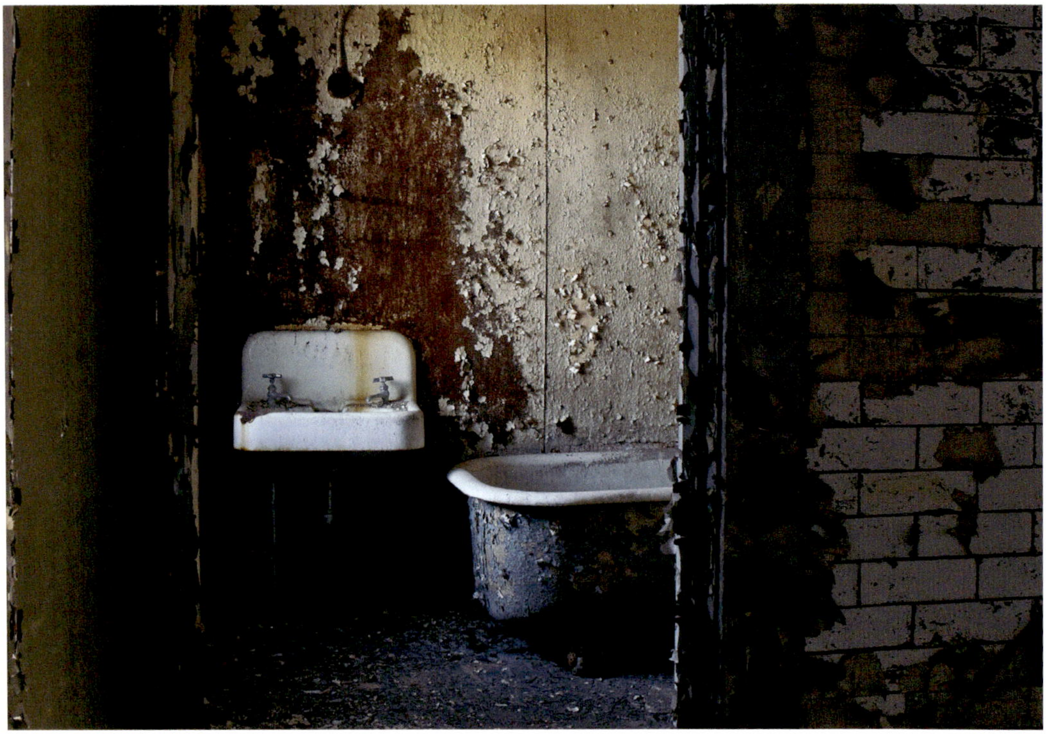

A claw-foot tub wasting away.

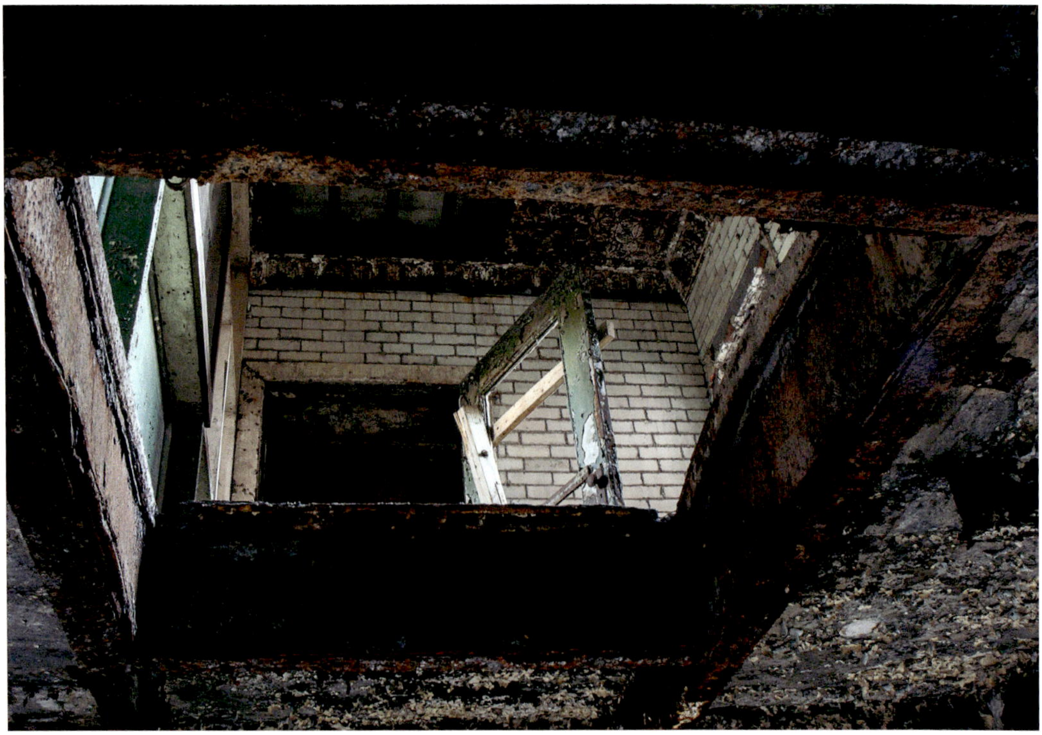

The hole in the floor that was reportedly used for hangings.

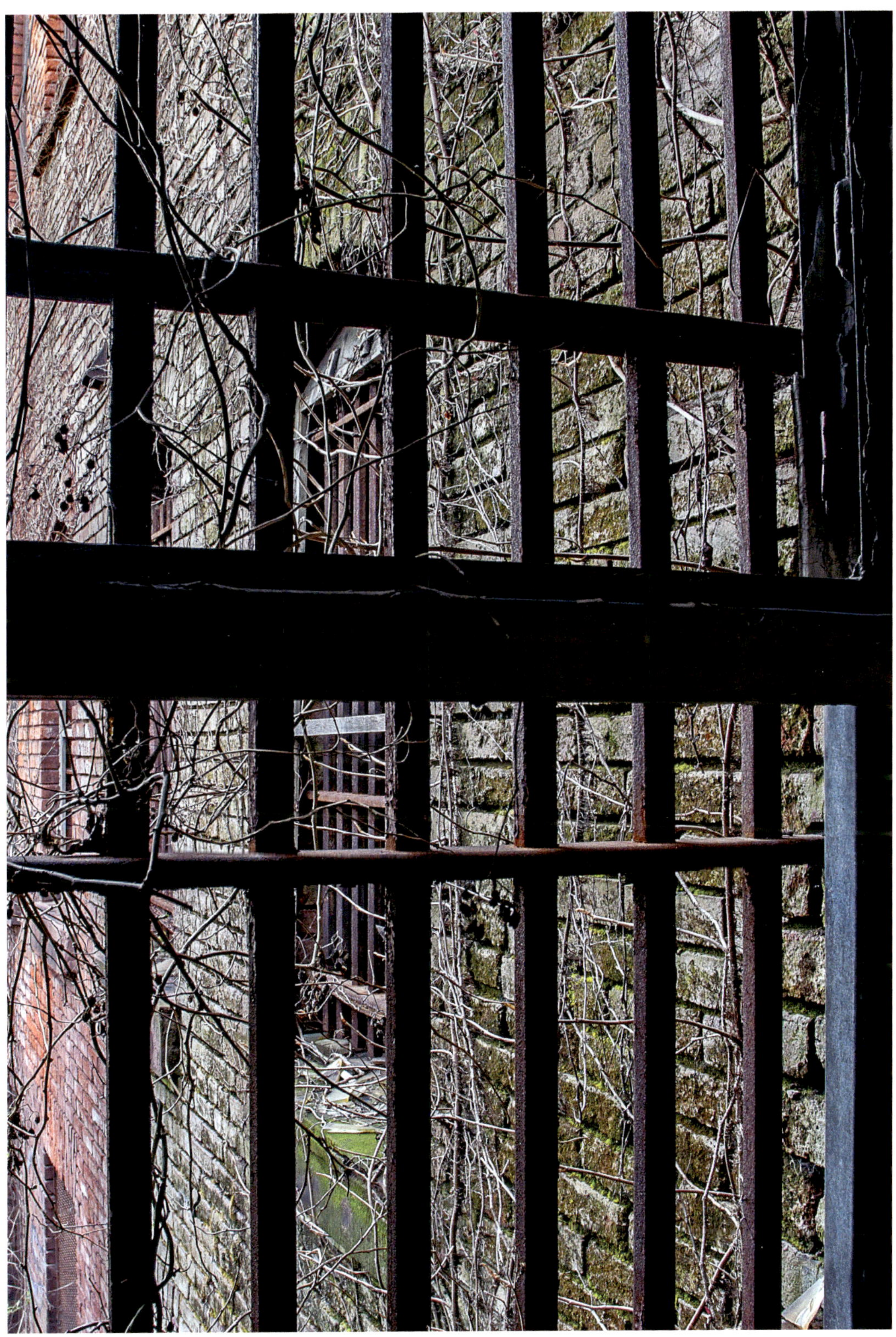

Vines and moss cover areas of the exterior.

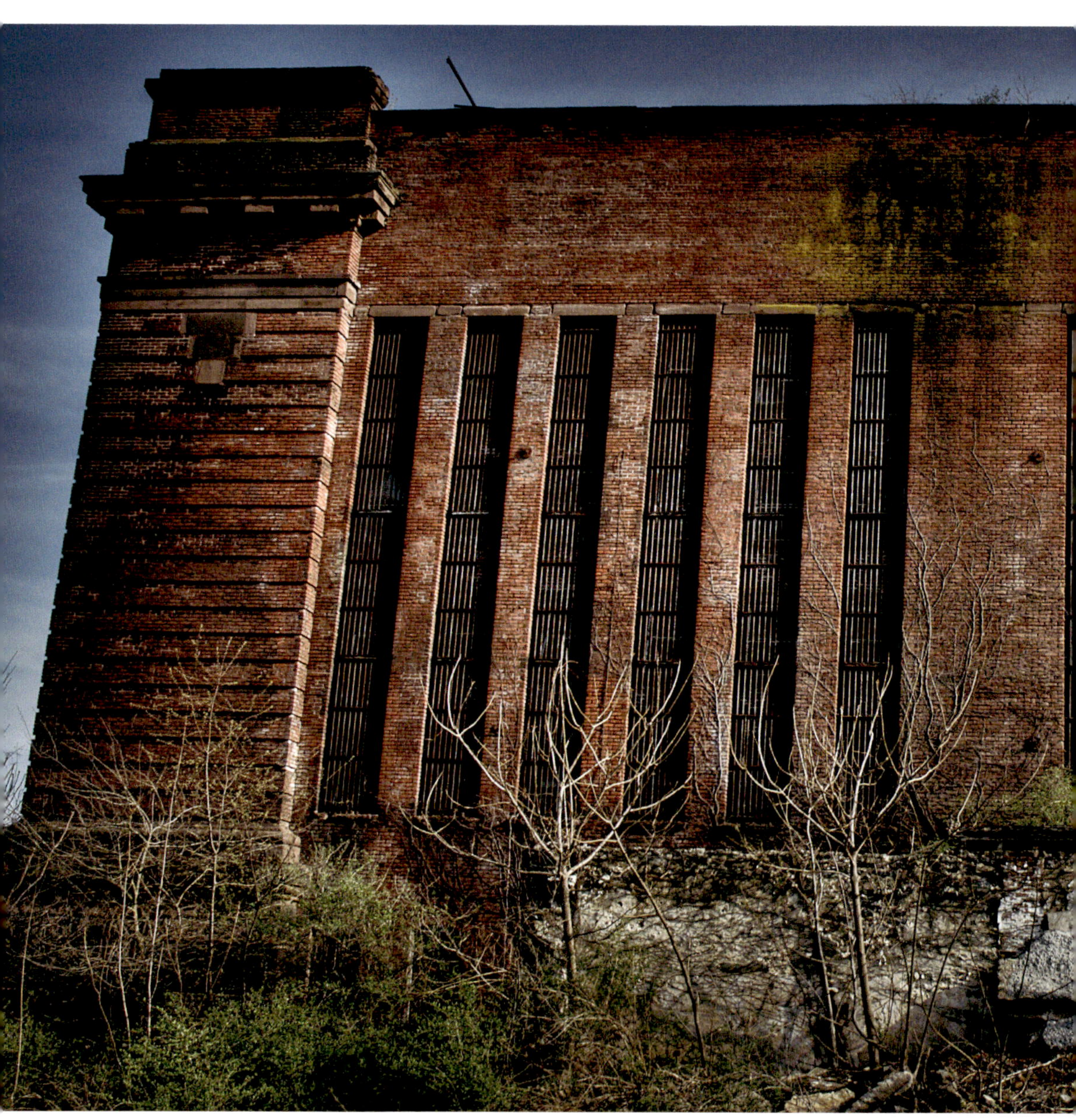

The walls of the former York County Prison no doubt hold countless, brutal secrets.

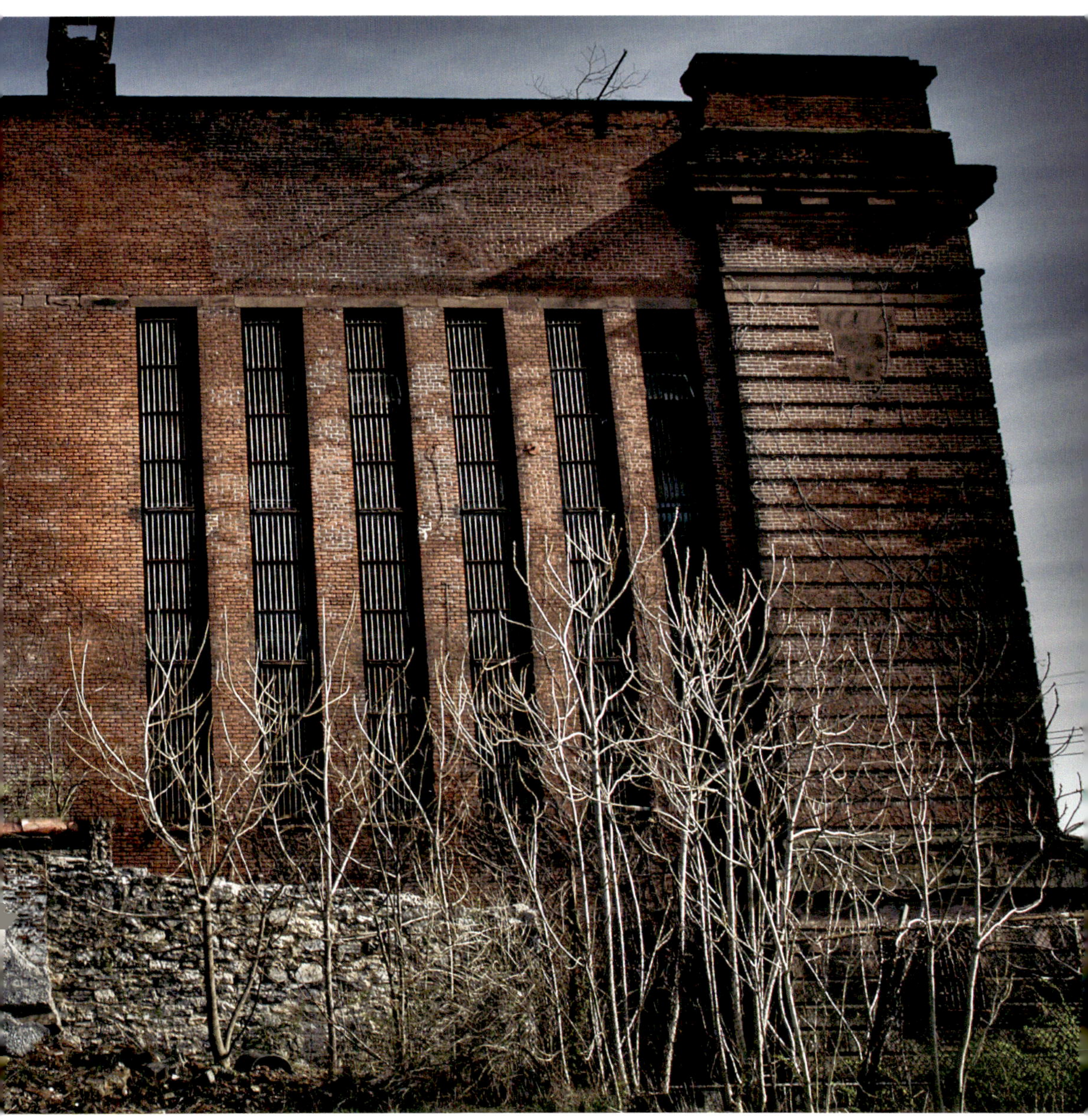

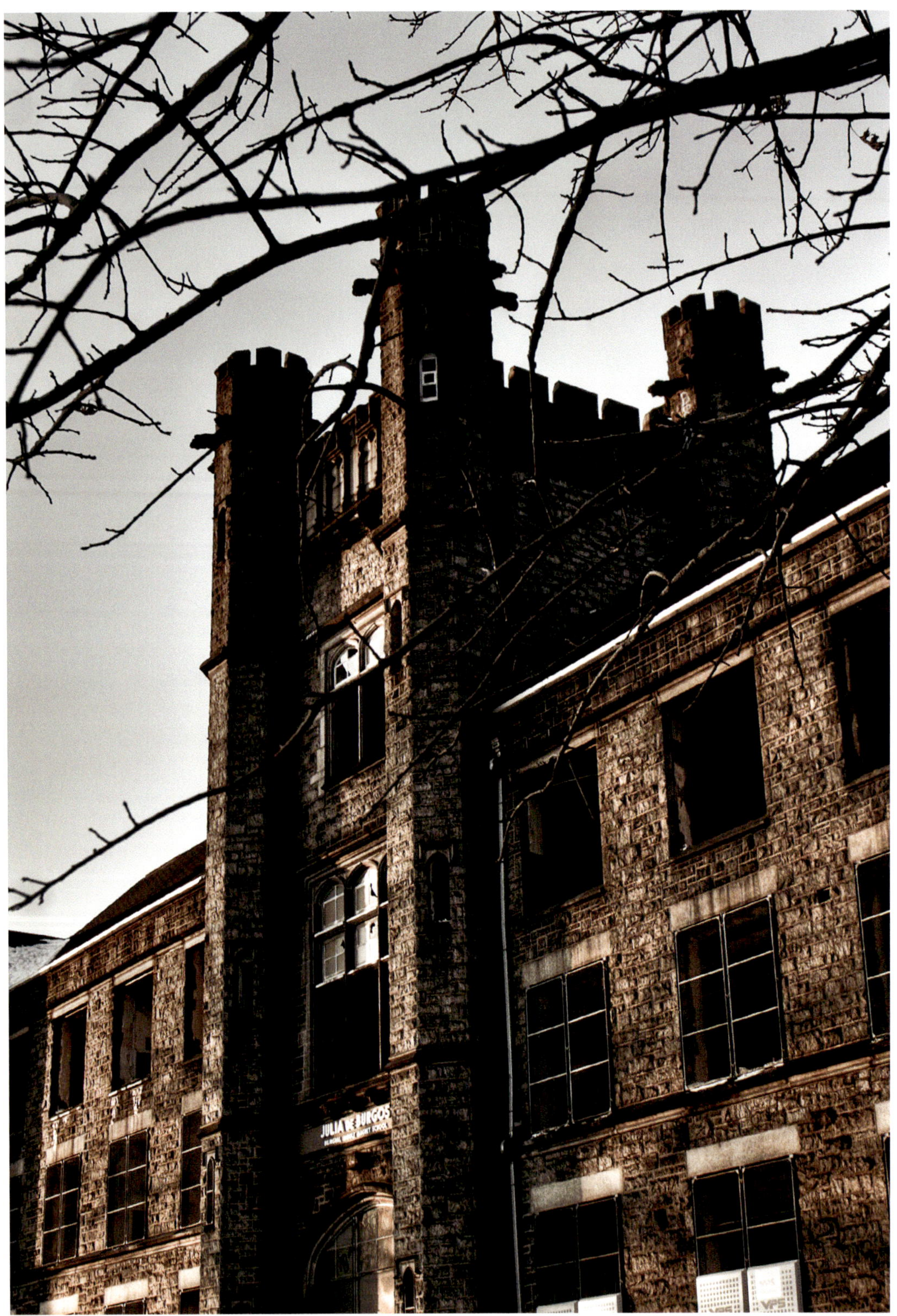

The castle-like structure that was once Thomas Edison High School.

THOMAS EDISON HIGH SHOOL (THE "CASTLE" SCHOOL)

Guarded by gargoyles, the once-castle-like former Northeast Manual Training School in Philadelphia bears witness to an astoundingly rapid decline in public education and the ugliness of racial segregation in Philadelphia during the 1950s and '60s. Built from 1903–1905, and designed by architect Lloyd Titus, the school was prized for its innovative design and academic excellence. During much of the nineteenth century, schools adhered to architect Samuel Sloan's interior plans: one large room able to be divided with moveable partitions into as many four classrooms. Titus, however, was not afraid to experiment, and he was the first to incorporate specialized classrooms into Northeast's design.

Titus's lauded design included twenty classrooms and seven shops planned around a U-shaped hallway with a central auditorium. The school was one of the first in Philadelphia to have specialized spaces and stood as a prototypical design and a move away from Sloan's designs of the previous century. While the interior may have been innovative, it was the exterior—with its deference to gothic architecture—that grabbed attention and inspired the imagination. In a 1986 application to the National Register for Historic Places, the building was described as "Collegiate Gothic Revival" and "built of random coarse granite, the building resembles an English castle with a battlemented center turret flanked by projecting, gable ends." It is no wonder the school on the corner of 7th Street and Lehigh Avenue was known the "Castle."

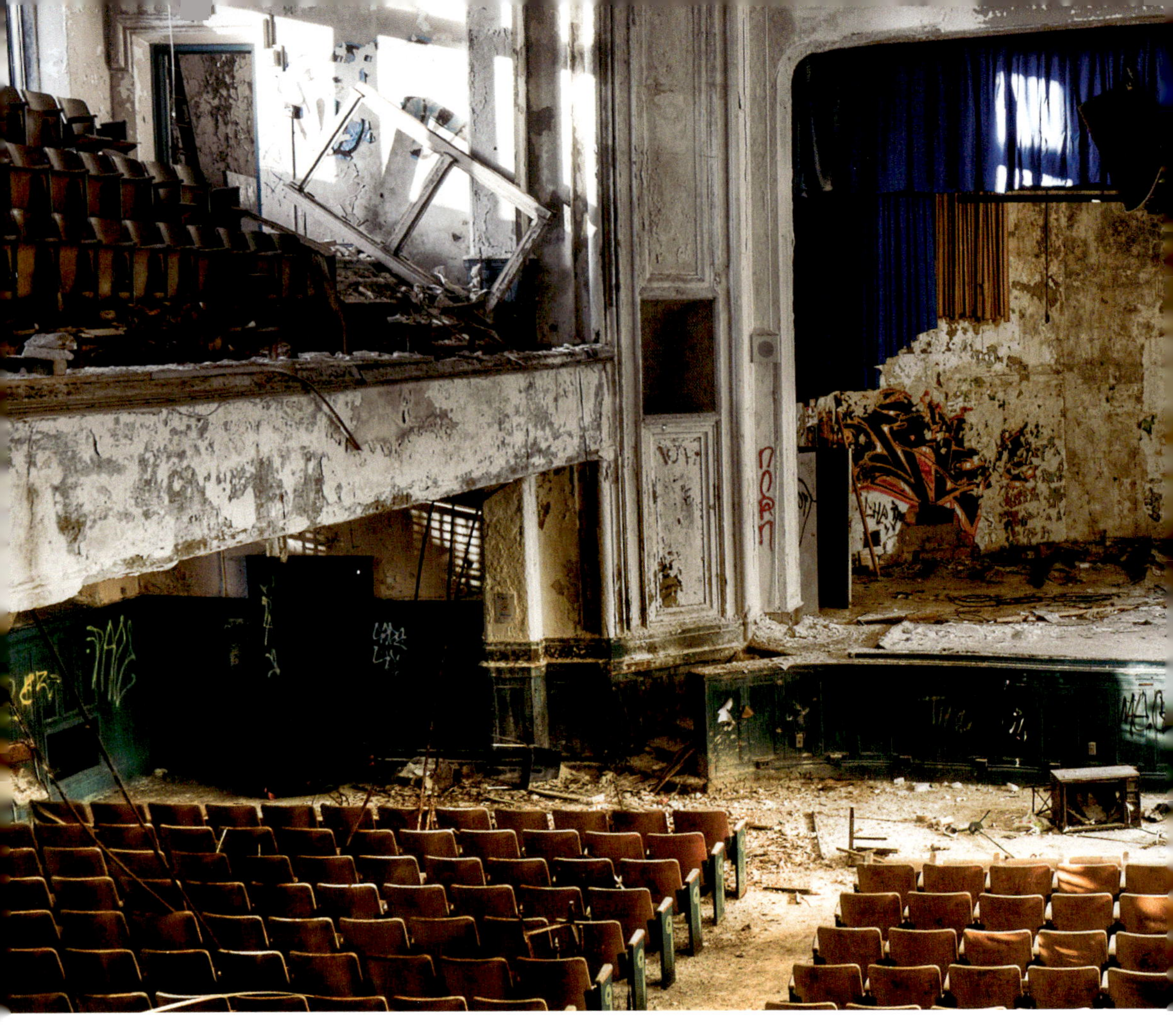

In 1911, Northeast Manual Training School became a four-year school and was renamed Northeast High School. Its title would remain in place until 1957 when a new school was built, taking with it the name and much of its legacy. The original Northeast High became Thomas Edison High School, and its decline began.

The decades preceding the school's renaming were prosperous. Northeast was considered one of the best public schools in Philadelphia, both academically and athletically. The well-established alumni network provided financial support, through fundraising, for college loans and awards for championship sports teams. By the mid-1950s, the school's demographic was changing in accordance with the neighborhood. A student body that began as predominantly white progressed to include an equal number of black students. At the time, the necessity for a new school was not questioned; it was simply explained away as due to increasing enrollment.

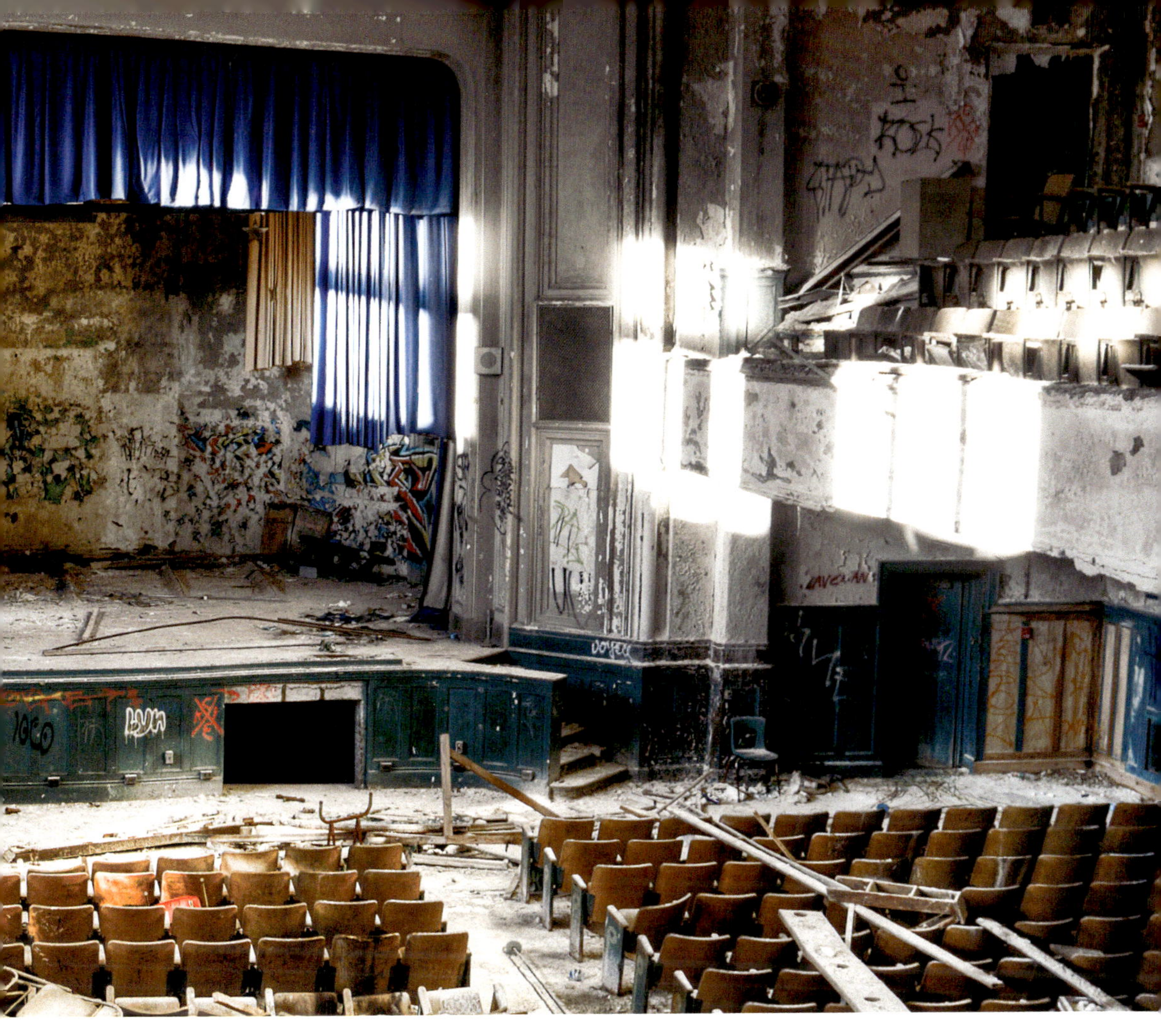

In 2001, almost five decades after Northeast High School was moved, a group of teenage detectives, students at Northeast High, set out to uncover more about the 1950s relocation of their school. Under the watchful eye of their social studies teacher, Donna Sharer, and supported by a Disney education grant, the students combed public records and conducted dozens of interviews with former alumni who graduated in the 1950s. Their painstaking research and analysis of data led them to uncover many uncomfortable truths about the 1957 move.

The most glaring falsehoods were revealed by high school yearbook data from 1945–1957 and census data from 1940, 1950, and 1960. The findings are irrefutable. Graduation rates had been steadily declining along with freshman registrations. In fact, in 1944, there were 1,400 freshman, and in 1956, there were 323. In 1947, 4.7 percent of graduates were African American, and in 1956, the percentage had risen to 36.6 percent. The Alumni Association's claims of a growing student body were clearly a ruse. Census data of the area showed racial diversity increasing steadily throughout the 1950s and 1960s, while the area where the new Northeast High School was built remained 99.9 percent white. It is difficult not to reach the conclusion that racial segregation was at the heart of the move and instigated the demise of Thomas Edison High School.

Much has been written about racial segregation in 1950s Philadelphia and the United States, and it is beyond the scope of this book's research to examine the abandonment of Edison High School and the negative effect it had on the surrounding neighborhoods—but it was catastrophic. The quality of education declined, and the condition of the buildings deteriorated to such a point that in 1988 it was closed. At some point during the 1990s, Thomas Edison High School was repurposed, becoming the Julia De Burgos Bilingual Magnet Middle School.

Less than a decade later, in 2003, the school closed once again. One of the last recorded descriptions of the school, in 2006, was written by journalist Julia A. Seymour. In an interview with a former Julia De Burgos emergency teacher, she describes the school building as crumbling and rat-infested. It is hard to understand how what was once a state-of-the-art educational facility, rivalling some university campuses, can be left to rot. In 2011, a fire ravaged the already slated-for-demolition structure. By 2013, nothing remained. Today, a Save-A-Lot store and parking lot occupies the area that was once guarded by gargoyles sitting atop their castle-like edifice.

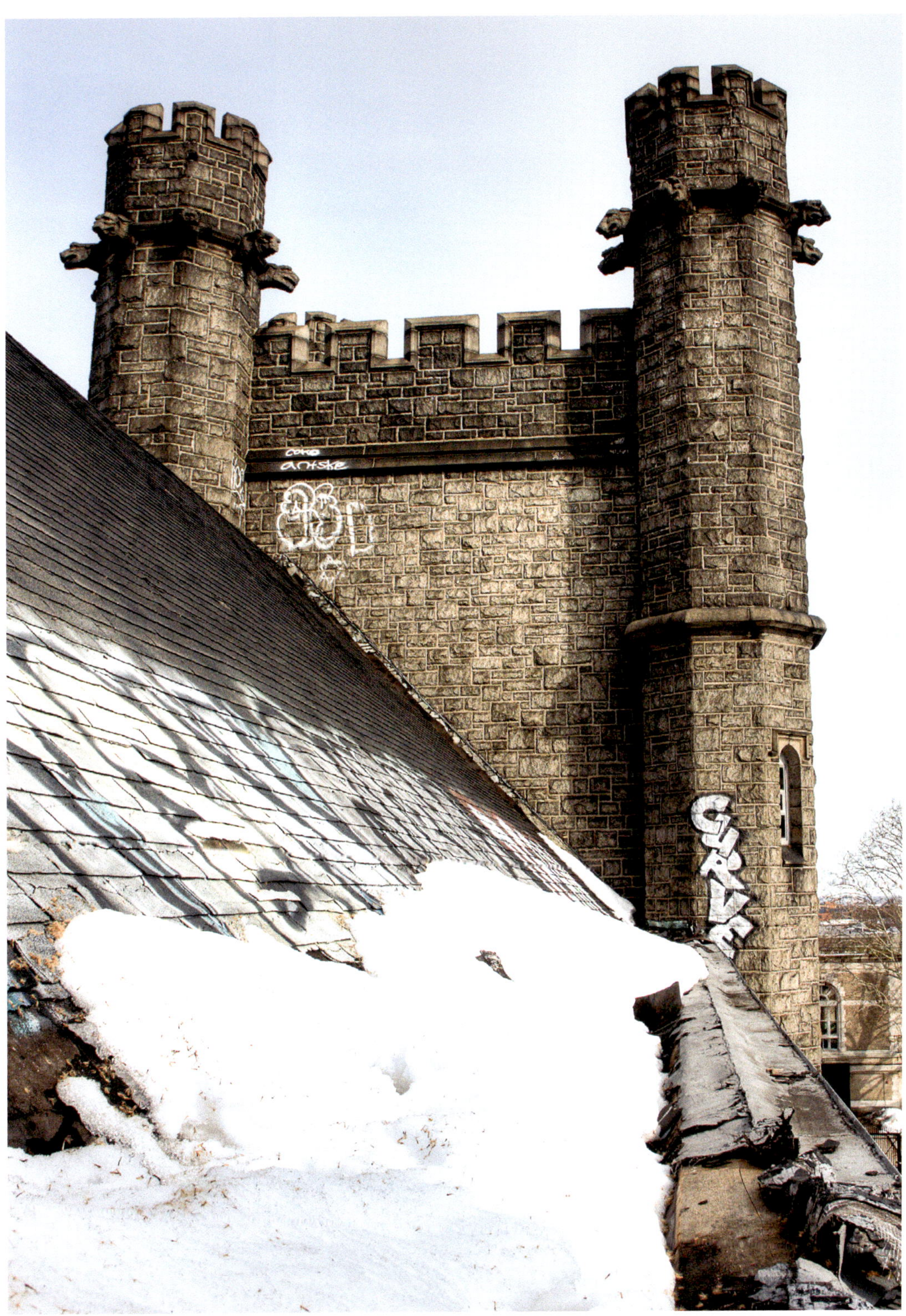

The snow-covered roof leading to the gargoyle-guarded turret.

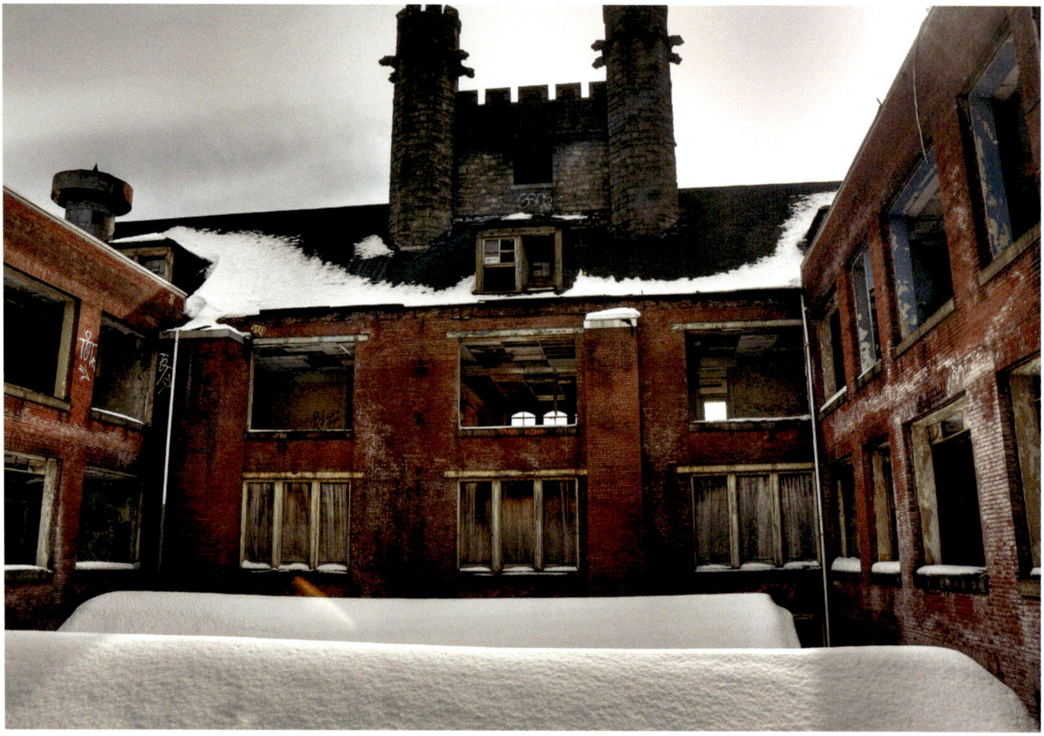

The snow-covered roof offering another view of the turret.

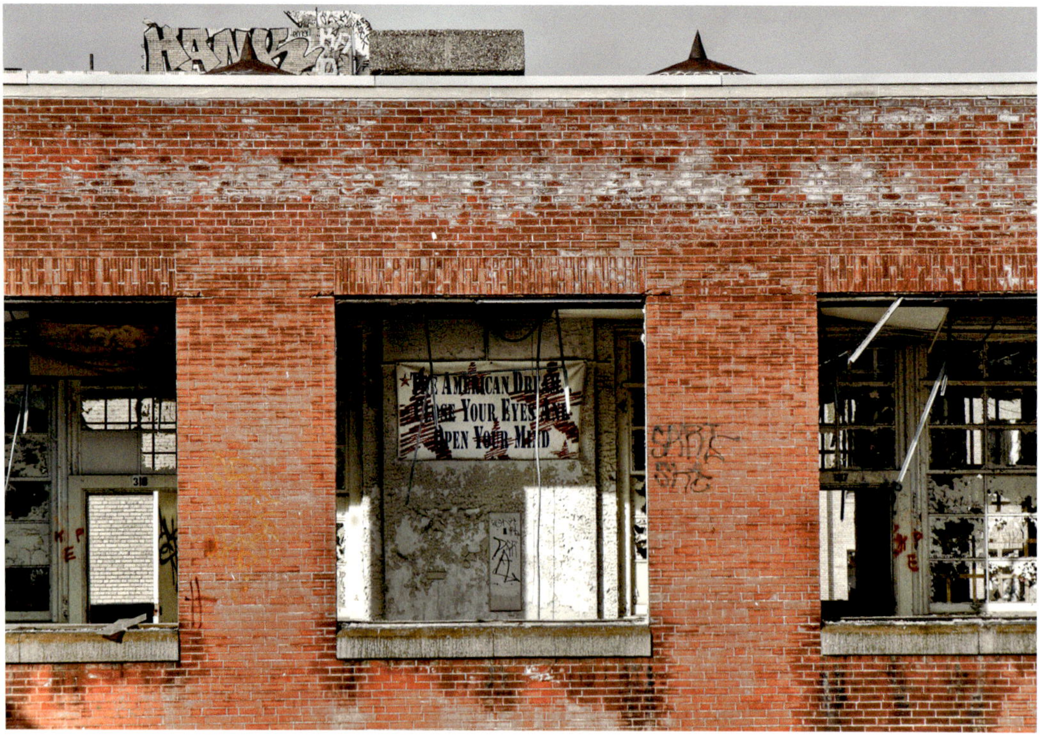

The view of classrooms that look as though they are part of a war zone.

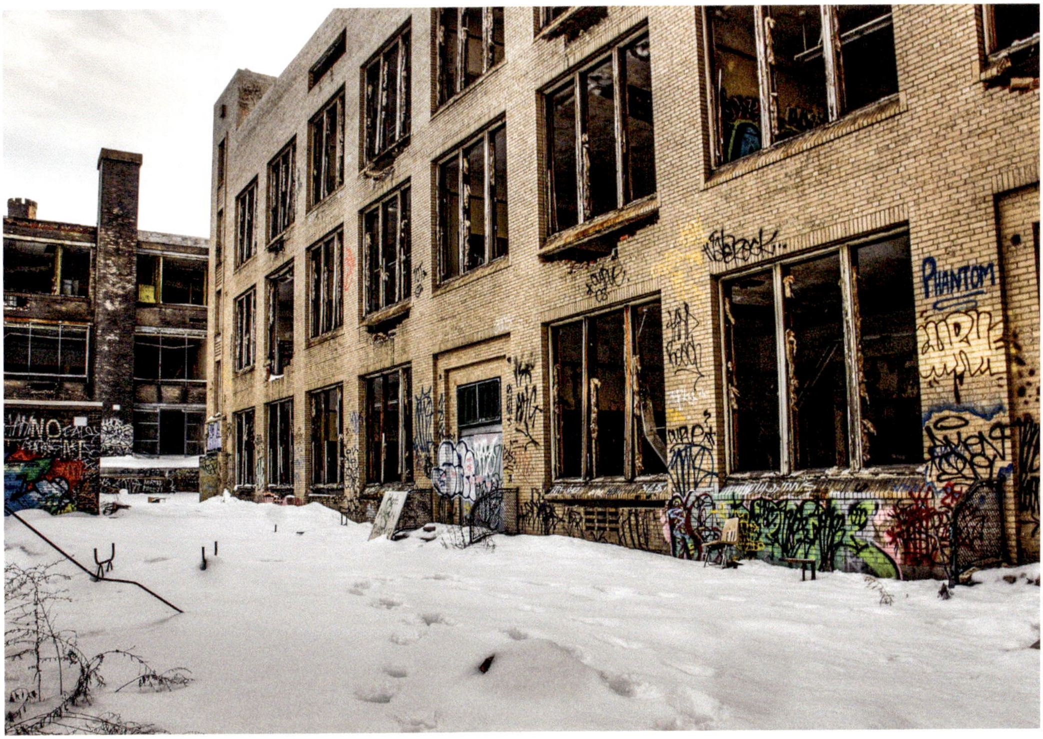

The heavily graffitied area within the courtyard.

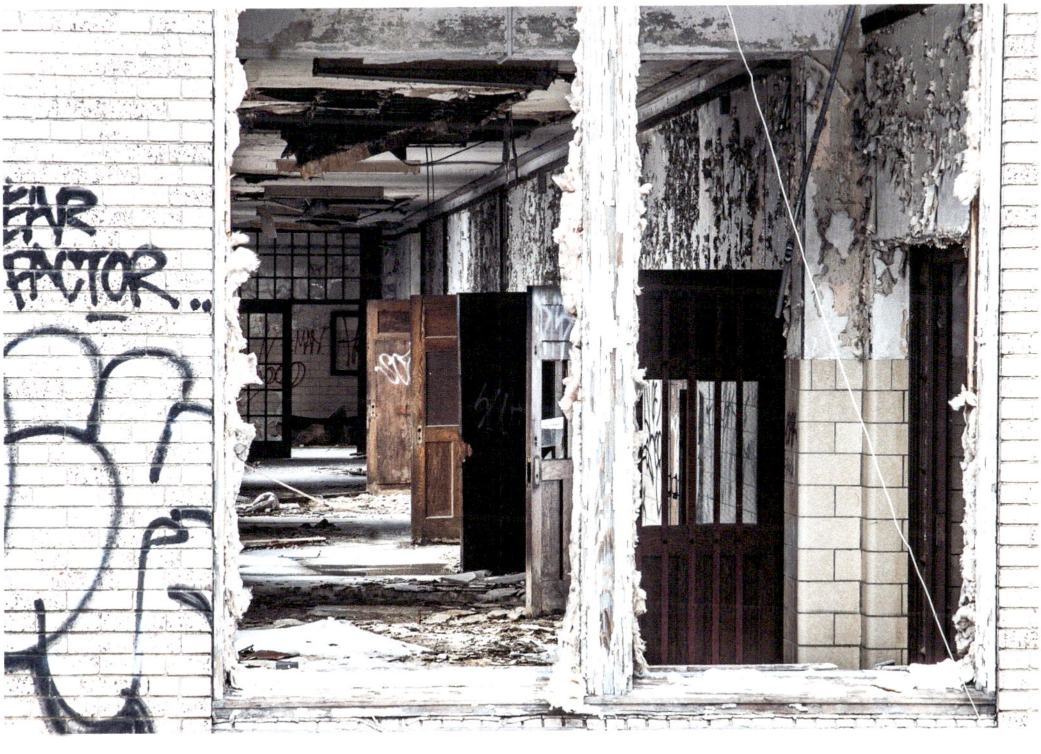

Another image showing the level of damage, both natural and man-made.

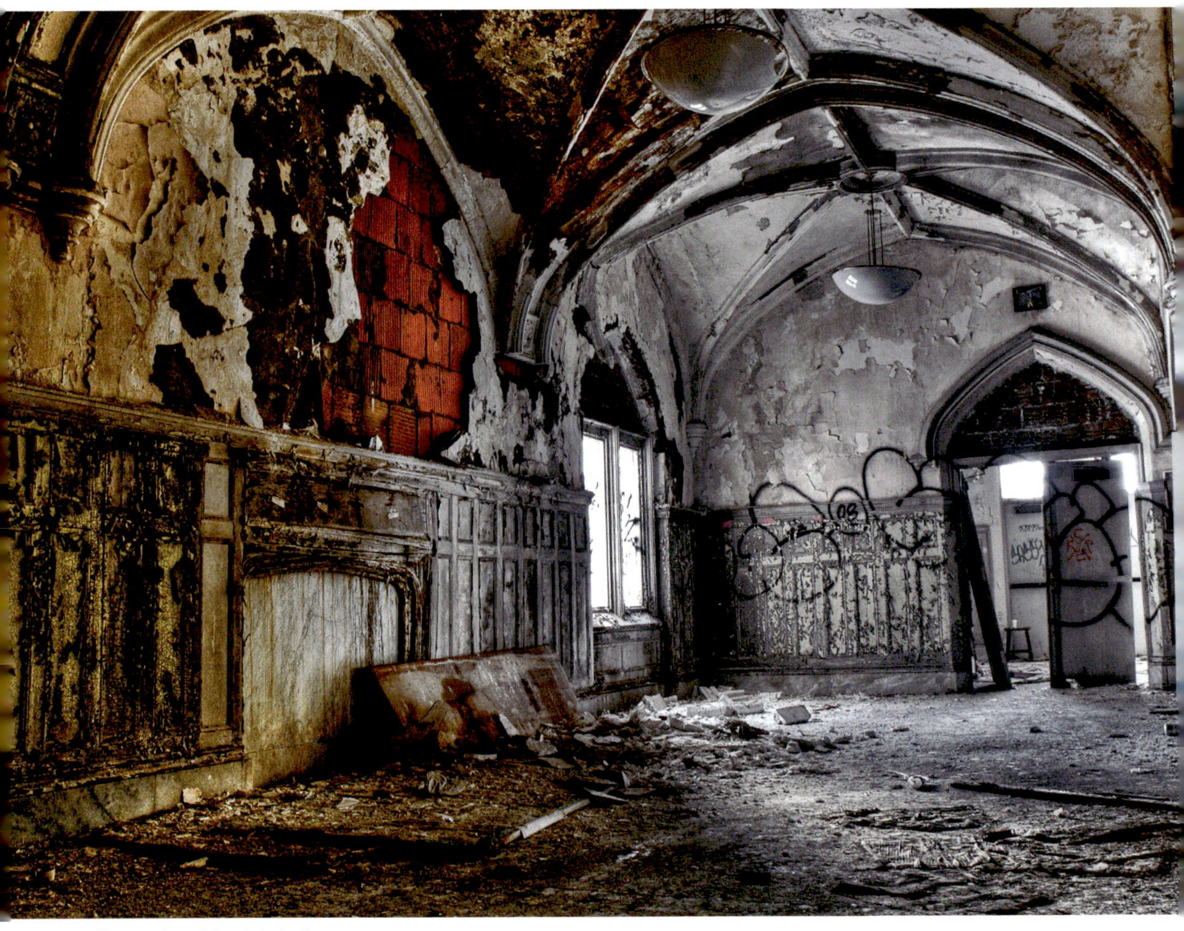

Above: A gothic-style hallway.

Opposite page: The interior stairwell.

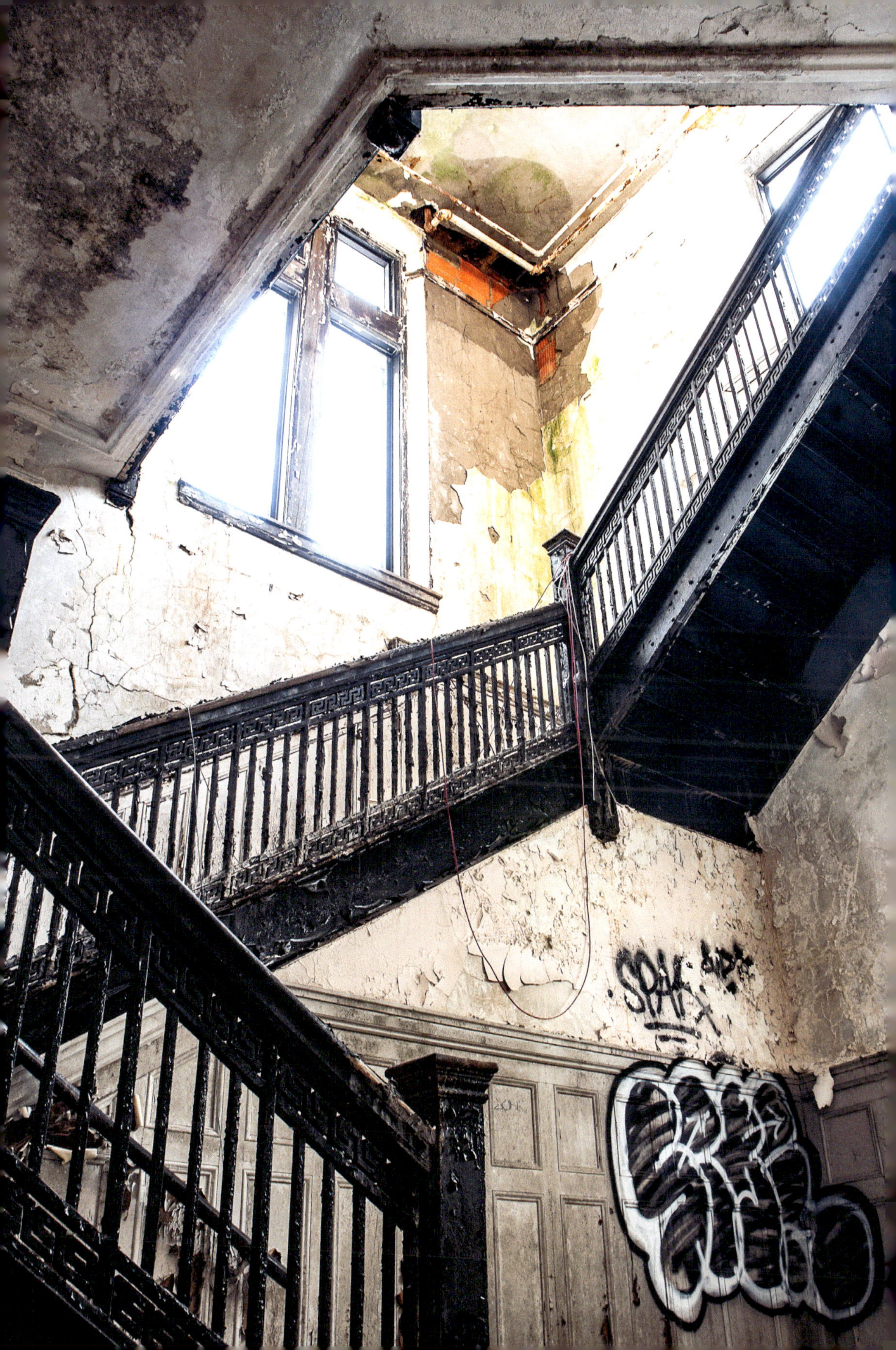

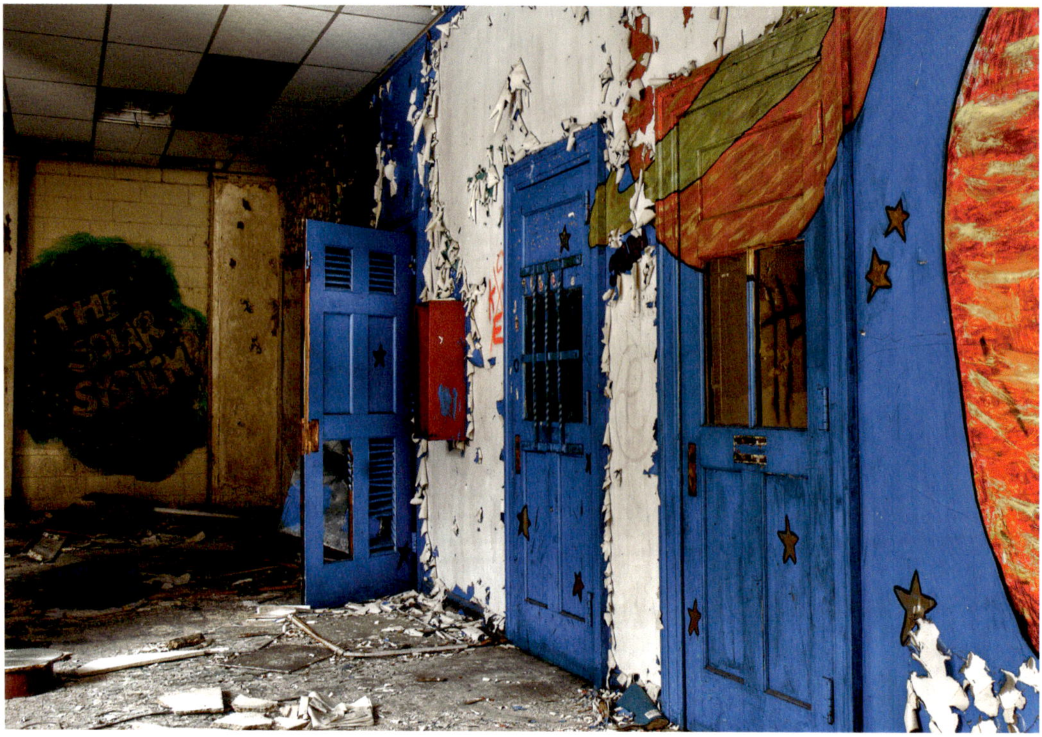

Brightly painted classroom doors.

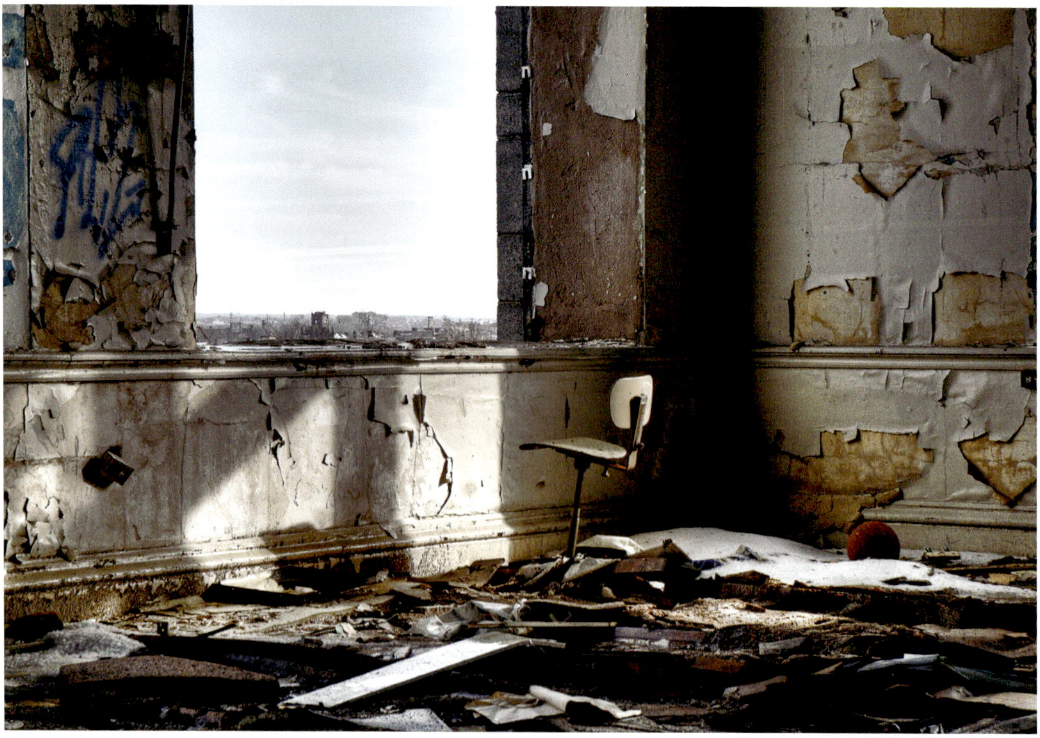

A lone chair and discarded basketball are all that remain in one of the classrooms.

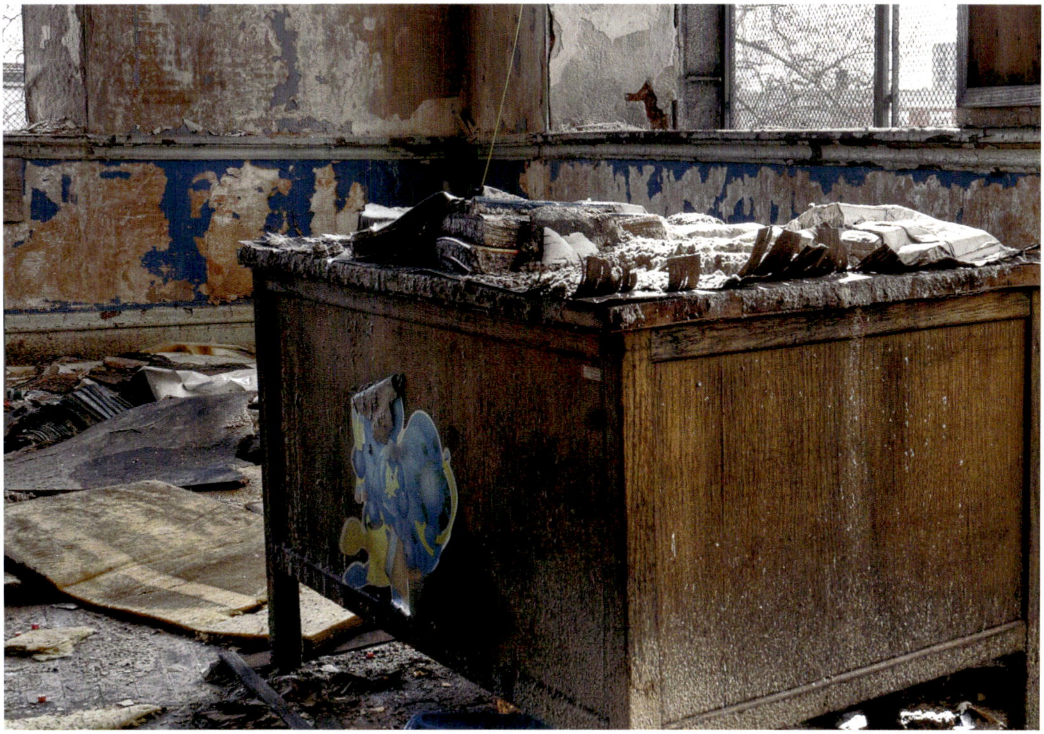

A teacher's desk succumbing to water damage.

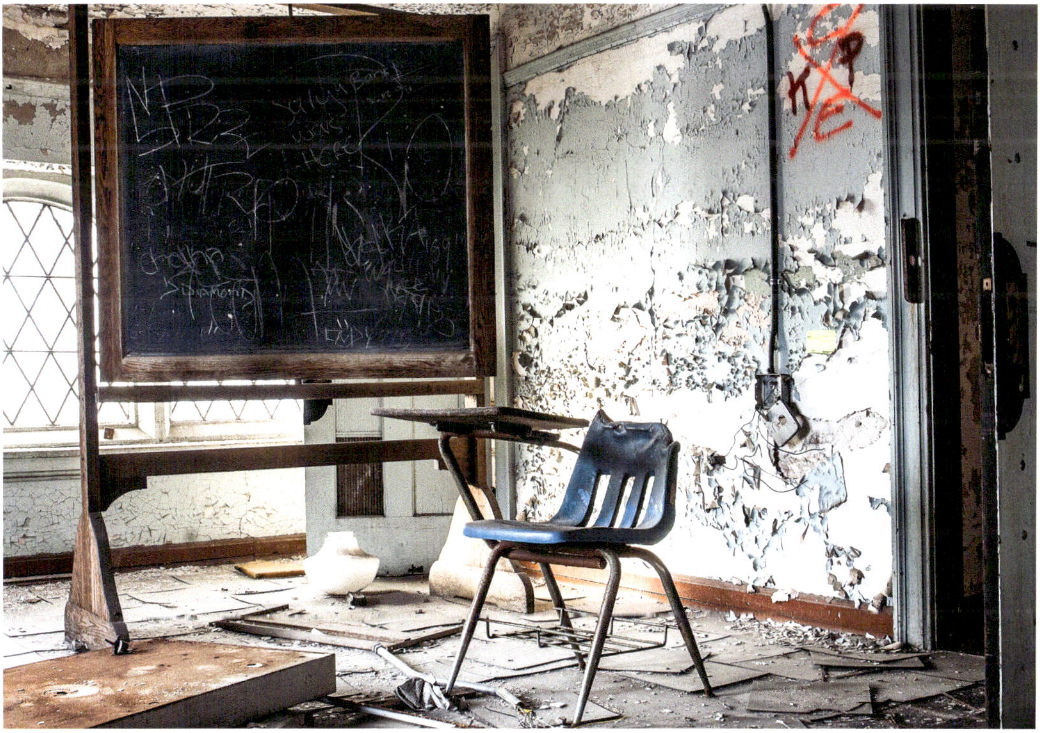

Paint peels from the walls of a long-abandoned classroom.

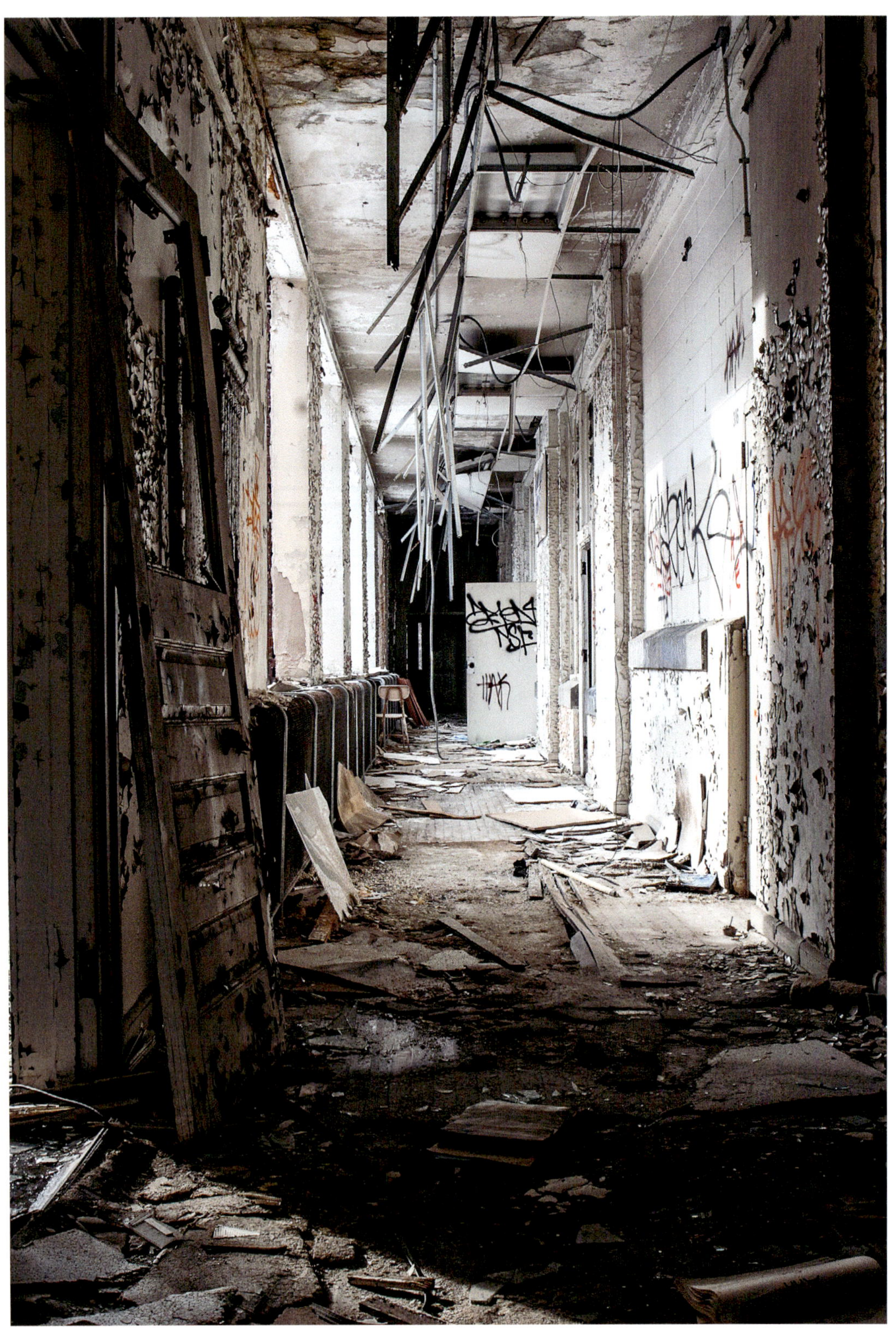

Debris litters a badly water-damaged hall.

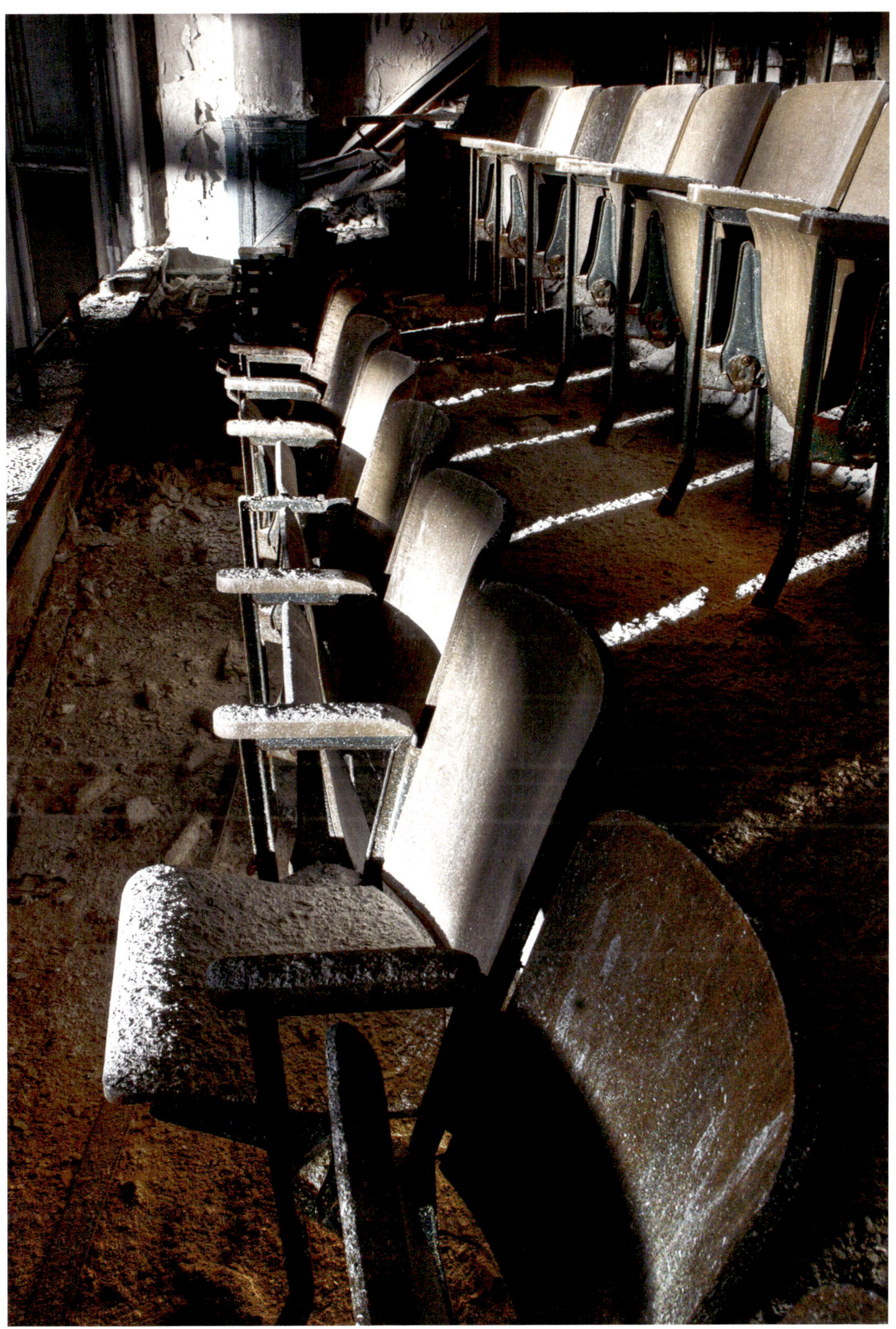

Plaster-covered seats in the auditorium.

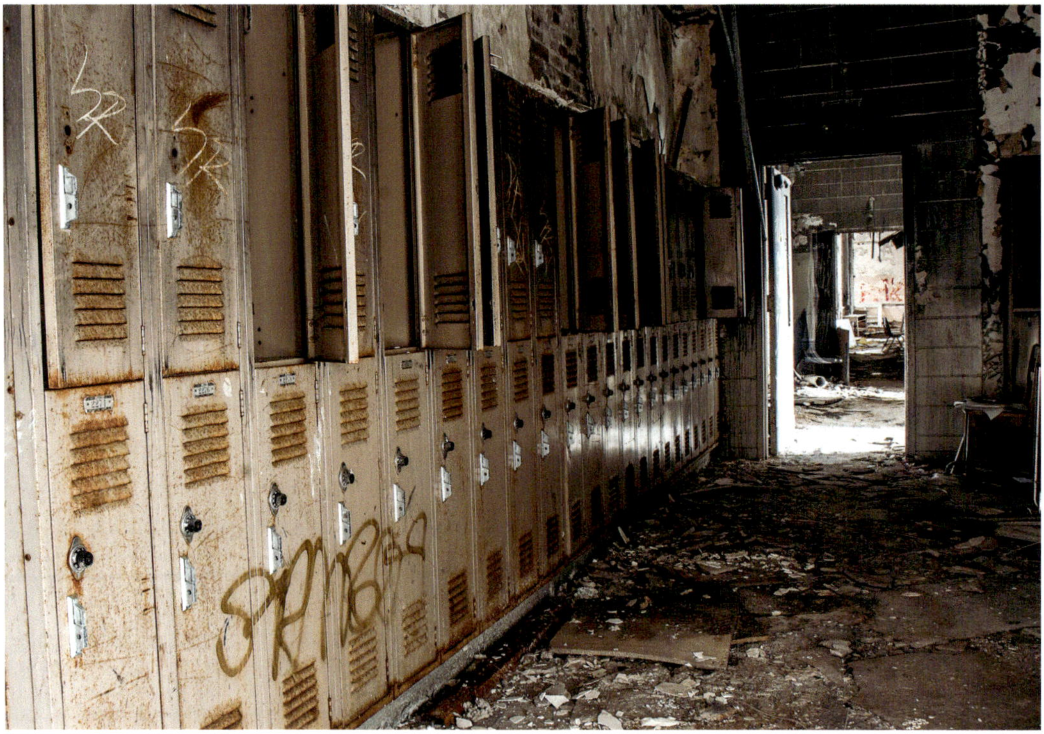

The locker room.

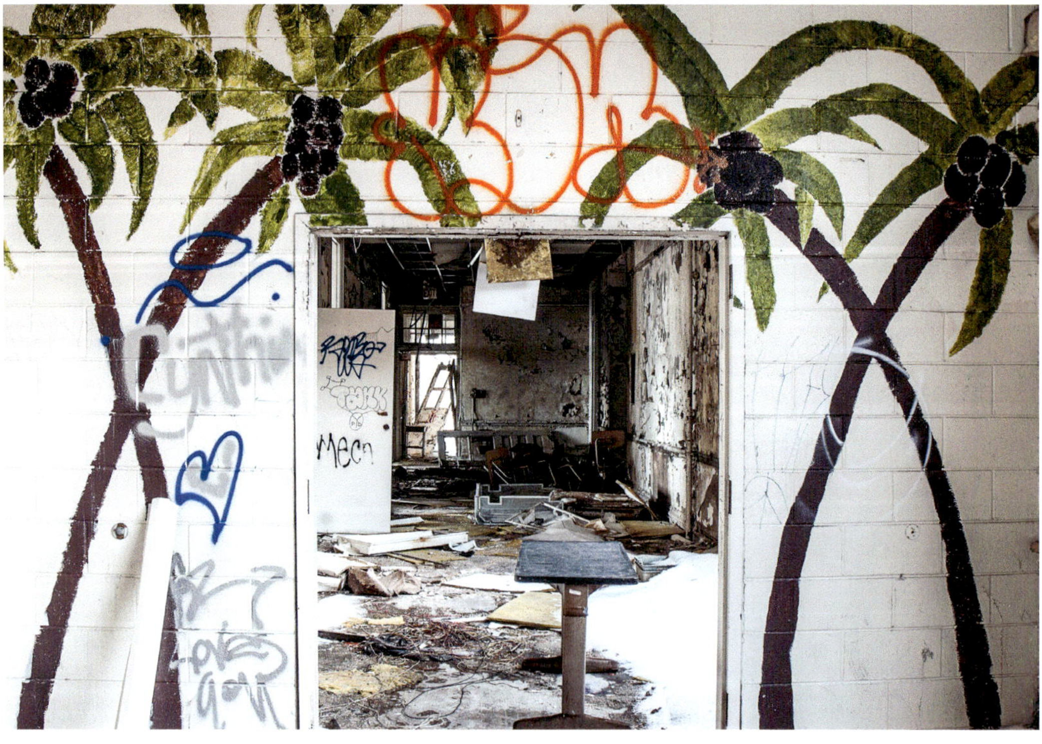

Colorful murals do little to disguise the wreckage.

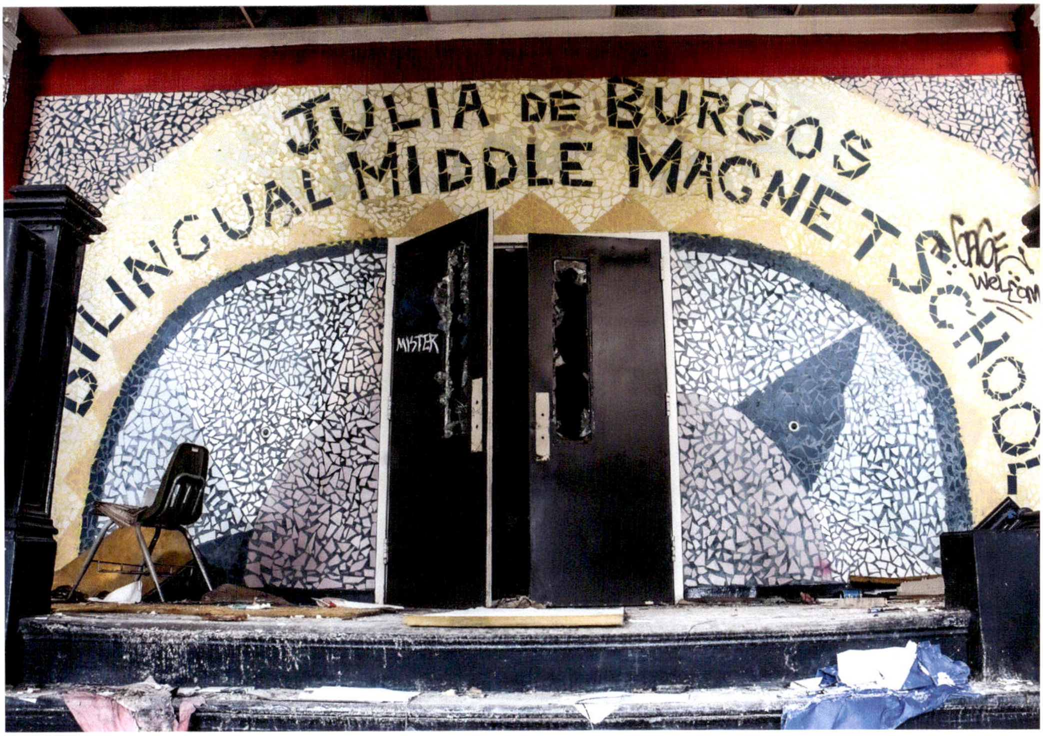

A mosaic representing the final phase in the school's life.

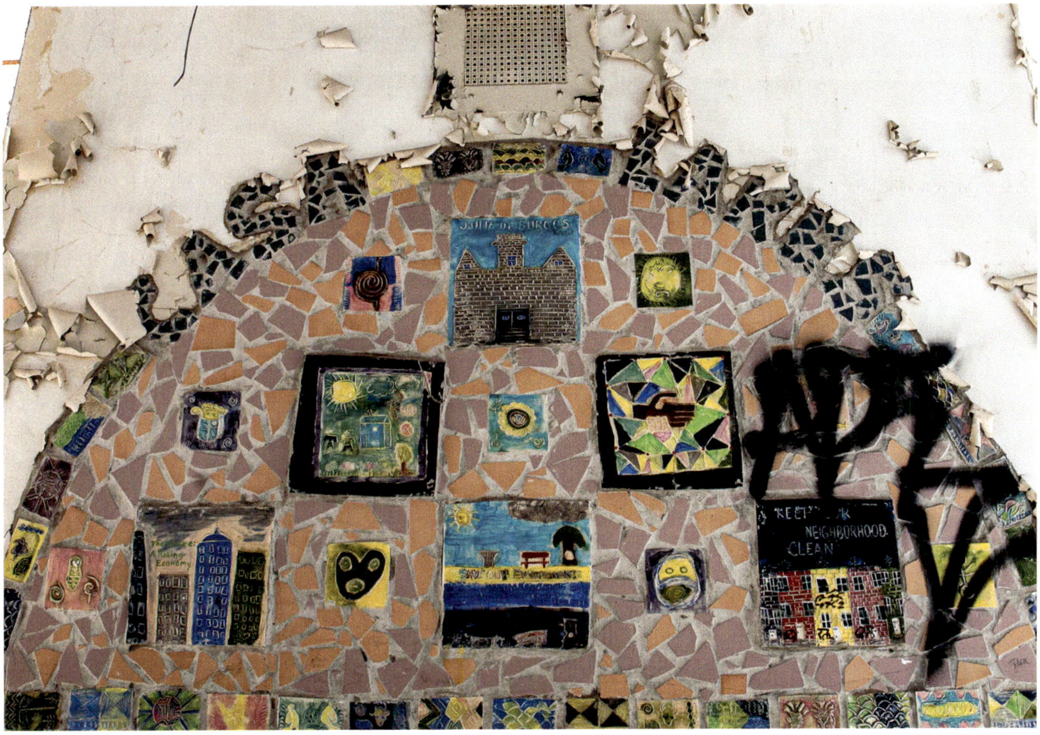

Bright mosaics inside the decaying building.

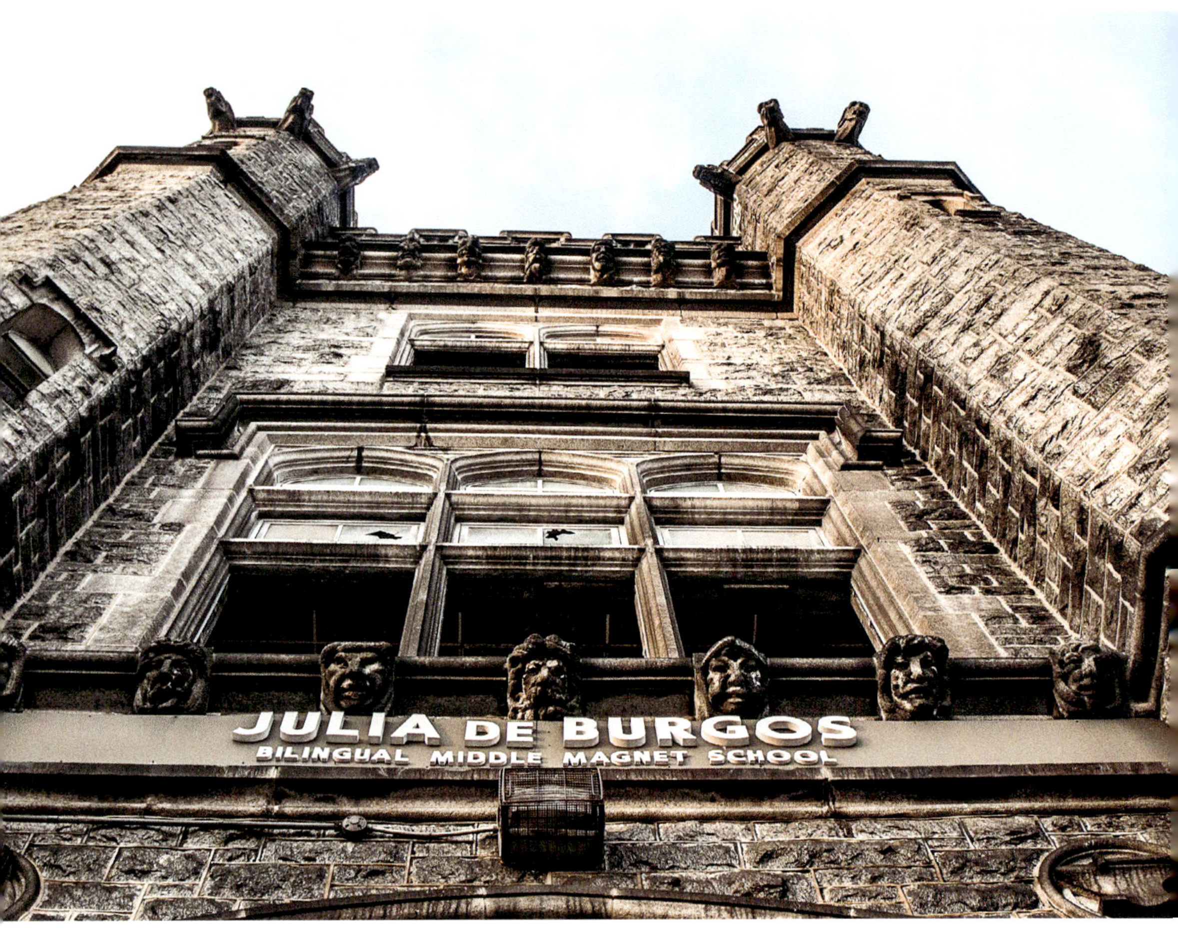

Above: Theatrical masks above the main entrance.

Opposite page: Sadly, the gargoyles no longer watch over their domain at the corner of 7th Street and Lehigh Ave. in Philadelphia.

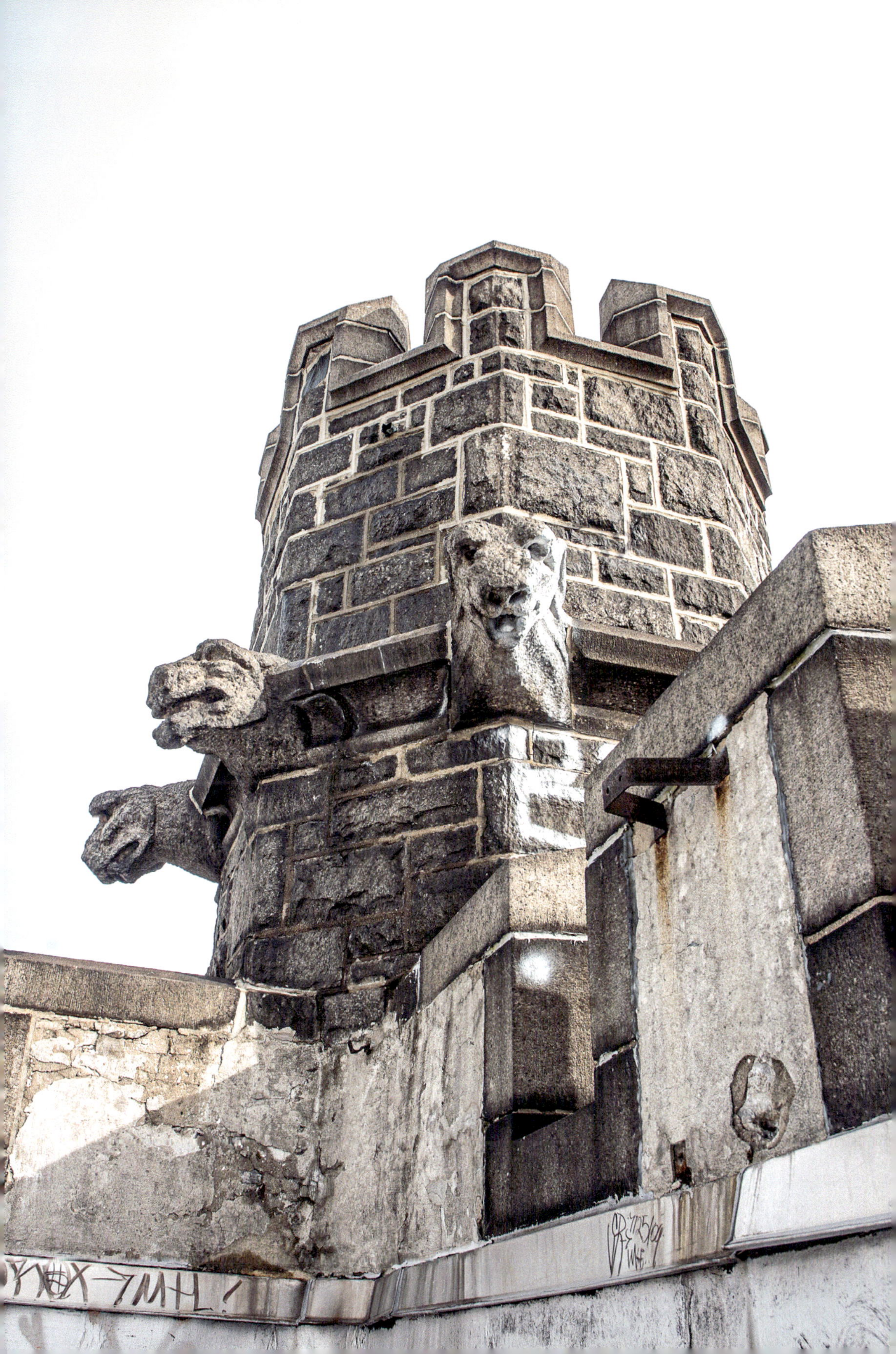

BOMBERGER'S (MICHTER'S) DISTILLERY

An idyllic country road in rural Pennsylvania winds through farmland and travels past what remains of one of America's agricultural and industrial gems—Michter's Distillery. The unassuming weatherboard stillhouse is all that remains, and it gives little indication of the importance the site played in whiskey distilling in the United States. By the 1800s, Pennsylvania led the nation in whiskey production, with more 3,000 distilleries producing more than 6.5 million gallons of whiskey, and it all began decades before, along that idyllic country road.

A Swiss Mennonite farmer, John Schenk, started America's first distillery in 1753 as an ancillary to his gristmill and other farming operations. When soldiers in the Revolutionary War were supplied with whiskey to help them through the unrelenting winters, the demand for distilling grew and local farmers from the area wanted their excess fruits and grains converted to alcohol. A popular rumor suggests George Washington may have stopped at Shenk's to buy whiskey for his troops, and although only a rumor, it is believed to be entirely possible as Washington would have passed through the area on his way to Valley Forge.

Whiskey became America's spirit of choice, surpassing its rival rum in sales and distilling operations and soon became a commercial rather than agricultural enterprise. Shenk's son-in-law, Rudolph Meyer, took over operation of the distillery during the 1780s and added two new stills. The business continued to grow and pass to Shenk relatives, and it was not until 1861 that the name Bomberger's Distillery

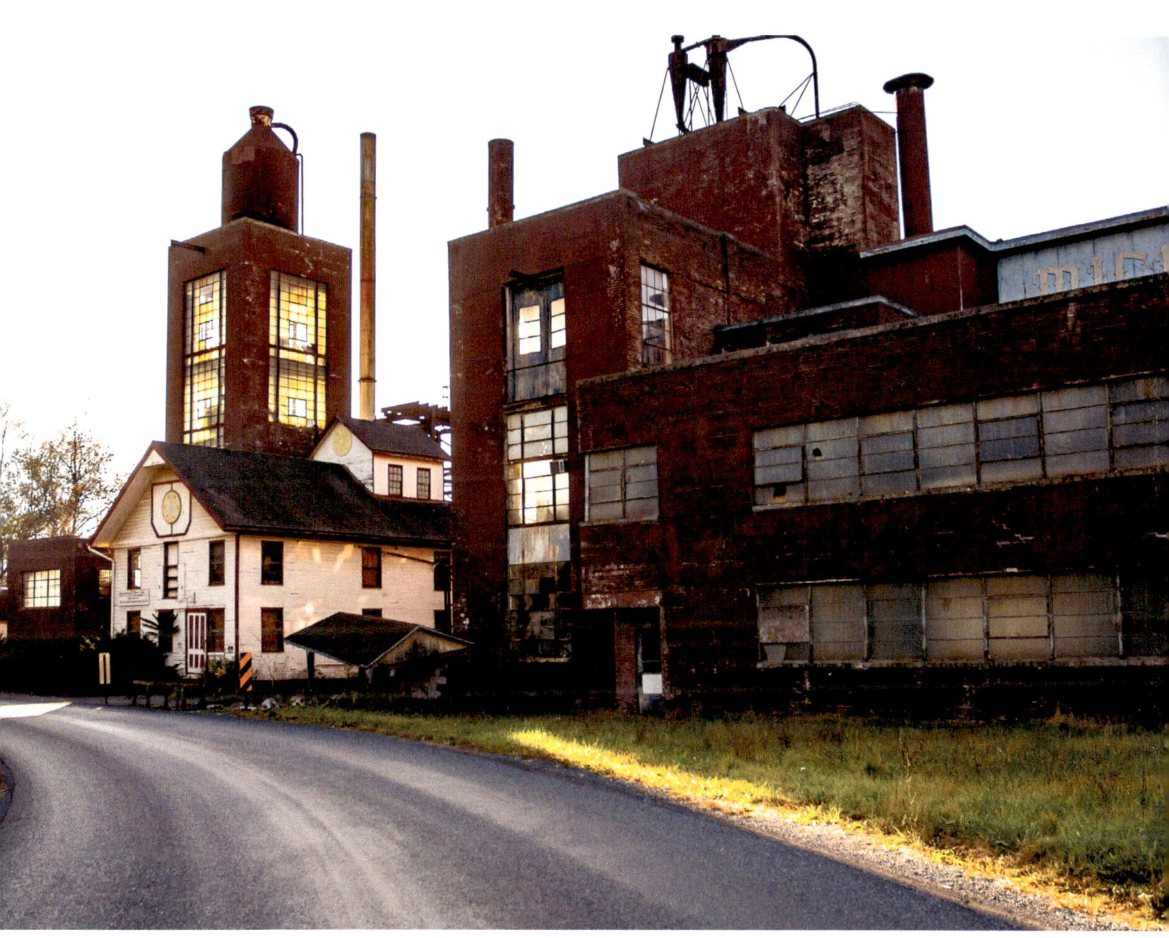

Michter's Distillery.

was put in place. Abe Bomberger and his sons successfully operated the distillery from 1861 until Prohibition forced its closure in 1920.

Information regarding the operation of the distillery between the decades 1930 through 1990, when the distillery closed permanently, are difficult to decipher. Whiskey enthusiasts are a passionate breed, and dedicated blogs and, supposedly, historically correct websites contradict one another, as do the reported interviews with former employees who are now elderly, and direct descendants who are relying on word of mouth. The National Register of Historic Places paperwork, which was filed successfully in 1980, offers an accurate overview of the founding of the distillery and a detailed inventory of the buildings on the site, but the missing decades are just that—missing.

How the name Michter's Distillery came to be appears to be agreed upon: Louis Forman took the names of his sons, Michael and Peter, and combined them; however, then the mystery begins. Many articles and blogs claim Forman purchased the distillery in 1950, and others claim the 1970s, but if either of those dates were correct, it does not explain the name Michter's on a 1942 ceramic whiskey jug. And in yet another interpretation of events, an interview with an elderly former employee claims Forman never owned the distillery, but only worked there.

Precise dates and names are not integral to the story of Michter's Distillery. Its rise and fall is the story of much of American manufacturing: mass production and large conglomerates forcing smaller manufacturers out of business; the public's need for quantity over quality; and, in the case of whiskey, a decline in customers, as the wine and spirit industry grew to encompass a staggeringly broad range of products.

America's first and, at one point, oldest operating distillery died a slow, quiet death alongside a rural Pennsylvania road. Its history, however inaccurate, will live on for decades to come as the resurgence in micro-distilling and the fanatical dedication by whiskey enthusiasts to keep its history alive continues. Its illustrious past also guarantees it a happy ending of sorts.

While the site may sit vacant, except for the lonely stillhouse, the Michter's name lives on. Joe Magliocco, a businessman and attorney, purchased the abandoned Michter's trademark in 1996 for $275 and began the process of rebuilding a proud heritage. Today, Michter's is a much-loved brand with a devoted following.

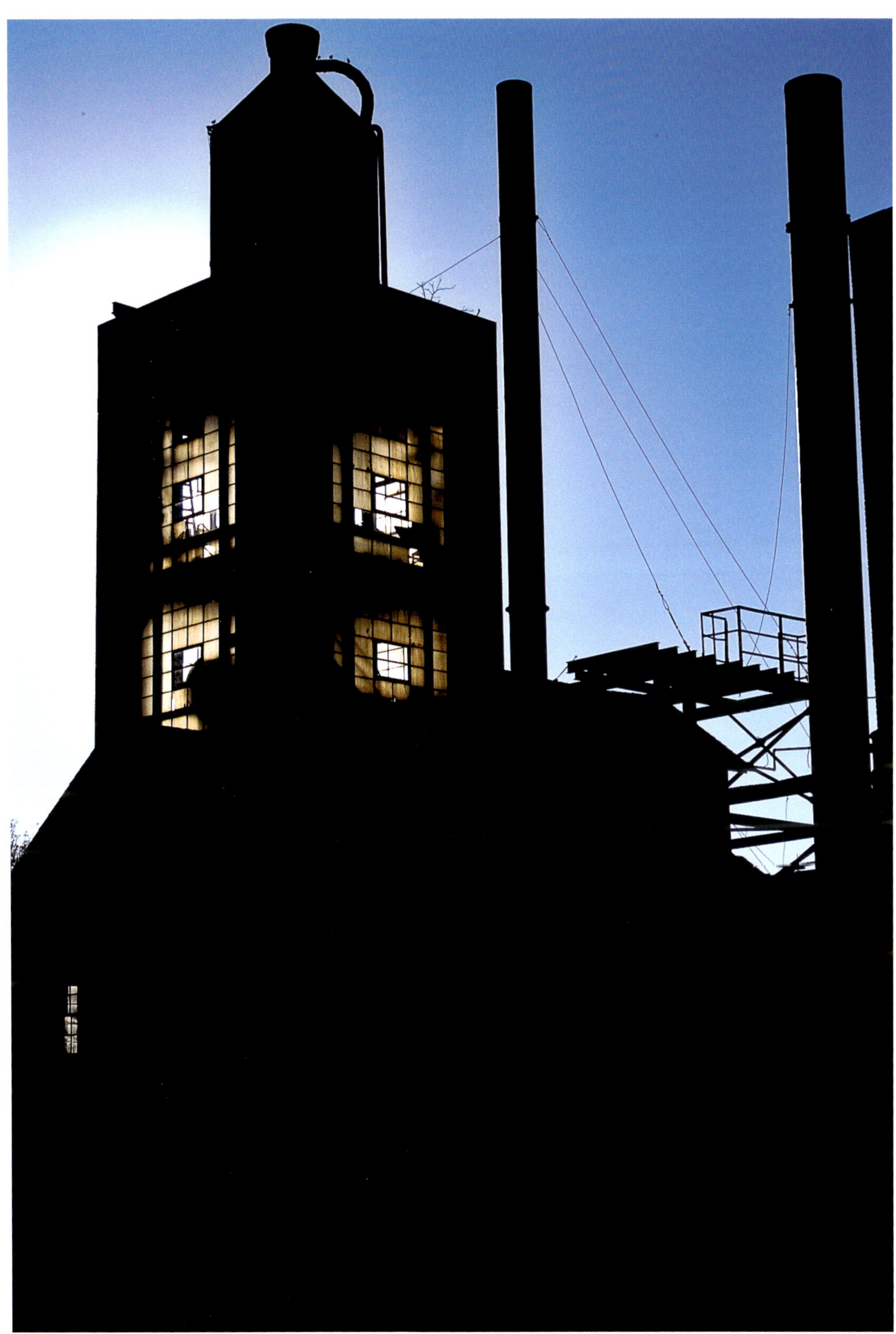

A silhouette of the old distillery tower and jug.

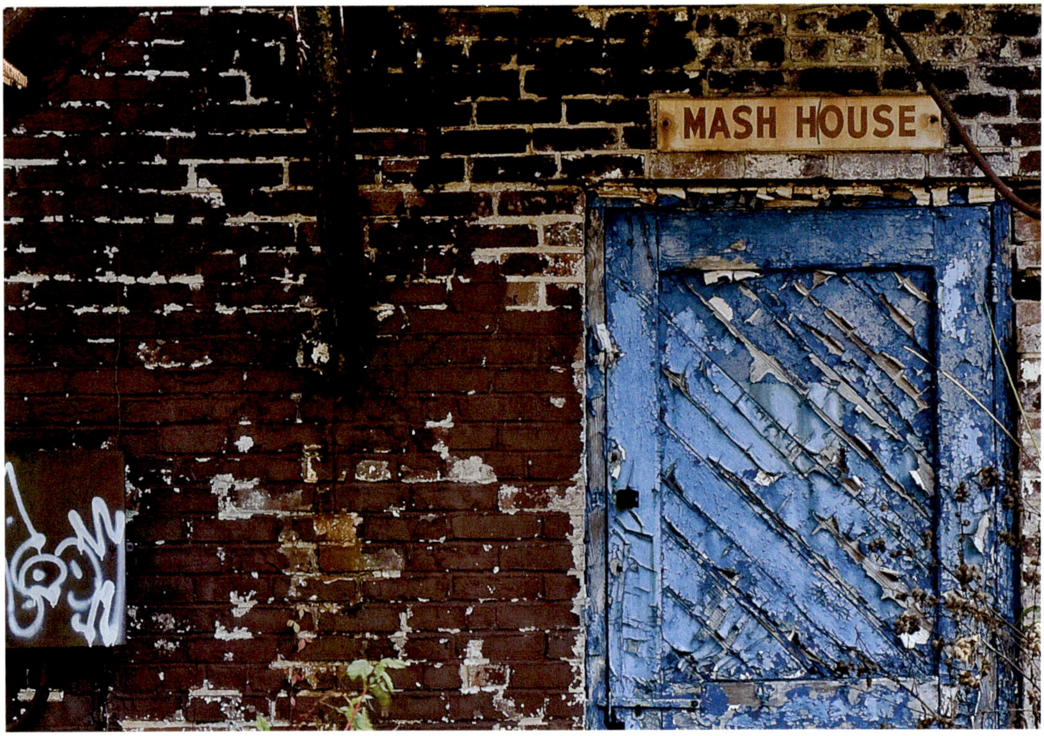

Peeling paint on the mash house door.

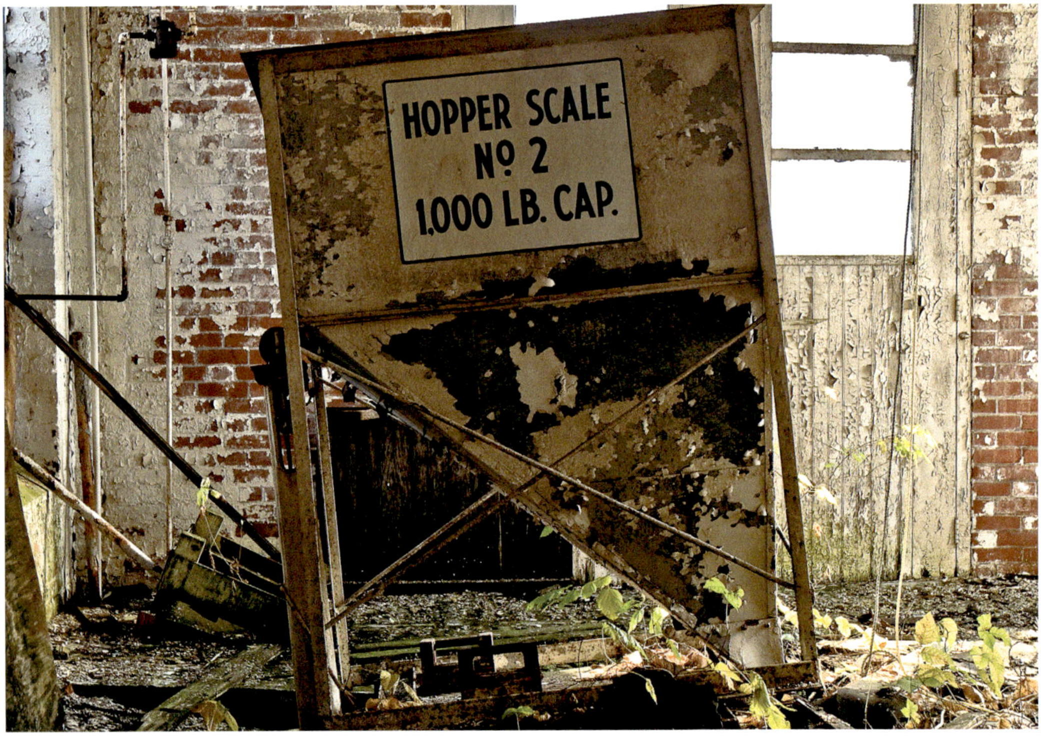

A hopper sinks into the rotting wooden floor.

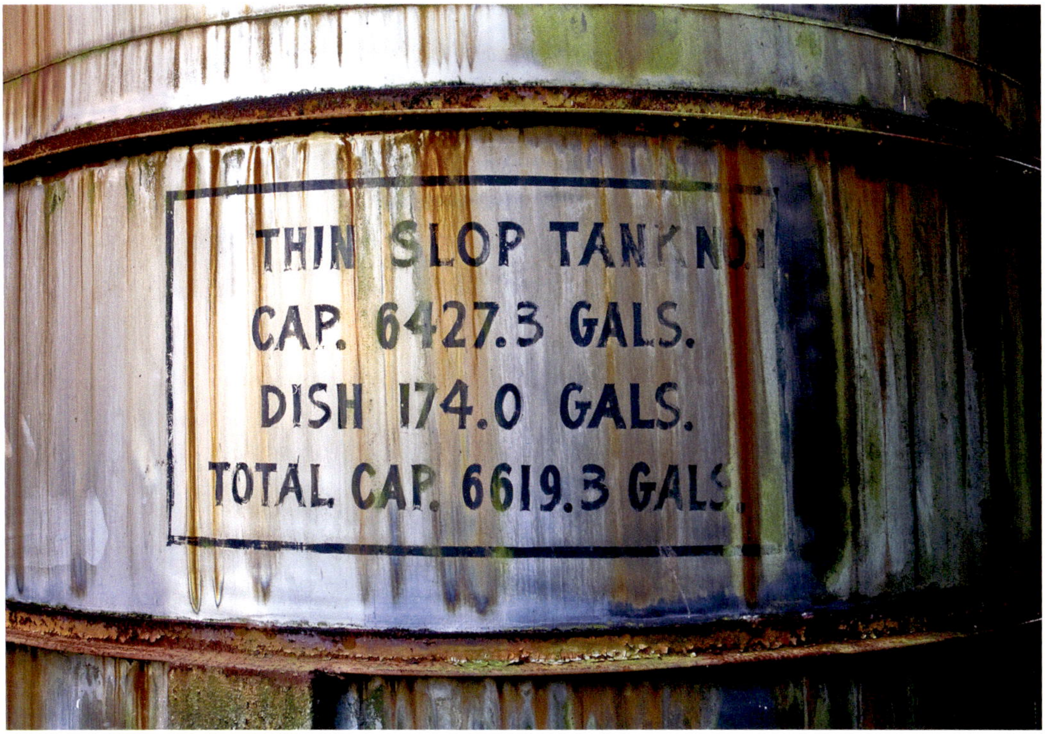

A rusting slop tank.

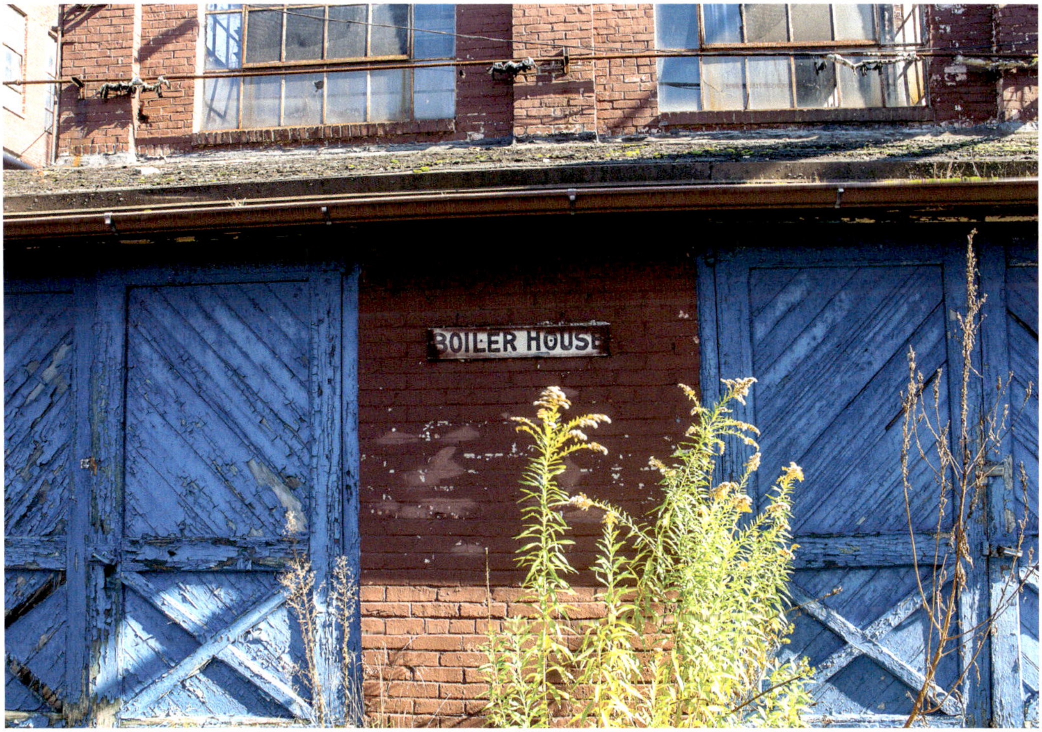

Bright blue doors contrast with the painted brown brick.

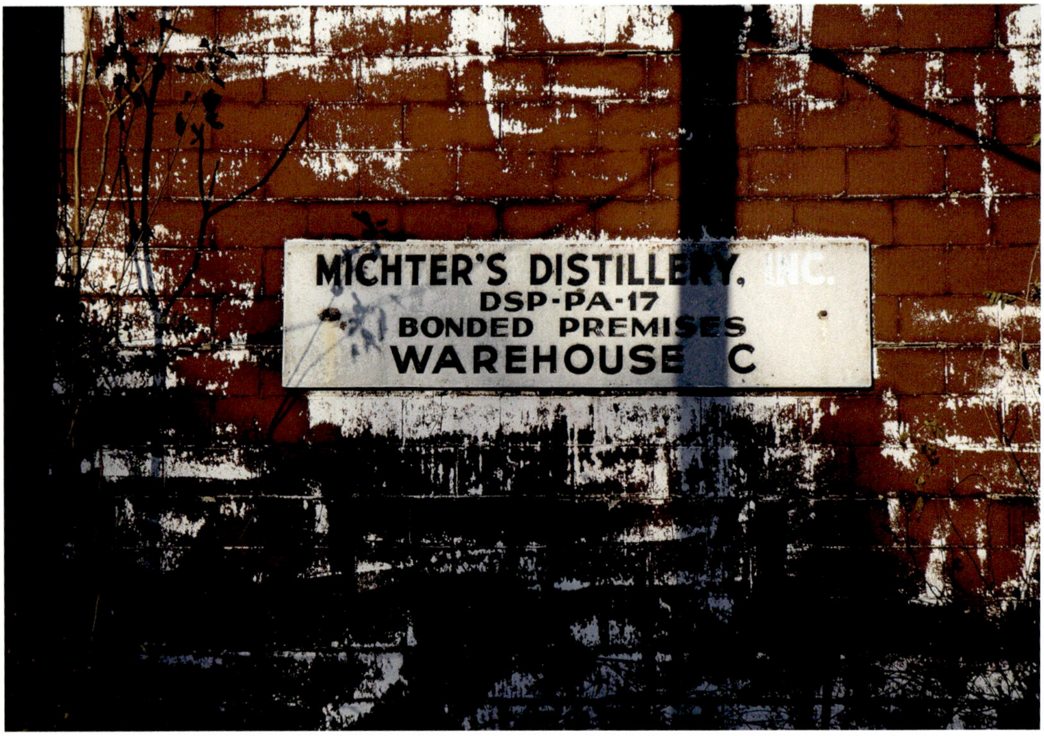

The warehouse sign.

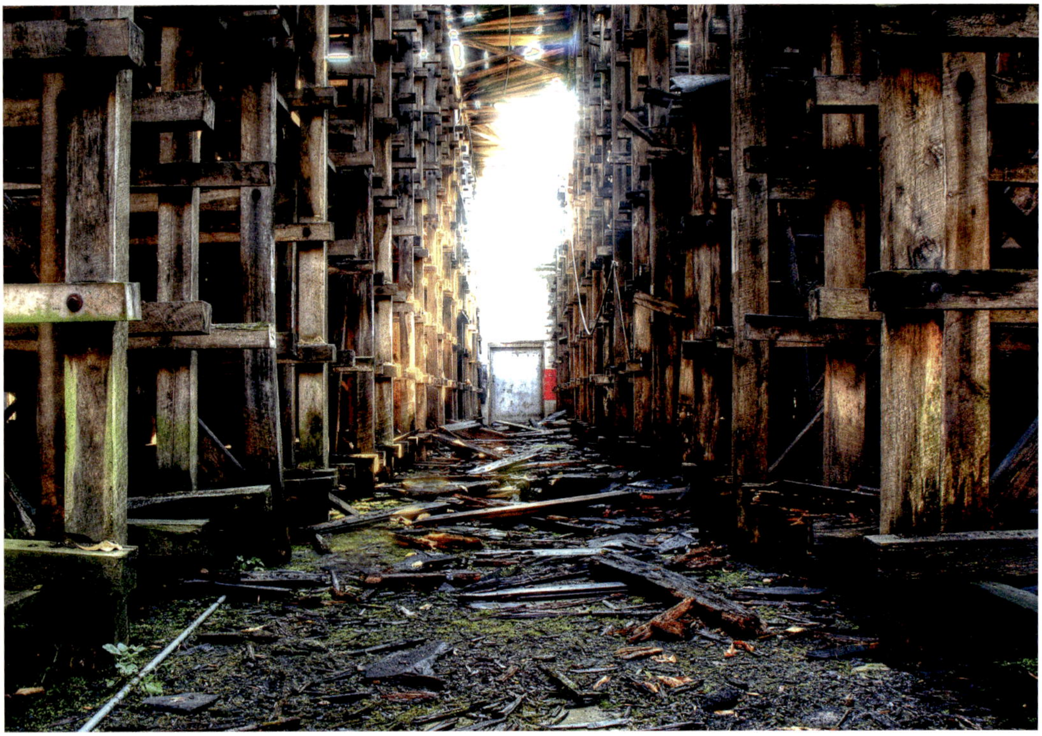

The interior of the warehouse where the whiskey barrels were once stored.

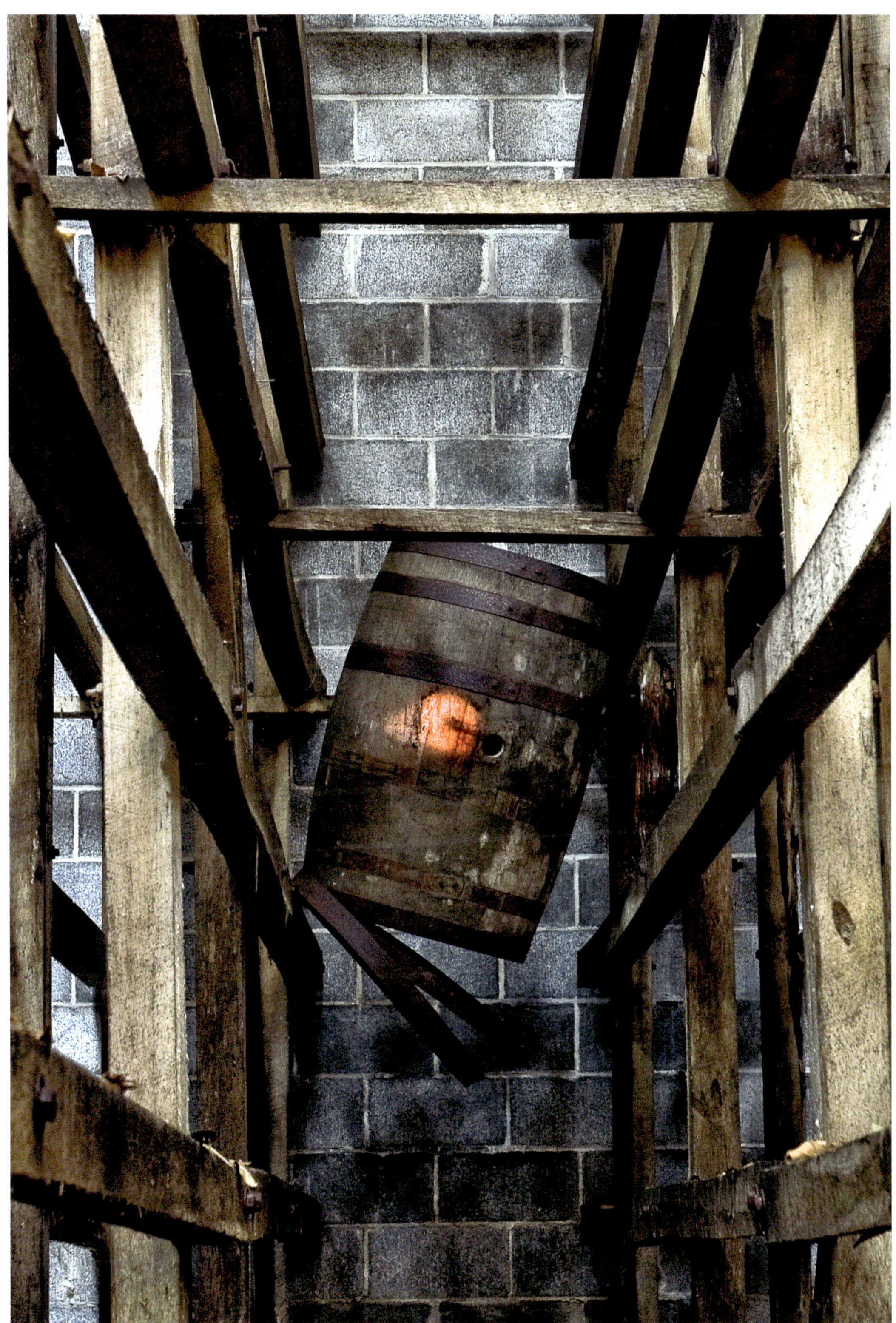

A lone barrel balances precariously.

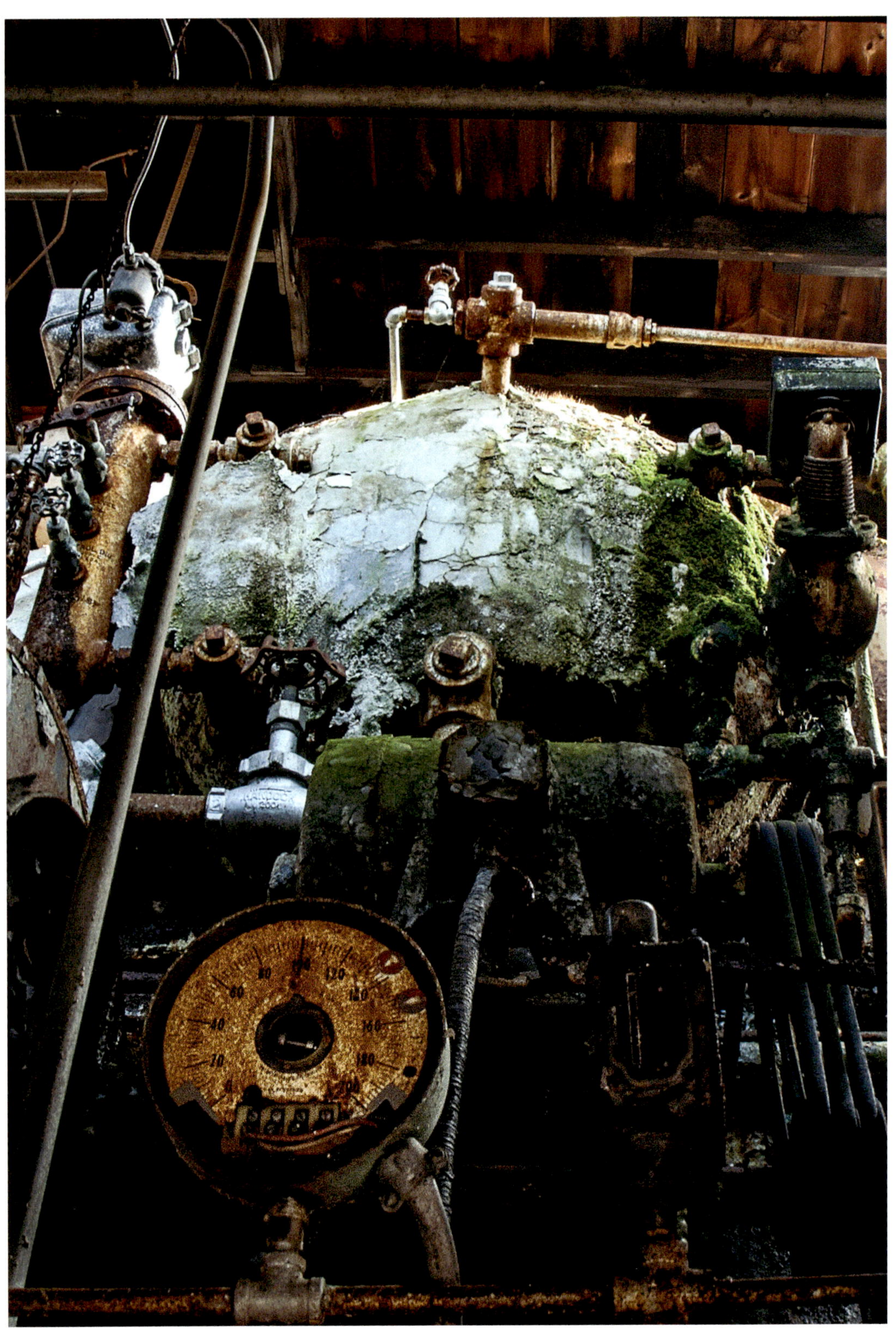

Moss-covered distilling equipment.

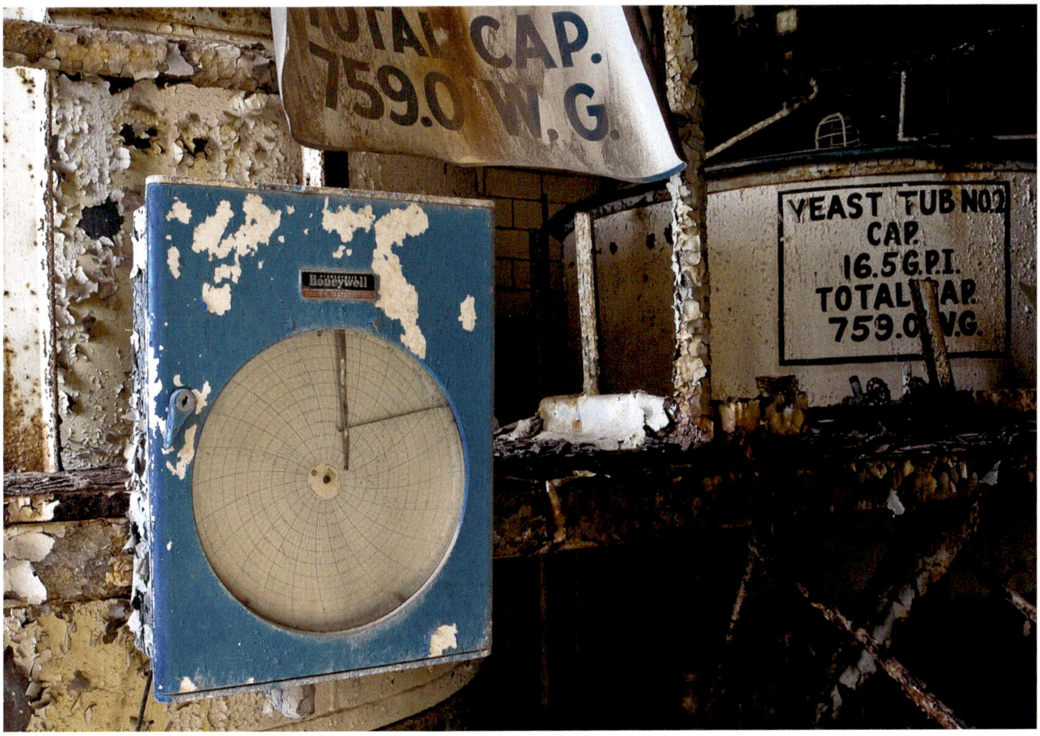

A disintegrating yeast tub.

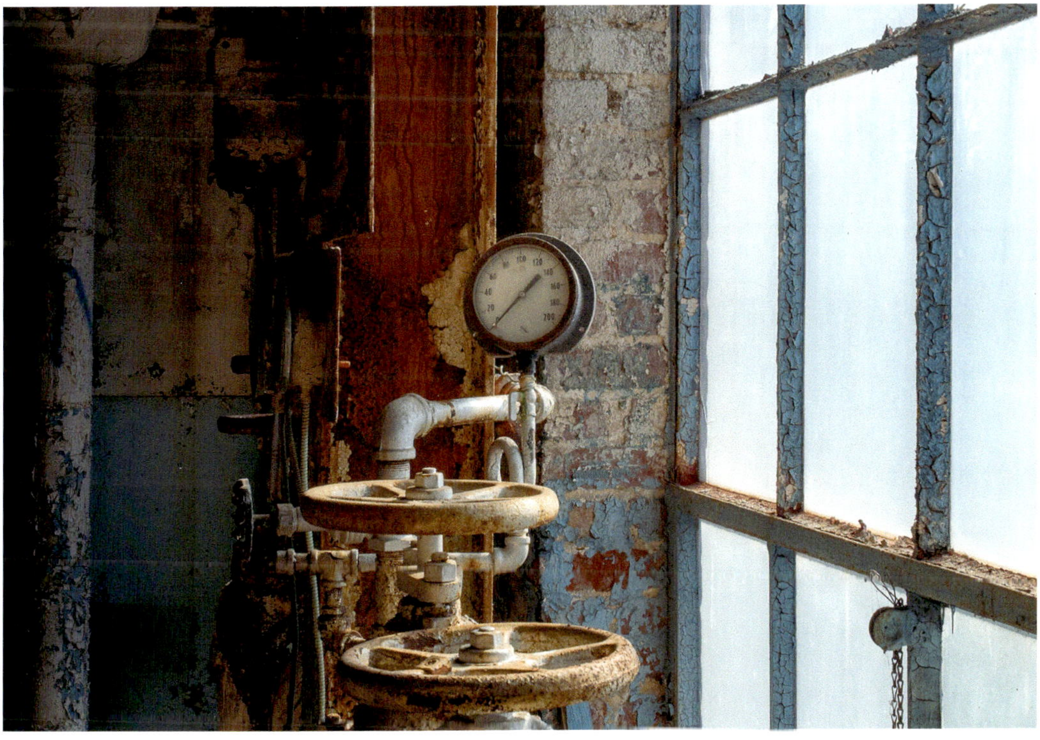

A gauge, no longer in use.

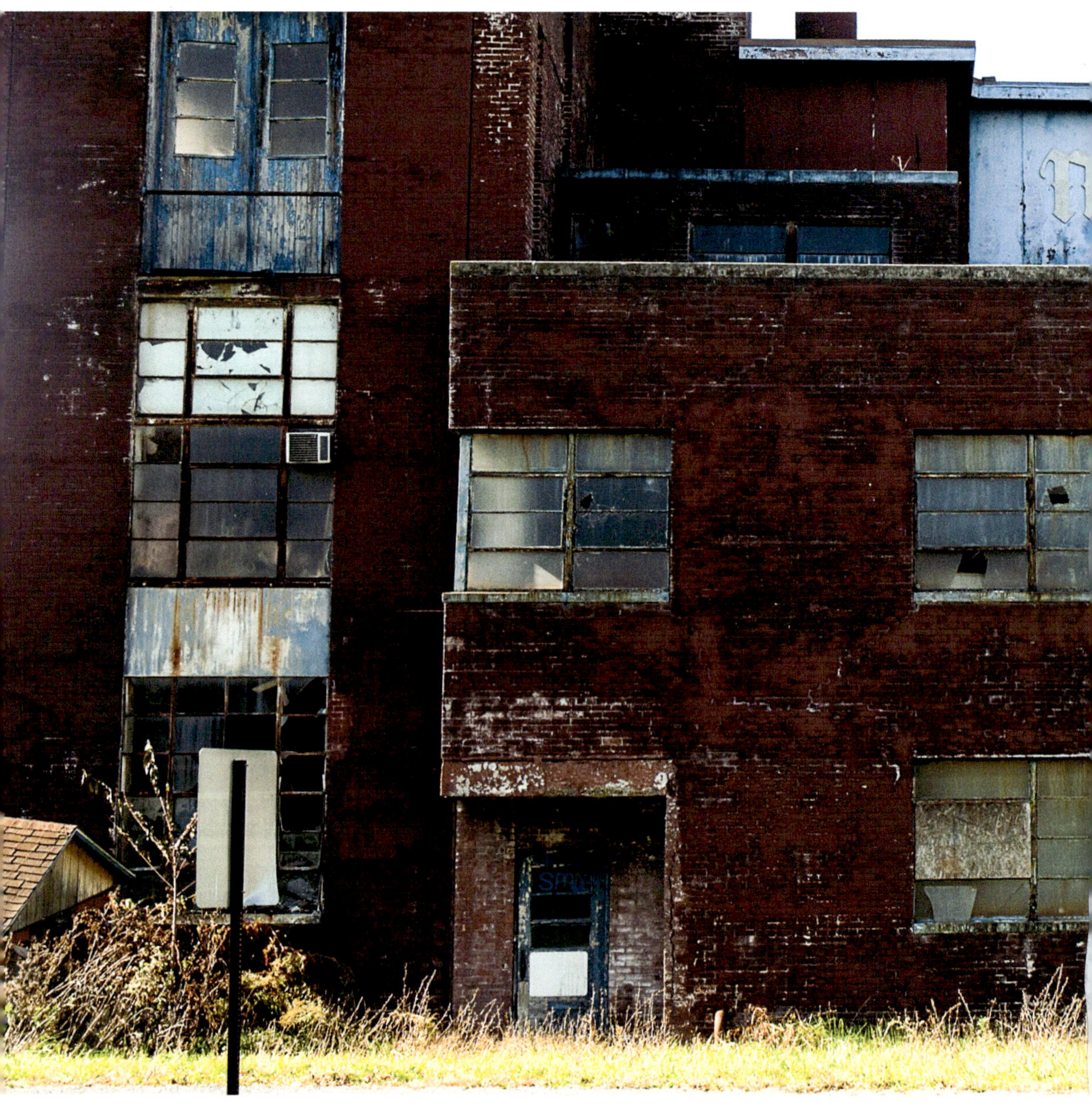

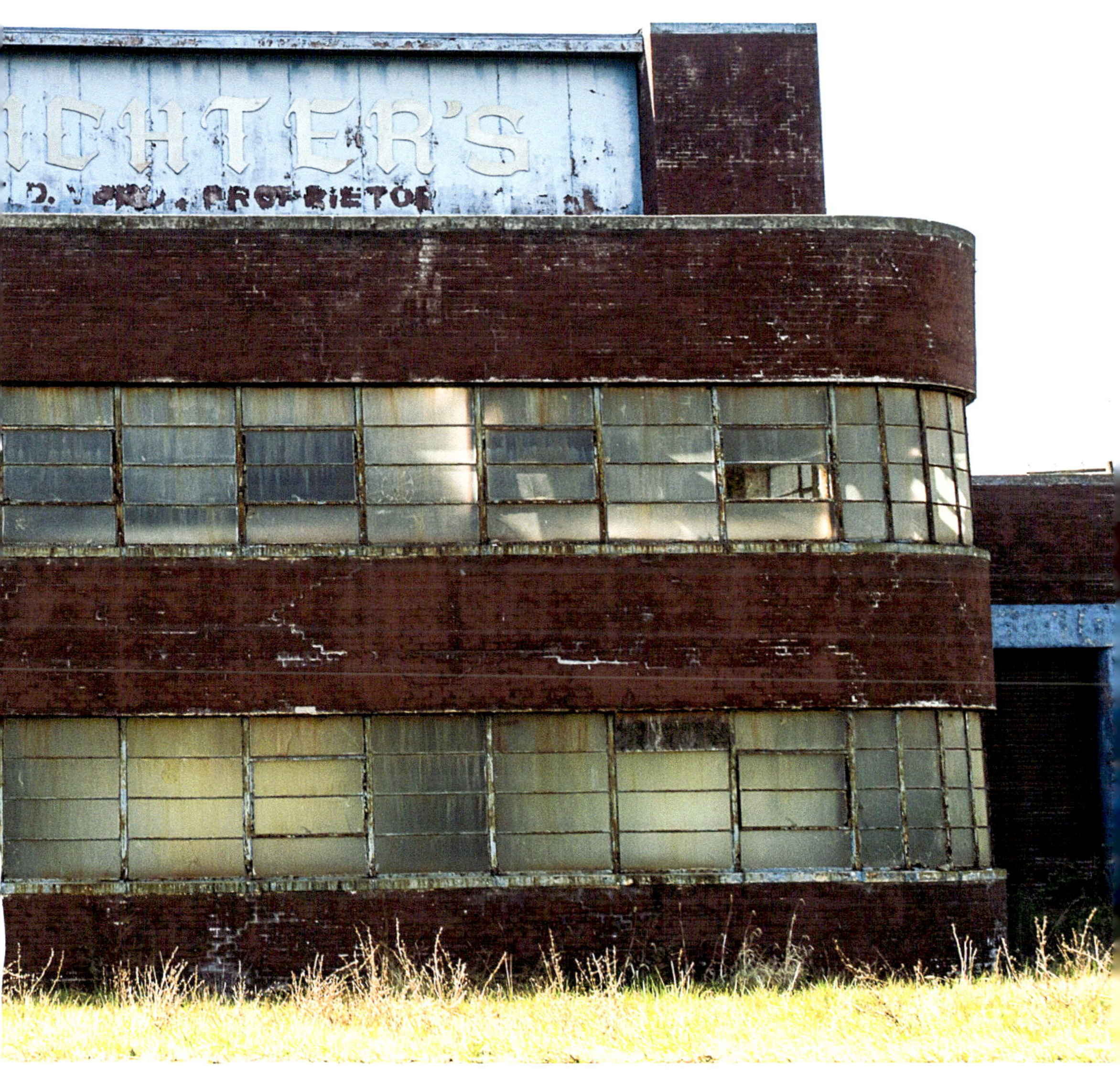

While this section of the distillery bears the Michter's name, it has since been demolished. All that remains is the original stillhouse, built in the 1840s.

BIBLIOGRAPHY

"Abandoned Poconos Legend: Buck Hill Inn," *Sometimes Interesting,* retrieved from sometimes-interesting.com/abandoned-poconos-legend-buck-hill-inn/

Addy, Jason, "Judge denies new trial in former prison lawsuit," *York Dispatch*, January 2017. Retrieved from www.yorkdispatch.com/story/news/local/2017/01/18/judge-denies-new-trial-former-prison-lawsuit/96736038/

Arthurs Kristin, Capanna Philip, Catallo Cortney, Cobette Antonio, Eck Russell, Golphin Tommy, Green Wil, Griffis Christine, Ivers Michael, Jean Elizabeth, Jennings Steven, Johnson Shanae, Keichline Katie, Ketter Krista, Lami Mohammad, Lessa Evan, Longenecker Michelle, Maron Casey, McGonagle Patricia, Melendez Vidal, Messer Greg, Miller Jennifer, Padus Oksana, Patel Janki, Pawlikowski Damian, Philip Jobby, Sanchez Michael, Stalmaster Joseph, Stoerrle Jillian, Szymula Agnieszka, Troy Jason, "Why did Northeast High School move from 8th and Lehigh Aves. to Cottman and Algon Aves. and become coeducational in 1957?" Service Learning Project, Class 161 2001–2002. Retrieved from dsharer.weebly.com/uploads/3/8/2/6/3826849/northeast_high_schools_move_1957.pdf

Bombergers Distillery, National Register of Historic Places. Retrieved from npgallery.nps.gov/NRHP/GetAsset/NHLS/75001649_text

Borek, Michael, "Scranton Lace,"Michael Borek Photography. Retrieved from michaelborek.com/portfolio/?album=&gallery=8&galname=SCRANTON%20LACE

Christopher, Matthew, "The Church of the Transfiguration,"*Abandoned America*. Retrieved from www.abandonedamerica.us/church-of-transfiguration

Calvert, Scott, "Philadelphia Illustrates Catholic Churches Dueling Dynamics in America," *Wall Street Journal*, September 2015. Retrieved from www.wsj.com/articles/philadelphia-illustrates-catholic-churchs-dueling-dynamics-in-america-1443346202

Davidson, Matthew, "How Philadelphia Moved a High School to Maintain Segregation," *The Nicest Kids In Town*, June 2009. Retrieved from https://whyy.org/articles/9117/

Delmont, Ken, "Why Remember Edison High School?" *York Daily Record*, April 2007. Retrieved from blog.phillyhistory.org/index.php/2011/08/why-remember-edison-high-school/

Finkel, Ken, "Why Remember Edison High School?" *York Daily Record*, April 2007. Retrieved from blog.phillyhistory.org/index.php/2011/08/why-remember-edison-high-school/

Freireich, Gordon, "Old York County Prison and all that's Alcatraz," The Philly History Blog, August 2011. Retrieved from www.ydr.com/story/archives/2007/04/29/old-york-county-prison-and-all-thats-alcatraz/74453346/

Friedman, Steven, "Outsiders Dine on Scranton Lace," *Lackawanna Historical Society Journal,* Spring 2009. Retrieved from www.lackawannahistory.org/newsletters/Volume39_No2.pdf

Haughney, Christine, "Vatican Ties Go Just So Far," *Wall Street Journal*, August 2006. Retrieved from www.wsj.com/articles/SB115447451640923957

Golak, Matt, "Fire Ravages Old Edison High." WHYY, PBS, NPR, August 2011. Retrieved from whyy.org/articles/9117/ "In Re: Condemnation by the Redevelopment Authority of the City of York," Casetext, Commonwealth Court of Pennsylvania. Retrieved from casetext.com/case/in-re-condemnation-by-the-redevelopment-auth-of-york-appropriating-in-fee-simple-certain-lands-of-john-e

Lipman John, "Michter's—The Jug House That Warmed The Revolution," EllenJaye Blog, September 2001. Retrieved from www.ellenjaye.com/michters.htm8

Lockwood, Jim, "Scranton Planners Hear Update on Laceworks Village Project" AP News, February 2019. Retrieved from apnews.com/article/92c9812011904dbe97f3e3d8020c6458

Mataloni, Carmella, "Buck Hill Inn Demolition Underway," WNEP16 The News Station, January 2018. Retrieved from www.wnep.com/article/news/local/monroe-county/buck-hill-inn-demolition-underway/523-1bbca333-f560-497c-b16b-c182de4cbd8f

McLure, Jim, "Old York County Prison holds prison art, other artifacts of historical value," *York Daily Record,* March 2014. Retrieved from yorkblog.com/yorktownsquare/old-york-county-prison-developers-should-be-sensitive-to-prison-art-other-artifacts/

Mike and Mike, "Michter's Distillery: Past, Present and Future," Bourbon Culture Blog, Retrieved from thebourbonculture.com/whiskey-info/michters-distillery-past-present-and-future/

Padwee, Michael, PA-Philadelphia Church of the Transfiguration, Historic US Tile Installations, Novemeber 2012. Retrieved from sites.google.com/site/tileinstallationdatabasemz/pa_philadelphia--church-of-the-transfiguration